Universities and Regional Economic Development

T0331293

In a knowledge-based economy, universities are vital institutions. This volume explores the roles that universities can play in peripheral regions, contributing to processes of regional economic development and innovative growth.

Including a series of case studies drawn from Portugal, Norway, Finland, the Czech Republic, Estonia and the Dutch-German border region, this will be the first book to offer a comprehensive comparative overview of universities in European economically peripheral regions. These studies seek to explore the tensions that arise in peripheral regions where there may not be obvious matches between university activities and regional strengths.

Aimed at academics, policy-makers and practitioners working on regional innovation strategies, this volume brings a much-needed sense of realism and ambition for all those concerned with building successful regional societies at the periphery of the knowledge economy.

Paul Benneworth is a senior researcher at the Center for Higher Education Policy Studies, University of Twente, the Netherlands, and Agderforskning, Kristiansand, Norway.

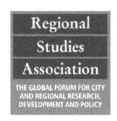

Regions and Cities

Series Editor in Chief
Joan Fitzgerald, *Northeastern University, USA*

Editors
Ron Martin, *University of Cambridge, UK*
Maryann Feldman, *University of North Carolina, USA*
Gernot Grabher, *HafenCity University Hamburg, Germany*
Kieran P. Donaghy, *Cornell University, USA*

In today's globalised, knowledge-driven and networked world, regions and cities have assumed heightened significance as the interconnected nodes of economic, social and cultural production, and as sites of new modes of economic and territorial governance and policy experimentation. This book series brings together incisive and critically engaged international and interdisciplinary research on this resurgence of regions and cities, and should be of interest to geographers, economists, sociologists, political scientists and cultural scholars, as well as to policy-makers involved in regional and urban development.

For more information on the Regional Studies Association visit www.regionalstudies.org

There is a **30% discount** available to RSA members on books in the *Regions and Cities* series, and other subject related Taylor and Francis books and e-books including Routledge titles. To order just e-mail Joanna Swieczkowska, Joanna.Swieczkowska@tandf.co.uk, or phone on +44 (0)20 3377 3369 and declare your RSA membership. You can also visit the series page at www.routledge.com/Regions-and-Cities/book-series/RSA and use the discount code: **RSA0901**

Universities and Regional Economic Development

Engaging with the Periphery

Edited by Paul Benneworth

Routledge
Taylor & Francis Group

LONDON AND NEW YORK

First published 2019
by Routledge
2 Park Square, Milton Park, Abingdon, Oxon OX14 4RN

and by Routledge
52 Vanderbilt Avenue, New York, NY 10017, USA

First issued in paperback 2020

Routledge is an imprint of the Taylor & Francis Group, an informa business

British Library Cataloguing-in-Publication Data
A catalogue record for this book is available from the British Library

Library of Congress Cataloging-in-Publication Data
A catalog record has been requested for this book

ISBN 13: 978-0-367-66579-1 (pbk)
ISBN 13: 978-1-138-05127-0 (hbk)

Typeset in Bembo
by Out of House Publishing

Dedicated to Martha Barbara Benneworth

Contents

Figures

Tables

Contributors

Paul Benneworth is a senior researcher at the Center for Higher Education Policy Studies at the University of Twente, Enschede, The Netherlands and at Agderforskning, Kristiansand, Norway.

Jos van den Broek is a senior researcher at the Rathenau Instituut, The Hague, The Netherlands.

Inna Čábelková is an assistant professor and the head of the Qualified Skills Department at the Faculty of Humanities, Charles University, Prague, the Czech Republic.

Franziska Eckardt is a PhD student at the Center for Higher Education Policy Studies at the University of Twente, Enschede, The Netherlands.

Manuel Fernández-Esquinas is a research scientist at the Spanish National Research Council (CSIC).

James Karlsen is an associate professor at the University of Agder, Norway, a senior researcher at Agderforskning, Kristiansand, Norway, and a senior associate researcher at Orkestra, Basque Institute of Competitiveness, Spain.

Anne Keerberg is a PhD student at Tallinn University of Technology (TTÜ), Finland, researching higher education institutions and regional development.

Jan Kohoutek is a senior researcher at the Centre for Higher Education Studies in Prague and an assistant professor at the Faculty of Social Sciences, Charles University, Prague, the Czech Republic.

Jari Kolehmainen is Research Director at the University of Tampere, Faculty of Management, Urban and Regional Studies Group (Sente), Finland.

Heli Kurikka is a researcher at the University of Tampere, Faculty of Management, Urban and Regional Studies Research Group (Sente), Finland.

Nina Kyllingstad is a PhD candidate at the Department of Working Life and Innovation at the University of Agder, Norway and a researcher at Agderforskning, Kristiansand, Norway.

Lisa Nieth is a PhD student at the Center for Higher Education Policy Studies at the University of Twente, Enschede, The Netherlands.

Rómulo Pinheiro is a senior researcher (part-time) at Agderforskning, Kristiansand, Norway and Professor of Public Policy and Administration at the University of Agder, Norway.

Hugo Pinto is a researcher at the Centre for Social Studies, University of Coimbra (Portugal) and Professor in the Faculty of Economics, University of Algarve.

Libor Prudký is an associate professor at the Faculty of Humanities, Charles University, Prague, the Czech Republic.

Michaela Šmídová is a researcher at the Centre for Higher Education Studies, Prague, the Czech Republic.

Markku Sotarauta is Professor of Regional Development Studies in the Faculty of Management at the University of Tampere, Finland.

Elvira Uyarra is Senior Lecturer in Innovation Management and Policy at Alliance Manchester Business School (University of Manchester).

Preface

The cliché is that science is a team game, with the result being more important than the individual who scores the goal. However, all of us in science know that we are all under immense pressure to perform as individuals. We are measured, monitored and managed as individuals, whilst the business of creating interesting and useful new knowledge is a collective affair. It has therefore been a great privilege to work as part of a dynamic, enthusiastic and dedicated group of scholars who are keen to explore the roles of universities in peripheral regions. Although ultimately it is my name that stands on the cover as editor, in this preface I wish to draw attention to and recognise the contribution of participants in our wider scholarly community that have made this volume possible.

This book reports results coming out of the PERIF-EU project, a collaboration between Agderforskning in Norway and a number of higher education research centres in the Czech republic. Many thanks are due to Rómulo Pinheiro, senior researcher at Agderforskning, for acquiring and overseeing the project and supporting my participation in the project through AF. The project was a fascinating opportunity to concentrate on truly peripheral regions, and the core set of case studies was sufficiently exciting to help enrol a list of other researchers with their own cases to contribute to this volume. The research leading to these results has received funding from the Norwegian Financial Mechanism 2009–2014 and the Czech Republic's Ministry of Education, Youth and Sports under Project Contract no. MSMT-5397/2015. I am a very demanding editor to work with, and I'd like to thank all the authors in this volume for their willingness to submit to my dictates as well as their patience as I suffered with RSI over the summer of 2017.

A word of thanks is certainly due to the publishers, Routledge, and in particular their dedicated staff on the Regions and Cities series who worked with me on this volume, namely Lisa Lavelle, Emily Kindleysides, Elanor Best and Natalie Tomlinson. This is my fourth volume in this series, something that reflects the great enthusiasm and support they provide their editors with, at a time when academic publishers are increasingly driven by profits rather than the nurturing of new ideas. It has been a great pleasure to work with them on this volume, and I hope to continue this relationship into the future.

The last year has also seen some rather unpleasant shocks. One year ago we received the unexpected news of the passing of Professor Susan Christopherson, editor of this series. She has been a great inspiration to all of us in the field of economic geography, and made a number of leading contributions to debates around innovation, universities and uneven development. As we were finalising the volume, we were also told of the untimely death of our colleague on the PERIF project Olga Šmídová. Although she was not a contributor directly to this volume, she was an enthusiastic participant in the project meetings and the email discussions in which the ideas presented in this volume emerged. Our thoughts have been with those nearest and dearest to Olga and Susan, and they are being sorely missed by us both professionally but also personally.

Finally, an acknowledgement is also due to Martha Barbara. When I submitted the proposal on 17 October 2016 to the publisher from the Coffee Bar in C pier of Schiphol en route to Lisbon for a meeting of the Forskningsrådet-funded Digitalize or Die project, we hoped that we'd not be seeing you for another six weeks. But you popped out at the end of the week, and thankfully you have grown as rapidly as the manuscript. Your growth has been an inspiration to me as I have sought to finalise this volume and I am delighted to have both a healthy happy daughter and my long-dreamed-of volume on universities and regional development in the periphery. The making of this volume was inextricably bound up with you, and for that reason, I dedicate this volume to you, Martha Barbara Benneworth.

1 Universities and regional development in peripheral regions

Paul Benneworth and Lisa Nieth

Introduction: the challenge of universities contributing to peripheral regions

Universities have been defined as important actors in today's knowledge economy since the 1990s, contributing to economic growth and development through knowledge production and collaboration with diverse stakeholders (Benneworth, Charles, & Madanipour, 2010; Etzkowitz & Leydesdorff, 2000). Nevertheless, universities' success is at least partly a function of their incredible organisational complexity (Lewis, Marginson, & Snyder, 2005) and there has been little consideration in conceptualising universities as regional organisations and how their complexity affects their regional engagement. In failing to consider this complexity, scholars and policy-makers implicitly assume that it is enough for universities to adopt a strategic regional engagement position, whilst in reality universities face various difficulties when asked to co-ordinate action around their knowledge production and circulation. It is this organisational complexity, and its implications for universities' regional contributions, that this volume seeks to address.

Universities are knowledge-producing organisations with very decentralised organisational structures, Weick (1976) describing them as being "loosely coupled". In this volume, it is not just institutions that have the formal title of university, but all kinds of higher education institution (HEI) that blend teaching and research, thereby also encompassing universities of applied science, university colleges, specialist higher colleges (e.g. for teachers, musicians or artists).[1] Accordingly, different academic disciplines and areas (Becher & Trowler's (2001) "academic tribes") have very different approaches to creating new knowledge (research), transmitting knowledge (teaching), and transferring knowledge (valorisation). Universities therefore have to find formal and informal ways to simultaneously accommodate these different practices within singular organisational structures. Attempts by universities to develop a singular knowledge transfer strategy risk failing to capture the diversity of engagement practices across these different academic communities. Indeed, it is particularly complicated for university managers to produce singular engagement strategies that will have the desired effect of encouraging and facilitating their staff to drive regional development and hence deliver engagement.

This complex situation is true for all kinds of external engagements, but can be particularly prevalent in regional engagement, where universities are co-operating with partners that are physically nearby, rather than those that are necessarily optimal for the knowledge creation at hand. In the last decade, there has been an emerging rhetoric that universities need to be world-class, excellent, and global citizens (Salmi, 2009) raising the risk that regional engagement is something for 'second rate' academics who cannot do this internationally excellent research (Akker & Spaapen, 2017). This can result in strong pressures on universities not to engage with their regional partners, tensions so strong that they cannot be overruled by the vague sense of 'public duty' that universities have. These tensions come particularly to the fore in less innovative regions, because there are natural pressures and demands that encourage and regularise regional engagement as a legitimate university activity. Likewise there are not naturally the world-leading innovative partners with whom universities can collaborate and claim it represents 'excellent research'.

To better understand these tensions, this volume presents a series of case studies drawn from regions where these problems have specifically come to the fore. To place these into a broader context, in this chapter we firstly contextualise the broader environment within which there have been these rising expectations that universities can contribute, as well as make an overview of the case studies that are presented. In the next chapter, we then explore the precise nature of the problematic, which is that these models are heavily dependent on well-functioning regional coalitions to achieve those effects, whilst universities do not necessarily see immediate benefits in participating in these coalitions. Together, these two conceptual chapters set out in detail the conceptual framework, of regions shifting their regional economic development trajectories by purposive interventions from regional innovation coalitions (RICs). This model in turn provides the basis for identifying where tensions might exist, and exploring them in the context of peripheral regions, where they might be the most extreme and hence amenable to study.

In the nine empirical chapters, these tensions are explored through a series of detailed case studies of how HEIs have contributed to these regions' development. Each of these empirical chapters follows a common format, although each of the chapters has been written to provide a free-standing contribution to our overall message. The chapters begin by setting out the regional development problem in that peripheral region, and conceptualising through a more precise specification of our overarching model. The chapters then each set out their method, also providing an overview of the region to characterise its precise form of peripherality. Each chapter then provides a distinct analytic step, setting out the history of how universities have tried to contribute to the region, which tensions these have raised in the particular context, and what kinds of solutions have been successful, and less successful in resolving these tensions. We then offer a more general reflection on how universities can contribute to solving particular kinds of peripherality problems whilst accounting for the engagement problems that peripherality can raise for universities. In the final chapter, we draw these elements together to reflect on what this means for theories of universities and regional development, as well as the policy and practical recommendations that arise.

Contemporary conceptual approaches to regional economic development

Policy concepts for universities' regional contributions

Our starting point for understanding the challenge of universities engaging in peripheral regions has been a family of concepts that have emerged in the last decade to better explain, predict, and steer regional change. This was the latest step in a much longer incorporation of notions of knowledge capital in theories of economic development in the context of neo-endogenous development theories, which seek to understand the roles that can be played by local actors in an increasingly globalised world. The answer to this came through an understanding of the increasing importance of knowledge capital to explaining economic growth (formally through the relationship of total factor productivity to productivity growth, see Romer, 1994; Solow, 1994; Temple, 1998). Knowledge capital emerged through interactive learning processes and these interactive processes were facilitated by the presence of different kinds of proximity (Benneworth, Irawati, Rutten, & Boekema, 2014). This regional characteristic of geographical coherence provided the starting point for the emergence of what Moulaert and Sekia (2003) were to call 'Territorial Innovation Models'. These provided explanations of how a region's specific characteristics could facilitate these interactive learning processes and thereby affect growth.

Where these models fell short was that they did not provide satisfactory models for making policy prescriptions, simply describing, sometimes in quite some conceptual details, the characteristics of regions that *had been successful in the past*. As policy-makers – particularly in the European Union and the Organisation for Economic Co-operation and Development – sought to operationalise these into policies, there was a realisation that their one-size-fits-all approach was problematic (Boschma, 2013). As every regional authority hastened to create a biotech cluster, policy-makers sought to identify how regions could exert agency and thereby improve their own prospects by building on their existing strengths and future opportunities rather than mimicking historically successful regions. Rooted in emerging concepts of evolutionary economic geography, these concepts sought to better elucidate the link between regional activity today and improved prospects tomorrow. Chapter 2 provides more detail on these concepts, as in this chapter, we restrict ourselves to a consideration of the explanations of how regions could improve their own situations.

We here focus on two distinct policy concepts that emerged in the course of the 2000s. One of these is likely to be familiar to many readers, that of smart specialisation, because of the European Union's requirement that territories in receipt of structural funding should have a valid smart specialisation strategy. By presenting two of them, we illustrate the more general point that policy-makers have been interested in how regions can 'create their own futures'. This interest is central to understanding evolving policy expectations on universities, which we address in this chapter, before turning in the next chapter to how this creates tensions for universities in terms of living up to those expectations. The two concepts to which we now turn are constructed regional advantage (CRA) and (the aforementioned) smart specialisation.

Constructing regional advantage

The first policy concept that we consider, constructed regional advantage, was launched by the Directorate-General for Research and Innovation in 2006 (European Commission, 2006). The CRA model sees proactive public–private partnerships applying existing knowledge in new ways to create regional economic advantages (Asheim, Coenen, Moodysson, & Vang, 2007). In this perspective, *regional advantage* and new regional pathways do not always arise spontaneously (particularly in peripheral regions!). These new regional pathways therefore have to be deliberately and proactively *constructed* in ways specific to regional economic and governance contexts. These models of constructed regional advantage typically comprise three key elements, namely 'related variety', 'differentiated knowledge bases', and 'platform policies', which affect regional learning and knowledge creation processes.

The 'related variety' concept derives from economic geography where a certain degree of cognitive proximity can support effective learning and communication between different industries. This means that knowledge transfer and learning are more likely to happen between sectors that are sufficiently technologically related but simultaneously not too cognitively proximate (where there are few opportunities for cross-industry learning). Emilia Romagna in northern Italy emblematised how related variety can significantly affect economic renewal and growth; its diffused engineering knowledge base provided the foundation for many high technology sectors to emerge in the post-war period, including robotics, car manufacturing, and agricultural machinery. Asheim, Boschma, and Cooke (2011, p. 898) attribute this knowledge accumulation as occurring because "these new sectors not only built and expanded on [the] extensive regional knowledge base, they also renewed and extended it".

The 'differentiated knowledge base' concept argues that companies with similar kinds of knowledge base organise their innovation processes (and their relationships with third parties) in similar kinds of ways. This literature differentiates three types of knowledge: analytical (science based), synthetic (engineering based), and symbolic (artistic based) and for each of these there are different kinds of interactions with knowledge suppliers. Analytic knowledge transfer involves acquiring scientific and technology knowledge, through patents, licenses, and contract research. Synthetic knowledge is acquired by shared learning involving knowledge suppliers and users 'doing and understanding' together. Symbolic knowledge is embedded through acts of creativity in which new products are created by interweaving the ideas and creativity into these products. These knowledge bases are analytic categories and most real innovation activities involve different kinds of knowledge base but the argument is that innovation support and policies need be mindful of these different kinds of innovation (Asheim *et al.*, 2011; European Commission, 2006).

The notion of platform policies emerged as a specific reaction to the aforementioned problem of thin policy-borrowing within earlier TIM-inspired policies that saw innovation policy become a sectoral support approach for existing industries (Pugh, 2014). Platform policies attempt to integrate different forms of support (for instance talent formation and environmental enhancement) applicable to many industries, and facilitate natural spill-overs between sectors and also the spontaneous emergence of new sectors. Platform policies seek to promote related variety, being "structured on the basis of shared and complementary knowledge bases and competences, the promotion of spin-off companies and the encouragement of labour mobility" (Uyarra, 2010b, p. 128). A good example for a platform policy is the 'Preseli Platform' in West Wales, which sought to advance the very heterogeneous sectors of food production and consumption, tourism, textiles, and maritime activities by activities such as connecting knowledge institutions to firms or training and attracting talented people (Cooke, 2006).

Smart specialisation

In parallel with the development of the constructed regional advantage approach, the EU advisory group 'Knowledge for Growth' (K4G) introduced the smart specialisation approach, proposing national and regional policy intervention and investments in areas that "create future domestic capability and interregional comparative advantage" (Foray, David, & Hall, 2009). The focus of smart specialisation is on 'entrepreneurial discovery processes' that identify the economic sectors with current and future potential to drive regional development (Foray *et al.*, 2009; McCann & Ortega-Argilés, 2013a). In an entrepreneurial discovery process, stakeholders identify potential R&D and innovation domains in their region, scan technological and market opportunities, recognise bottlenecks, and articulate obstacles to development (Boschma, 2013, p. 6). These entrepreneurial stakeholders can be any private or public actors (inventors, companies, HEIs, etc.) with suitable accurate knowledge to identify future potential.

Those at the European level that introduced smart specialisation were seeking to force policy-makers to make clear choices regarding which sectors to specialise into. It was hoped this would likewise compel policy-makers to select policy interventions tailored to specific regional settings and opportunities rather than following the latest fads. Regional actors are critical within the 'entrepreneurial discovery processes' by collectively defining specialisation areas and serving as 'entrepreneurial path finders', leaving policy-makers with the more modest roles to "allow and help economic agents to find their own ways in a decentralized and bottom-up process and then carefully observe what is happening" (Foray, David, & Hall, 2011, p. 10). From this perspective, policy-makers do have responsibilities for incentivising entrepreneurial discovery processes, selecting suitable public investments to complement emerging specialisations, and evaluating subsidy effectiveness (Foray et al., 2009). In the 2014–20 programming period for the European Structural Funds having a smart specialisation strategy in place was an eligibility criterion to receive funding, and the approach is widely implemented and understood across Europe.

It is this "clear policy-prioritization logic which is well suited to promoting innovation in a wide variety of regional settings" (McCann & Ortega-Argilés, 2013b, p. 1292) that has made smart specialisation an appealing approach to European policy-makers seeking to stimulate innovation in all regions (Foray, 2017; Foray et al., 2009, p. 3). Nevertheless, there remains some dispute over its applicability to all kinds of regions, notably less-favoured regions with unfavourable economic structures that have a low potential to diversify (Boschma, 2014). There is also evidence that regional policy-makers have in many cases been resistant to this nudge towards discontinuing older sectoral support strategies sometimes merely badging their older clusters as an entrepreneurial discovery-led network (Pugh, 2014). More generally, policy-makers have often pre-identified economic activities with regional potential, restricting entrepreneurial discovery process to these predefined areas, rather than it being fully open-ended as intended (Crespo, Balland, Boschma, & Rigby, 2017).

The roles of universities in regional partnerships

The role of universities in these processes is immediately clear, participating as regional actors that shape the particular future-creating activities. As knowledge creators and circulators (Yigitcanlar, 2010), universities are expected to be part of these partnerships and contribute to the region by having a significant impact on its innovation capacity and economic development (OECD, 2007). The European University Association (2014, p. 9) indeed goes further, claiming that there is an urgent need to recognise "the role of universities as a key partner in taking forward successful Smart Specialisation Strategies in partnership with other stakeholders in the region". The factors identified for the success of smart specialisation strategies, "dialogue, trust and alignment of university portfolio and regional strategies" (European University Association, 2014, p. 17), exemplify the complexity of reaching successful partnerships.

Universities can directly affect a region's development by producing new knowledge and educating the regional workforce. The production and distribution of knowledge with economic value can happen through commercialisation of this knowledge (e.g. in form of patenting or spin-offs), through collaboration with companies (e.g. in joint projects or consulting), and through informal knowledge exchange (e.g. through networking activities). Nevertheless, cooperation between different partners is not a straight-forward process realised in a 'happy family setting' (Lagendijk & Oinas, 2005), particularly where actors have different strategic goals, and make their own strategic decisions depending on variables defined by themselves. Policy-makers often encounter the practical problem that universities are regularly reluctant or problematic partners within regional collaborative activities, undermining the potential impact of their engagement.

Our diagnosis in this volume is that these problems only make sense when understood in the context of a mushrooming number of policy goals to which universities are expected to contribute (de Boer *et al.*, 2017). The resultant 'mission stretch' (Scott, 2007) can accentuate the tensions between global competition, based on academic excellence defined by international standards, and regional demands, following policy agendas for societal impact and relevance, (Krücken, Kosmützky, & Torka, 2007). With these multiple missions for universities, the argument has been made that the regional mission runs the risk of being 'crowded out' by universities' core missions of teaching and research and in particular pressures to be internationally excellent in these core activities (Benneworth, Young, & Normann, 2017; Pinheiro, Benneworth, & Jones, 2012). Across our case studies we are able show how diverse policies demand attention from HEIs which in return do not have the capabilities to concentrate on university regional engagement policies.

To a certain degree, there is a common understanding that universities are loosely coupled organisations, compiling different units and individuals with particular goals and identities, and dependencies on history and resources. Nevertheless, diverse challenges have been identified with respect to the varied missions and intentions that pressure universities. One challenge is that higher education institutions have been featured as manageable and strategic organizations, able to respond in a well-articulated (i.e. strategic), efficient, and socially accountable manner to demands that are not only complex, but often contradictory (Pinheiro *et al.*, 2012; Uyarra, 2010a). Regional actors expect that HEIs are able to 'help the region' and cooperate seamlessly to reach common goals. Diverse factors – for instance the degree of alignment between research topics and the needs of the region, the history of engagement, and the types of regional businesses – have an impact on the degree of engagement advance (Gunasekara, 2006). The high quantity of these potential impact factors highlights the diversity of missions an HEI can face in a region. Finally, from a policy perspective, there is an urgent need to understand effective combinations of policies that help HEIs to engage within regional innovation coalitions (RICs).

The contributions from the chapters to this volume

To illustrate and analyse the pressures that higher education's regional contributions face, we present a set of empirical case studies reflecting the diversity of economic peripherality across European regions. Each of these regional chapters sets out the precise nature of the regional development problem and the involvement of regional HEIs in solving that problem. In identifying the pathways through which solutions emerge, the specific tensions that hinder solutions, and the strategies adopted by actors to deliver successful outcomes, each chapter provides its own insights into this overall problematic. In Chapter 2, we provide a more specific categorisation of which problems arise in which specific chapter, and here we provide an overview of the cases we present and the main issues they raise for our research.

Chapter 3 presents the case of Agder, an old industrial region in the south of Norway seeking to capitalise on the growth benefits offered by Norway's booming oil and gas sector. A once highly regionally focused set of regional colleges were merged to create a new university. That university has faced the uncomfortable balancing act of establishing its academic bona fides in terms of globally excellent research whilst sustaining regional partners' political support. This chapter illustrates the limits to strategic approaches to university regional engagement and highlights the importance of allowing staff the flexibility to manage their own engagement activities.

Chapter 4 deals with the efforts in a region dominated by a set of low-technology processing and service industries, the Algarve, to profile itself as a knowledge region by building on competencies in its university and poly-technic. The main challenge for the Algarve has been the total dominance of all innovation policy processes by HEIs in the absence of other kinds of innovative actors. The universities have therefore had to carefully negotiate between dom-inating innovation policies and investments for their own benefits, and losing sight of their teaching and research activities. This chapter illustrates the mul-tiple roles that universities are sometimes called upon to play as a consequence of their internal complexity.

Chapter 5 presents the case of an extremely remote and sparsely populated Arctic region, Finnmark, in Norway's far north, which has suddenly been expected to become a knowledge-intensive region as part of Norway's wider geopolitical claims within the Barents region. Higher education colleges have long been a part of the national regional development strategy, but their merger into a single regional university college has revealed the limits to HEIs and regional development. The chapter illustrates their highly localised and place-specific nature, bringing benefits to the larger settlements but with almost no effect on the more remote inland and coastal locations most at threat from development trends.

Chapter 6 presents a case from the 'ordinary periphery', Telemark, lying just outside Norway's capital region, a region with an industrial history where there was a very low natural demand for higher-level and innovation skills. The cre-ation of a new university college has, as with Finnmark, had very localised benefits, but has not been able to change the overall regional development trajectory by addressing problems of demographic ageing, unemployment, and outmigration. The chapter illustrates that for some regions with smaller HEIs, the totalising nature of these problems can hinder taking the first steps towards regional engagement, highlighting that there is nothing wrong with very 'ordinary' modes of innovation in these ordinary regions.

In Chapter 7 we present the case of Vysočina in the Czech Republic, a region whose peripherality has also represented a real strength in terms of permitting a very high quality of life provided by a high level of environmental development and social capital. The regional development strategy therefore sought to leapfrog industrial development and find a way to transform the region into a post-industrial economy, thereby maintaining this high quality of life. The main issue this raises is that there is no strong regional pull for university knowledge activities, and this has left the region's HEI making many ad hoc contributions with no overall sense of how it could be 'regionally engaged'.

Although Chapter 8 is also drawn from the Czech Republic, it is hard to imagine a sharper contrast between Vysočina and Usti, a classic Eastern European region long dominated by heavy engineering and extractive industries but now seeking to upgrade those activities to provide a sustainable development path. Given that the University of Jan Evangelist Purkyne (UJEP) was only founded in 1991, it is perhaps surprising that it has been able to create a dominant position for itself in regional strategies, but it has established itself as a reliable, stable partner. The case highlights the need to create strategic institutional spaces where partners can meet, share ideas, and develop relationships that outlive policy and parliamentary cycles.

Chapter 9 looks at efforts by Estonia to diffuse the benefits of its more established universities to drive regional development in its periphery through creating a network of regional colleges with associated centres of excellence linked backed to the three main universities in Tallinn and Tartu. These were relatively small activities that created a bridge between urban university research groups and particular local industries that could use the university knowledge as part of their own upgrading and innovation efforts. The issue was in ensuring the degree of specificity and focus in the technology transfer activities with suitable teaching activities that had a salience beyond the immediate assisted firms.

Chapter 10 presents an example from a cross-border region, spanning the east of the Netherlands and western Germany, the EUREGIO, both regions once dominated by a textiles industry which disappeared from the late 1960s. The main potential benefits lie in developing cross-border activities with more cross-border fertilisation, but in this case these are continually undermined by pressures from their respective national systems that inhibit co-operation. The chapter highlights the importance of 'fuzzy governance spaces' for reconciling these tensions and allowing the creativity and flexibility to encourage knowledge spill-over across national borders.

The final empirical chapter, Chapter 11 presents a case study from a region that was once the best practice example of industrial transition, Tampere, in Finland, once the home of Nokia and a thriving ICT sector closely linked to regional HEIs. However, overspecialisation and lock-in led to the collapse of Nokia and also hurt other actors who had arranged their activities to closely align with Nokia. A similar regional coalition to that that had driven the first transformation emerged to try to create new development pathways. Universities found themselves having to balance between the urgent need to replace lost courses and research programmes to investing in activities that could support the newly emerging software services and automation sector.

Acknowledgements

This chapter received funding from the Norwegian Financial Mechanism 2009–2014 and the Ministry of Education, Youth and Sports under Project Contract No. MSMT-5397/2015. This chapter also reports findings from the RUNIN project (The Role of Universities in Innovation and Regional Development) that received funding from the European Union's Horizon 2020 research and innovation programme under Marie Skłodowska-Curie grant agreement No. 722295.

Note

1   There is some ambiguity about third-cycle provision in non-third-cycle institutions, such as the delivery in the UK of foundation degrees within Further Education colleges. There is some evidence that non-higher vocational colleges are starting to consider their regional role more systematically. In the Netherlands, there have been efforts – through for example the Centers of Innovative Craftsmanship – to build knowledge bases within the further education (Middle Professional Education) sector. Paralleling what has been done in Higher Professional Education these seek to educate better professionals by incorporating knowledge creation in syllabi in the form of applied research and reflection activities (OECD, 2014).

References

Akker, W. v. d., & Spaapen, J. (2017). *Productive interactions: Societal impact of academic research in the knowledge society*. Retrieved 17 April 2018, from www.leru.org/files/Productive-Interactions-Societal-Impact-of-Academic-Research-in-the-Knowledge-Society-Full-paper.pdf.

Asheim, B., Boschma, R., & Cooke, P. (2011). Constructing regional advantage: Platform policies based on related variety and differentiated knowledge bases. *Regional Studies, 45*(7), 893–904.

Asheim, B., Coenen, L., Moodysson, J., & Vang, J. (2007). Constructing knowledge-based regional advantage: Implications for regional innovation policy. *International Journal of Entrepreneurship and Innovation Management, 7*(2/3/4/5).

Becher, T., & Trowler, P. (2001). *Academic tribes and territories: Intellectual enquiry and the culture of disciplines*. New York: McGraw-Hill Education.

Benneworth, P., Charles, D., & Madanipour, A. (2010). Building localized interactions between universities and cities through university spatial development. *European Planning Studies, 18*(10), 1611–1629. doi:10.1080/09654313.2010.504345.

Benneworth, P., Irawati, D., Rutten, R., & Boekema, F. (2014). The social dynamics of innovation networks: From learning region to learning in socio-spatial context.

In R. Rutten, P. Benneworth, D. Irawati, & F. Boekema (Eds), *The social dynamics of innovation networks*. London: Routledge.

Benneworth, P., Young, M., & Normann, R. (2017). Between rigour and regional relevance? Conceptualising tensions in university engagement for socio-economic development. *Higher Education Policy, 30*(4).

Boschma, R. (2013). *Constructing regional advantage and smart specialization: Comparison of two European policy concepts*. Papers in Evolutionary Economic Geography (PEEG), Utrecht University, Section of Economic Geography.

Boschma, R. (2014). Towards an evolutionary perspective on regional resilience. *Regional Studies, 49*(5), 733–751.

Cooke, P. (2006). Constructing advantage in Preseli, Pembrokeshire. In J. Osmond (Ed.), *The Preseli papers*. Cardiff: Institute of Welsh Affairs.

Crespo, J., Balland, P.-A., Boschma, R., & Rigby, D. (2017). *Regional diversification opportunities and smart specialization strategies*. European Commission. Retrieved 17 April 2018, from https://ec.europa.eu/research/openvision/pdf/rise/crespo-balland-boschma-rigby_regional_diversification.pdf.

de Boer, H., File, J., Huisman, J., Seeber, M., Vukasovic, M., & Westerheijden, D. F. (2017). *Policy analysis of structural reforms in higher education: Processes and outcomes*. Cham: Springer International Publishing.

Etzkowitz, H., & Leydesdorff, L. (2000). The dynamics of innovation: From national systems and 'Mode 2' to a triple helix of university–industry–government relations. *Research Policy, 29*(2), 109–123. doi:10.1016/S0048-7333(99)00055-4.

European Commission. (2006). *Constructing regional advantage: Principles – perspectives – policies*. Retrieved 17 April 2018, from www.dime-eu.org/files/active/0/regional_advantage_FINAL.pdf.

European University Association. (2014). *The role of universities in Smart Specialisation Strategies*. Retrieved 17 April 2018, from http://eua.be/Libraries/publication/EUA_Seville_Report_web.pdf?sfvrsn=2.

Foray, D. (2017). *Smart Specialisation Strategies*. Paper presented at the 12th Regional Innovation Policies Conference, Santiago.

Foray, D., David, P., & Hall, B. (2009). *Smart specialisation – the concept*. Knowledge for Growth expert group, Europa. Retrieved 17 April 2018, from http://ec.europa.eu/invest-in-research/pdf/download_en/kfg_policy_brief_no9.pdf.

Foray, D., David, P., & Hall, B. (2011). *Smart specialisation: From academic idea to political instrument, the surprising career of a concept and the difficulties involved in its implementation*. MTEI working paper. Retrieved 17 April 2018, from https://pdfs.semanticscholar.org/29ad/6773ef30f362d7d3937c483003d974bc91c5.pdf.

Gunasekara, C. (2006). The generative and developmental roles of universities in regional innovation systems. *Science and Public Policy, 33*(2), 137–150.

Krücken, G., Kosmützky, A., & Torka, M. (2007). *Towards a multiversity? Universities between global trends and national traditions*. Bielefeld: Transcript Verlag.

Lagendijk, A., & Oinas, P. (2005). *Proximity, distance, and diversity: Issues on economic interaction and local development*. Aldershot, Hants, England: Ashgate.

Lewis, T., Marginson, S., & Snyder, I. (2005). The network university? Technology, culture and organisational complexity in contemporary higher education. *Higher Education Quarterly, 59*(1), 56–75.

McCann, P., & Ortega-Argilés, R. (2013a). Modern regional innovation policy. *Cambridge Journal of Regions, Economy and Society, 6*(2), 187–216.

McCann, P., & Ortega-Argilés, R. (2013b). Smart specialization, regional growth and applications to European Union cohesion policy. *Regional Studies, 49*(8), 1291–1302.

Moulaert, F., & Sekia, F. (2003). Territorial innovation models: A critical survey. *Regional Studies, 37*(3), 289–302.

OECD. (2007). *Understanding the regional contribution of higher education institutions: A literature review.* Retrieved 17 April 2018, from http://dx.doi.org/10.1787/161208155312.

OECD. (2014) *Territorial reviews: The Netherlands.* Paris: Organisation for Economic Co-operation and Development.

Pinheiro, R., Benneworth, P., & Jones, G. (Eds). (2012). *Universities and regional development: A critical assessment of tensions and contradictions.* London: Routledge.

Pugh, R. E. (2014). 'Old wine in new bottles'? Smart specialisation in Wales. *Regional Studies, Regional Science, 1*(1), 152–157.

Romer, P. M. (1994). The origins of endogenous growth. *Journal of Economic Perspectives, 8*(1), 3–22.

Salmi, J. (2009). *The challenge of establishing world-class universities.* World Bank.

Scott, P. (Ed.). (2007). Back to the future? The evolution of higher education systems. In B. Kehm (Ed.), *Looking back to look forward: Analyses of higher education after the turn of the millennium.* Kassel: INCHER.

Solow, R. (1994). Perspectives on growth theory. *Journal of Economic Perspectives, 8*(1), 45–54.

Temple, J. (1998). The new growth evidence. *Journal of Economic Literature, 37*(1), 112–156.

Uyarra, E. (2010a). Conceptualizing the regional roles of universities, implications and contradictions. *European Planning Studies, 18*(8), 1227–1246.

Uyarra, E. (2010b). What is evolutionary about 'regional systems of innovation'? Implications for regional policy. *Journal of Evolutionary Economics, 20*(1), 115–137.

Weick, K. E. (1976). Educational organizations as loosely coupled systems. *Administrative Science Quarterly, 21*(1), 1–19.

Yigitcanlar, T. (2010). Making space and place for the knowledge economy: Knowledge-based development of Australian cities. *European Planning Studies, 18*(11), 1769–1786.

2 Universities and neo-endogenous peripheral development

Towards a systematic classification

Lisa Nieth and Paul Benneworth

Introduction

In the previous chapter we argued that there are a variety of pressures in peripheral regions that can hinder universities from becoming involved in regional development. Nevertheless, as the empirical chapters in this book are able to compellingly demonstrate, there are universities managing to overcome these barriers and support processes of regional growth. In this volume, we seek to create a wider conceptual framework and a set of policy recommendations to better understand and ultimately shape the participation of universities in regional development processes. The challenge that all the regions in this volume face is that they are trying to radically change their course, whether it is Tampere (see Chapter 11) which is seeking to deal with the overnight closure of its largest industry, mobile telephony, or Vysočina (see Chapter 7) which is trying to build a service economy without driving industrialisation. This means that there are not always strong well-configured partners in the region articulating clear demands to which universities can respond. As Benneworth, Sanchez-Barrioluengo, and Pinheiro (2016) argue elsewhere there are no 'one-size-fits-all' models for understanding university contributions, so in this chapter, we seek to develop a more systematic classification of the ways in which universities do contribute, as well as the barriers and tensions around these contributions.

The starting point for this chapter is that we propose an evolutionary economic geography approach to understanding these regions' overall developmental trajectories. In this perspective, regional development is a process of change based on the contemporary structure, and the ways that different elements of that structure interact, grow, and evolve. In this perspective, these radical course changes in peripheral regions are conceptualised as switches of evolutionary path. What drives that path switching can be when new paths are created, when existing paths are altered, and when old redundant paths are killed off. These peripheral regions are in many cases locked-in to developmental pathways that do not lead to knowledge-based development, and yet regional partners lack the opportunities to create new paths – they are 'locked-in' (see Chapter 1). A clear opportunity for universities in peripheral regions is to contribute to breaking this lock-in as part of a wider 'coalition' of interested actors, in the public, private, and societal sectors.

But what the empirical chapters also demonstrate is that these coalitions are resource-restricted, and university resources may not always be compatible with or complementary to other regional assets. Universities face the challenge of investing substantially in activities for regional benefit that may in turn leave them overspecialised in regional-facing activities for which there is no obvious partner (see Chapter 11). Or universities might face other more urgent pressures (such as internationalisation) that see them unable to devote adequate resources to these local-facing activities (see Chapter 3). Universities might become unintentionally strategic actors in development processes, with other actors placing high expectations on them simply because they are so important to regional innovation processes (see Chapter 4). Smaller universities may have a primarily local, town-level impact, and for countries with large natural regions (such as Norway), they may face a tension in managing between this local and their wider regional impact (see Chapter 5). We therefore present a more systematic overview of the opportunities, the barriers, and the solutions that have been adopted to accommodate them, as a lens by which to read the empirical chapters that follow.

The evolutionary economic geography perspective

Economic geographers have increasingly come to realise that traditional economic analysis is inadequate to understand increasingly complex regional development processes. Evolutionary economic geography (EEG) (Boschma & Martin, 2010; Kogler, 2015) has emerged in response in order to understand and track regional adaptation and evolution capacities, conceptually combining regional science, geography of innovation, heterodox economics, and natural sciences. Kogler (2015, p. 709) argues that EEG "highlights the important factors that initiate, prevent or consolidate the contextual settings and relationships in which regions and their respective agents … change over time". EEG explains how regions self-transform from within according to place- and time-specific factors and processes (Boschma & Martin, 2010; Hassink, 2010). This focus on developmental transformation and the capacity to adapt allows what is an ostensibly hybrid nomothetic approach to provide comparative analysis. EEG focuses on regional-specific features that determine and shape whether some regions have been able to develop successfully and even renew themselves, while others have not (Gong & Hassink, 2017).

One of the main concepts within EEG is that the present configuration of individuals, entities, and localities is determined by past experiences and competencies, 'path dependency'. This concept explains phenomena like regional growth disparities, the development of specific technologies in certain locations, and the degree of adaptability of regions (Martin & Sunley, 2010). The long-term development of a region depends upon its capability "to diversify into new applications and new sectors while building on their current knowledge base and competences" (Tödtling & Trippl, 2012, p. 15). Understanding radical regional reorientation, the focus of this chapter, requires us to understand how paths of development can be renewed, formatted, or created in regions whilst accounting for their dependence on the past (sometimes referred to as 'creating a space for history' or 'taking history seriously' (Boschma & Martin, 2010; Martin & Sunley, 2010)).

Martin and Sunley (2010) define various ways of how new regional pathways can be created within regionally dependent development paths. Path creation is influenced by various variables, most significantly (a) whether the past trajectories are enabling or constraining, and (b) whether the origins of change are intended/deliberate or accidental (Table 2.1). This is a conceptual distinction to make, and in individual regions the situation will be influenced by a mixture of different and interwoven variables that have an impact on each other and might not be clearly separated easily. Meyer and Schubert (2007, p. 29) believe formation of new pathways can be found somewhere between "an emergent and completely unplanned process" and "deliberately and strategically controlled processes".

New sectors may evolve simply through creative breakthroughs unrelated to existing activities happening in the region (IV). Another mechanism might be that new activities emerge as off-shoots through innovations and discoveries in already existing industries, for example the way that ICT emerged out of electrical engineering industries (II). Existing companies might also create spinoffs/new companies that ultimately become more successful than the parent companies themselves (III). This case is specifically recurrent where large companies detect potentially promising new branches, but don't want to take the risk themselves (e.g. NXP spinning out of Philips). And finally, an external strong

Table 2.1 Varieties of path creation

(a) Place and path effects	(b) Origins of new path of development	
	Deliberate and intentional	*Chance and accidental*
Enabling new paths	I. Agents' search for opportunities, re- use resources, transfer competences as basis of new growth	II. Agents gain assets and experience, but accidents and events trigger new path
Constraining to existing path	III. Designed interventions to break path or switch location to overcome lock- in	IV. Unpredictable external shocks and random events break old trajectory and launch new path

Source: Authors' own articulation from Martin and Sunley (2010).

technology firm might choose to locate in another region and create an organic cluster around itself (I).

Tödtling and Trippl (2012) attribute path transformation to the cumulative outcome of actions and events involving diverse actors from within and outside the region, proposing three key paths. *Path renewal* implies the upgrading or revitalisation of an existing industry, with a specific industry's trajectory changing without a totalising shift in the regional industrial structure. This modification can take different forms and is commonly linked to changes in the regional knowledge infrastructure (for instance, firms introduce new technologies or update existing ones due to the knowledge exchange with a newly established HEI). More significant change is achieved through *path formation*, where a region's economic base is broadened: this may be driven exogenously (for instance through investment from actors outside the region) or endogenously (for instance through the activities of diversification of existing firms). Finally, *path creation* infers a substantial shift in the regional development trajectory, often from previous or existing paths (Martin & Simmie, 2008; Martin & Sunley, 2010), with new pathways created as new industries arise out of changes in technological and organisational structures. This "requires the existence of assets, resources or competencies rooted in the area" (Tödtling & Trippl, 2012, p. 6) such as a highly skilled work force or an excellent scientific base.

Regional lock-in and peripheral regions

Although path dependence is not necessarily problematic for a region, particularly for regions with high-technology industries that are performing well, it can be highly problematic for others when there is an opportunity cost that path continuation in one sector prevents a diversification into other sectors. In the case of the pharmaceuticals industry, path dependence may be positive in leading to path continuation, as has been seen with the emergence of biotech industries. But what has also been observed in other regions is that declining industries seek to secure their own survival, and fail, rather than pursuing new interests and innovations. It has been empirically observed that, in these situations, the declining sectors can influence policy-makers to support the attempts at path continuation, rather than investing in new sectors, what is commonly referred to as lock-in. In work predating the rise of EEG, the coal, iron, and steel industry in German Ruhr in the 1970s and 1980s became 'locked-in' to its past trajectory and was prevented from overcoming this path dependency as "strongly embedded regional networks turned from ties that bind to ties that blind" (Grabher, 1993, p. 24). Hassink (2010, p. 450) defines this regional lock-in state, as situations in which "initial strengths based on geography and networks, such as industrial atmosphere, highly specialized infrastructure, close inter-firm relations and strong support by regional institutions, turned into barriers to innovation". These conditions are said to occur most frequently in less advanced regions like old industrial or peripheral regions.

Tödtling and Trippl (2005) differentiate between the three kinds of problems that can limit regions' capacity to create new innovations: as well as this problem of lock-in, they identify that problems may be caused by a shortage of actors (institutional thinness) or fragmentation (where partners are unwilling to co-operate because of internal boundaries). The kinds of peripheral regions with which this volume is concerned are, as will be seen, facing primarily problems from their organisational and institution thinness as well as lock-in. These situations are typified by the absence of strong overlapping clusters, a shortage of development agencies able to mobilise clusters of innovation, and whose economies are dominated by sectors with low innovation levels often primarily in smaller firms mainly concerned with incremental innovation. HEIs in these regions may be part of the institutional thinness, offering medium- or low-level qualifications, and with few key knowledge competencies on which to base effective knowledge transfer services, which are rarely closely linked to regional knowledge demands.

Universities have received much attention as knowledge capital creators and circulators (Yigitcanlar, 2010), that are expected to contribute to the region and have a significant impact on its development (OECD, 2007). Nevertheless, universities are often oversimplified as institutions that are strategic and manageable organisations, underplaying the difficulties universities face in developing and implementing (external and internal) missions or strategies of universities (Pinheiro, Benneworth, & Jones, 2012; Uyarra, 2010). Although universities could potentially play active, constructive roles in creating new regional futures, the tensions they face hinder making those contributions and restrict them all too often to directly contributing academic knowledge (Benneworth, Coenen, Moodysson, & Asheim, 2009).

A first challenge is the fact that many times the academic knowledge of universities is not in line with the knowledge that could help the region, thereby transforming universities into 'cathedrals in the desert' (Morgan, 1997). Charles (2016) explains that it can be even more difficult for universities in rural/peripheral regions to support the local economy, because businesses tend to be smaller, the economic base is diverse, and because there tends to be a lower presence of knowledge institutions. Clear articulation of what is demanded by business and industry is a prerequisite for any interaction or knowledge transfer, which specifically SMEs (often the main economic players in peripheral regions) cannot live up to. Jongbloed, Enders, and Salerno (2008) argue that SMEs face particular challenges when they articulate their needs properly, often hindering successful knowledge exchange.

In Table 2.2, we identify the kinds of problems that can lead to lock-in and path dependency in peripheral regions, and link them to the tensions and challenges this can pose for universities in these regions.

With the increasing emphasis on public sector actors supporting these path-shifting processes with deliberate policy interventions, there is an increasing assumption that public policy actors will mobilise groups of regional partners who will deliberatively reflect and make choices to break locked-in paths and

Table 2.2 Possible challenges for peripheral regions identified by diverse scholars

Tensions that can lead to lock-in situations in peripheral regions	Author
• Lack of actors and support organisations that enhance technological change and innovation • SME dominance	Tödtling and Trippl (2005)
• Less developed in terms of the innovation interface backed by the resources and support necessary for networking, training, technological transfer, and other knowledge support systems	Doloreux and Dionne (2008)
• Mismatch between the regional supply of innovation and the demand for it	Cooke, Boekholt, and Tödtling (2000)
• Small-scale innovations that are incremental in nature • Innovation takes place through the application of existing knowledge or through new combinations of knowledge	Asheim and Coenen (2005)

• Fewer possibilities of entrepreneurial growth due to:
  • the comparative absence of regional competition;
  • the limited scale and scope of local market opportunities;
  • the distance from the largest/larger markets.
	North and Smallbone (2000)

Tensions/challenges related to the role of universities	Author
• Cooperation and transfer of technologies between R&D centres, HEI, and the private sector are less developed	Doloreux (2003)
• Imbalance in science and technology in favour of the public sector, the academic sector in particular	Landabaso and Reid (1999)
• Few or low-profile knowledge generation and diffusion through universities/research organisations • Education/training with an emphasis on low- to medium-level qualifications • 'Thin' structure of knowledge transfer; lack of more specialised services, often too little orientation on demand	Tödtling and Trippl (2005)

Source: Authors' own elaboration.

create new development trajectories (see Chapter 1). Asheim, Boschma, and Cooke (2001) conceptualise this process as 'constructing regional advantage', whilst the concept of 'entrepreneurial discovery' is central to Europe's smart specialisation activities (McCann & Ortega-Argilés, 2013). In this book, we focus on the dynamics of these groups of actors seeking to create new positive regional futures, which following Benneworth (2007) we refer to as regional

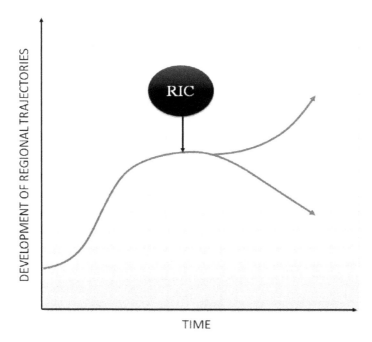

Figure 2.1 The role of RICs in developing new trajectories
Source: Authors' own elaboration.

innovation coalitions, that exert what Sotorauta (2014) has called soft regional leadership in these creative processes.

These 'regional innovation coalitions' are groups of actors from different organisations (regional authorities, companies, universities, etc.) who work together around this collective creative process. Lester and Sotorauta (2007) highlighted how the regional innovation coalition of the Tampere region constructed a new future for itself following the collapse of the Finnish economy in the early 1990s. They highlighted how various coalitions worked as "strong mobilizing forces" and reached common goals, like the attraction of a new regional university which later played a major role in the region's development (Lester & Sotorauta, 2007). These coalitions come together at a particular point in time and seek to steer the regional trajectory, ideally leading to an upgrading process through path extension and creation.

How can universities contribute to new path trajectories in peripheral regions?

When looking at the role of universities from an EEG perspective, we can see that universities are actors that do create new development paths, stimulate the transition from old to new paths, and help to avoid lock-in scenarios (Benneworth, Young, & Normann, 2017). Universities are important within regional innovation coalitions seeking to create new regional pathways, and their constituent of academics can be proactive in establishing, developing, and even leading specific coalitions. However, Benneworth and Pinheiro (2015) highlight that the process of creating these type of strategic partnerships is not straightforward as stakeholders within coalitions are very heterogenous, have different goals, and make their own strategic decisions depending on variables defined by themselves. Therefore, synergies and a supportive environment for all participants need to be created for strategic management to work successfully.

Lagendijk and Cornford (2000, p. 210) highlight that knowledge is seen as being "highly tacit, localised and untraded, embedded in localised networks of individuals and institutions" and therefore has the potential to form specific competitive advantage of a particular region. The coalitions are vital here, because this knowledge can be advanced and exchanged within them. But it is not only the exchange of knowledge that matters, but also the creation of new knowledge within these 'knowledge communities'. The new knowledge created through cooperation is also made available to other regional partners, a process that upgrades the region significantly (Benneworth & Pinheiro, 2015).

Any kinds of renewal, formation, and creation processes are directly related to changes in the knowledge infrastructure, in which universities can represent major players (Tödtling & Trippl, 2012). Path renewal is directly linked to changes in the knowledge infrastructure of the region, and may see new HEIs being created to support emerging sectors with highly skilled staff and knowledge transfer. New path formation may be associated with HEIs if they have particular technological breakthroughs that can be exploited closely, if they help bring new technologies into the region to create new sectors, or if firms and universities work together closely and dynamically to drive forward the technological frontier through the creation of these new sectors. Path creation, as the most fundamental method of change "preconditions a major transformation of the regional knowledge infrastructure" (Tödtling & Trippl, 2012, p. 7), often by regional universities being actively reconfigured by the emerging new sector, or supported with the location of particular government-funded research laboratories that can complement what universities and other HEIs can contribute.

We see here an additional dimension of the problem for peripheral regions, in that universities are not expected to do this by themselves, but instead are dependent on well-configured regional partners to push the universities to reflect on these evolving economic circumstances. Table 2.3 sets out some of the tensions in peripheral regions, potential university contributions, and the way that these situations have played out in the empirical material that follows.

Table 2.3 Possible responses of universities to lock-in scenarios

Tensions that can lead to lock-in situations in peripheral regions	University contribution to ease lock-in and transform pathways	Lessons from the empirical chapters
• lack of actors and support organisations • SME dominance	• upgrading of the capacity of existing SMEs and creating improvements in the regional skills base through offering specialised courses that are in line with the needs of regional companies	Chapter 4: when HEIs in the Algarve became too dominant, they were part of the lock-in and so addressing the lock-in demanded addressing institutional needs. Chapter 11: Tampere: an informal regional innovation coalition helping new ICT companies to move away from the shadow of Nokia; the innovative Demola platform and new incubation activities. Chapter 5: Finnmark brought primarily local benefits to the towns and villages it was located in, and its impact on the more rural parts of the region is more restricted.
• mismatch between the regional supply of innovation and the demand for it • less developed in terms of the innovation interface: incremental small-scale innovations, innovation through the application of existing knowledge/through new combinations of knowledge	• focus research on regional contents • make research agreements with regional actors	Chapter 6: Telemark benefits from having lots of small campuses each with a distinct profile tailored to local needs. Chapter 3: although the university management in Agder found the pressures difficult, there were staff who nevertheless found their own effective way to collaborate. Chapter 8: the creation of a strategic regional space to allow the HEI in Usti to bring together several small activities to add up to a 'regional contribution'.
• cooperation and transfer of technologies less developed • few or low-profile knowledge generation and diffusion • education/training with an emphasis on low- to medium-level qualifications • 'thin' structure of knowledge transfer • lack of more specialised services, often too little orientation on demand	• creation of a suitable business support infrastructure (technology transfer centres, regional development agencies, universities, etc.) with active participation of the university • knowledge exchange in regional innovation coalitions led by universities • creation of new kinds of knowledge in coalitions and sharing this knowledge	Chapter 7: the role of the university in building social capital and supporting effective regional institutions in Vysočina. Chapter 9: creating regional competence centres in Estonian regional colleges to improve local innovation systems. Chapter 10: the role of HEI institutional entrepreneurs in breaking down internal boundaries in regional innovation systems.

Source: Authors' own elaboration.

Conclusions

This chapter has proposed a conceptual framework for understanding the contribution of universities to regional economic development in peripheral regions, specifically focusing on the ways they contribute to path-breaking processes as well as the barriers they can face. These barriers and potentials interface in different ways in different regions, so in order to provide a commonality to the very different regional chapters, we propose three main areas of attention for regional studies of university contributions. The first relates to the challenge of institutional thinness, and the way that universities operate as institutional actors in the periphery. The second relates to the challenges of fragmentation, and in particular when there are not automatic synergies and matches between regional innovators and the knowledge base in regional HEIs. The third relates to the institutional entrepreneurial nature of universities, and the repertoires they exercise in peripheral regions to create new innovation support activities in what are otherwise institutionally sparse environments. These three areas of focus, and potential policy responses to them, are returned to in the final two chapters of this volume.

The first area of interest relates to the nature of universities as institutions, and the way that they operate in peripheral regions. It is not that universities are always part of innovative coalitions: in sparse regions they may actually be so tightly linked to old sectors and practices that they are actually part of the lock-in. These innovative coalitions do not have to be formal and work around particular planning processes; the case of Tampere illustrates how the informality of the new coalitions was vital in order to allow it not to be disrupted by the collapse of the old industry, so it is important not to reduce these activities and the necessary institutional leadership to purely administrative structures. Finally, universities have strongly local benefits but may have only weakly regional benefits, and that can create problems for regional innovation coalitions in which it becomes assumed that outlying municipalities and communities will be pleased at towns and universities deciding strategies that primarily benefit these places.

The second issue relates to a common problem in the periphery, namely that HEIs rarely have precisely the correct skills and knowledge portfolio that is demanded by existing regional clusters, nor do they have the competencies to create new clusters to exploit that relevant knowledge. We see a number of cases where regional HEIs have emerged out of the amalgamation of many local colleges into HEIs, whilst allowing them to retain their local rather than regional orientation. Of course this can create a strategic problem at the level of the university, in terms of how those divergent campuses can be united under a common strategic vision. The case studies show that the absence of a strategy for the university need not be a problem for those academics who are engaging regionally. What a good strategy or regional plan can do, however, is allow the university to create a bigger narrative around lots of tiny fragmented activities and help connect them up more effectively to potential regional beneficiaries.

The final element relates to the way that universities are not just transferring technologies, but through acts of what we might consider as institutional entrepreneurship, creating new kinds of assets and networks that raise the overall quality of the regional innovation coalition. They can help to build a common regional culture and to build social capital, and build more general support for the collaborative approach demanded by these new creative innovation methodologies. They can create new kinds of regional innovation intermediaries, most archetypically being the regional competence centres in the Estonian regional colleges which were so highly specialised to local activities that they did not demand substantive additional investments from the already stretched regional colleges. Finally, universities can work to break down boundaries in fragmented regional innovation systems, the most obvious example here being in the EUREGIO, where dynamic and engaged HEI academics and leaders were able to build projects, networks, and relationships across the national borders despite very strong disincentives arising from different national systems for education, research, and innovation.

Acknowledgement

This chapter received funding from the Norwegian Financial Mechanism 2009–2014 and the Ministry of Education, Youth and Sports under Project Contract No. MSMT-5397/2015. This chapter also reports findings from the RUNIN project (The Role of Universities in Innovation and Regional Development) that received funding from the European Union's Horizon 2020 research and innovation programme under Marie Skłodowska-Curie grant agreement No. 722295.

References

Asheim, B. T., Boschma, R., & Cooke, P. (2011) Constructing regional advantage: Platform policies based on related variety and differentiated knowledge bases. *Regional Studies, 45*(7), 893–904.

Asheim, B., & Coenen, L. (2005). Knowledge bases and regional innovation systems: Comparing Nordic clusters. *Research Policy, 34*(8), 1173–1190.

Benneworth, P. (2007). *Leading innovation: building effective regional coalitions for innovation.* Retrieved 16 December 2007, from www.nesta.org.uk/sites/default/files/leading_innovation.pdf.

Benneworth, P., Coenen, L., Moodysson, J., & Asheim, B. (2009). Exploring the multiple roles of Lund University in strengthening Scania's regional innovation system: Towards institutional learning? *European Planning Studies, 17*(11), 1645–1664.

Benneworth, P., & Pinheiro, R. (2015). *Involving universities in regional upgrading in the periphery.* CHEPS Working Paper 10/2015. University of Twente, Enschede.

Benneworth, P. S., Sanchez-Barrioluengo, M. S., & Pinheiro, R. (2016). One size does not fit all! New perspectives on the university in the social knowledge economy. *Science and Public Policy*, 43(6), 731–735. doi:10.1093/scipol/scw018.

Benneworth, P., Young, M., & Normann, R. (2017). Between rigour and regional relevance? Conceptualising tensions in university engagement for socio-economic development. *Higher Education Policy, 30*(4).

Boschma, R., & Martin, R. (2010). The aims and scope of evolutionary economic geography. In R. Boschma & R. Martin (Eds), *The handbook of evolutionary economic geography*. Cheltenham, UK: Edward Elgar Publishing.

Charles, D. (2016). The rural university campus and support for rural innovation. *Science and Public Policy, 43*(6), 763–773.

Cooke, P., Boekholt, P., & Tödtling, F. (2000). *The governance of innovation in Europe: regional perspectives on global competitiveness.* London: Pinter.

Doloreux, D. (2003). Regional innovation systems in the periphery: The case of the Beauce in Québec (Canada). *International Journal of Innovation Management, 07*(01), 67–94.

Doloreux, D., & Dionne, S. (2008). Is regional innovation system development possible in peripheral regions? Some evidence from the case of La Pocatière, Canada. *Entrepreneurship & Regional Development, 20*(3), 259–283.

Gong, H., & Hassink, R. (2017). Regional resilience: The critique revisited. In N. Williams & T. Worley (Eds), *Creating resilient economies: Entrepreneurship, growth and development in uncertain times* (pp. 288). Cheltenham, UK: Edward Elgar Publishing.

Grabher, G. (1993). The weakness of strong ties: The lock-in of regional development in the Ruhr area. In G. Grabher (Ed.), *The embedded firm: On the socioeconomics of industrial networks.* London: Routledge.

Hassink, R. (2010). Locked in decline? On the role of regional lock-ins in old industrial areas. In R. Boschma & R. Martin (Eds), *The handbook of evolutionary economic geography.* Cheltenham, UK: Edward Elgar Publishing.

Jongbloed, B., Enders, J., & Salerno, C. (2008). Higher education and its communities: Interconnections, interdependencies and a research agenda. *Higher Education, 56*(3), 303–324.

Kogler, D. F. (2015). Editorial: Evolutionary economic geography – theoretical and empirical progress. *Regional Studies, 49*(5), 705–711.

Lagendijk, A., & Cornford, J. (2000). Regional institutions and knowledge: Tracking new forms of regional development policy. *Geoforum, 31*, 209–218.

Landabaso, M., & Reid, A. (1999). Developing regional innovation strategies: The European Commission as animator. In K. Morgan & C. Nauwelaars (Eds), *Regional innovation strategies: Key challenge for Europe's less favoured regions* (pp. 19–39). London: The Stationary Office.

Lester, R., & Sotarauta, M. (Eds). (2007). *Innovation, universities, and the competitiveness of regions.* Helsinki: Tekes.

McCann, P., & Ortega-Argilés, R. (2013). Modern regional innovation policy. *Cambridge Journal of Regions, Economy and Society, 6*(2), 187–216. doi:10.1093/cjres/rst007.

Martin, R., & Simmie, J. (2008). Path dependence and local innovation systems in city-regions. *Innovation: Management, Policy & Practice, 10*(2–3), 183–196.

Martin, R., & Sunley, P. (2010). The place of path dependence in an evolutionary perspective on the economic landscape. In R. Boschma & R. Martin (Eds), *The handbook of evolutionary economic geography* (pp. 576). Cheltenham, UK: Edward Elgar Publishing.

Meyer, U., & Schubert, C. (2007). Integrating path dependency and path creation in a general understanding of path constitution: The role of agency and institutions in the stabilisation of technological innovations. *Science, Technology & Innovation Studies, 3.*

Morgan, K. (1997). The learning region: Institutions, innovation and regional renewal. *Regional Studies, 31*(5), 491–503.

North, D., & Smallbone, D. (2000). Innovative activity in SMEs and rural economic development: Some evidence from England. *European Planning Studies, 8*(1), 87–106.

OECD. (2007). *Understanding the regional contribution of higher education institutions: A literature review.* Retrieved 17 April 2018, from http://dx.doi.org/10.1787/161208155312.

Pinheiro, R., Benneworth, P., & Jones, G. (Eds). (2012). *Universities and regional development: A critical assessment of tensions and contradictions.* London: Routledge.

Sotarauta, M. (2014). Reflections on 'Mobilizing leadership in cities and regions', *Regional Studies, Regional Science, 1*(1), 28–31.

Tödtling, F., & Trippl, M. (2005). One size fits all?: Towards a differentiated regional innovation policy approach. *Research Policy, 34*(8), 1203–1219.

Tödtling, F., & Trippl, M. (2012). *Transformation of regional innovation systems: From old legacies towards new development paths.* Paper presented at the 52nd Congress of the European Regional Science Association: 'Regions in Motion – Breaking the Path', Bratislava, Slovakia. Retrieved 17 April 2018, from http://hdl.handle.net/10419/120516.

Uyarra, E. (2010). Conceptualizing the regional roles of universities, implications and contradictions. *European Planning Studies, 18*(8), 1227–1246.

Yigitcanlar, T. (2010). Making space and place for the knowledge economy: Knowledge-based development of Australian cities. *European Planning Studies, 18*(11), 1769–1786.

3   Towards a strategic alignment

Regional challenges and university
tensions in peripheral geographies

Rómulo Pinheiro

Introduction

Universities located in peripheral regions face two major challenges. The first
challenge pertains to path dependencies and the endogenous nature of the
region (Lambooy & Boschma, 2001). In contrast to more dynamic geographies,
peripheral regions face difficulties in moving from one economic model to
another (Lagendijk & Lorentzen, 2007), often resulting in 'lock-in' effects
(Crespo, Suire, & Vicente, 2014). The second challenge is internal to the universities, referring to resource dependencies and legitimacy issues (Oleksiyenko,
2012). Universities located in less central or dynamic geographies are heavily
dependent on recruiting regional student audiences and face difficulties in
attracting talented students and staff (Charles, 2001), who tend to converge to
more cosmopolitan/urban settings (Smith, Glasson, & Chadwick, 2005). Largely
due to their institutional profiles, more geared towards professional/vocational
fields and applied research, universities located in peripheral regions also suffer
from a 'legitimacy deficit' in terms of market reputation or status (Dahllöf &
Selander, 1994). They are often perceived by the established university players
and other stakeholders in the domestic higher education field as 'second rate',
not 'real universities' in the classic sense (Pinheiro, 2012).

Research on universities and regional development is increasingly beginning to stress the importance of the nature of the university organisation for
the way that those regional impacts are produced. This work dates back to the
1990s, when Burton Clark (1998) pointed to the five critical elements of a
university organisation that were necessary in order for it to become entrepreneurial, including strategic leadership and an empowered academic community. Clark identified the importance of engagement infrastructure within
universities, what he called the 'extended development periphery', as an essential part of universities creating regional impacts. More recent research identified that what is important is the way that those elements cohere to give what
Goddard first referred to as a 'strategic interface' between universities and their
surrounding regions (Chatterton & Goddard, 2000; Goddard, 1997). In these
activities, universities come together with regional partners to plan strategic
co-operation around joint projects and activities and dovetail their investment

plans and ongoing activities to collectively deliver regionally beneficial outputs (OECD, 2007). Indeed, most recently, Goddard and Vallance (2013) have argued that strategic co-operations are leading to the reinvention of the idea of the university with a more explicit territorial leadership role, what they call the 'civic university'.

This body of work, however, has been critiqued by some as not taking into consideration the fact that both universities and regions are complex entities and are faced with a multiplicity of tensions that, when taken together, are likely to determine the nature and scope of regional engagement (Pinheiro, Benneworth, & Jones, 2012a). The dual challenges of excellence and relevance in research are not easily resolved, particularly in the case of higher education institutions (HEIs) that have more traditionally had a 'relevant' profile (Perry, 2012). Pinheiro *et al.* (Pinheiro, Benneworth, & Jones, 2012c; Pinheiro, Benneworth, & Jones, 2015) suggest that, before any strategic interface can occur, it is imperative to, first, take into account the distinct nature of the entities in question (universities and regions), and second, take stock of the key challenges facing each of these entities. There is a risk that these practical tensions for co-operation are downplayed as this idea of university-regional co-operation becomes regarded as straightforward, and ultimately undermining the effectiveness of that co-operation. Likewise, there is often an assumption made that a strategy is sufficient; whilst although it may be an important first step, it is not sufficient to change academic behaviour (Breznitz & Feldman, 2012; Gunasekara, 2006). Pinheiro (2012) demonstrated that successfully institutionalising the third mission requires a wider set of structural mechanisms at multiple levels; from national policy to institutional strategies to departmental cultures.

Peripheral regions are often regions that have substantive policy problems that cannot easily be solved, and therefore this places additional pressure on seeking to develop those university-regional partnerships. Why would a university that is seeking to perform and excel choose to work together with regional partners that themselves may be suffering problems? This issue of how peripherality undermines university-regional co-operation is the subject of this chapter, which seeks to provide an overview of the kinds of tensions that arise in strategic interfaces between universities and peripheral regions. This chapter specifically poses two research questions, namely:

1. *What are the main challenges and/or tensions that the local university and the region face?*
2. *To what extent do these tensions determine the strategic interface between the university and the surrounding region?*

To address these two questions, we use a case study from Southern Norway, Kristiansand; its university was formed through a merger of several regional colleges and has been seeking to demonstrate its quality as a global institution, whilst industry and local government in the region have sought increasing impacts from the university. First, we provide an overview of the key challenges facing Southern Norway as a region. We then move on to shed light on the methodological aspects underpinning the study. Next, in the fourth section, we illuminate the sets of tensions facing the university and the surrounding region. This is followed by a discussion of the possibilities for moving from internal tensions toward an external (strategic) alignment against the backdrop of recent developments. Finally, we conclude our analysis by providing a series of recommendations, including on future research endeavours.

The regional challenge in Southern Norway

Southern Norway, or 'Agder', as it is commonly known, is home to around 300,000, representing 5.7% of Norway's total population; Norway's mountainous geography means that the majority of this population live along the coastline. Although just 300 km from Norway's capital of Oslo, this geography has also meant that the region has remained peripheral within the Norwegian economy. Administratively, the region is split between the two counties of East and West Agder, reflecting a cultural cleavage between the more industrialised east (around the city of Grimstad) and the more conservative-religious west (centred around Kristiansand). Most recently, the national government decided to merge these counties into a single county, part of a much wider set of national administrative reforms seeking to create fewer, larger, and ultimately more efficient regions. The region hosts a number of energy-intensive industry clusters, most notably around the gas and oil equipment and the process (aluminum) industries, as well as in areas of ICT as well as being a popular (domestic) tourist destination during the summer and host to many music festivals.

The University of Ager was formally awarded university status in 2007, as the culmination of a process of merger and upgrading of a number of traditional tertiary vocational colleges located in the Agder region since the 1960s (see the third section for more details). The orientation of these colleges reflected the underlying economic structures of their cities, with Grimstad in the industrial east hosting an engineering college, and Kristiansand in the west providing training for schools, local hospitals, and public administration. Prior to 2007, these were almost exclusively teaching activities without a formal research role, although there was extensive engagement with external actors as part of delivering their wider mission. This research mission was upgraded in the mid-1990s when the organisation that emerged from these mergers was granted university college title, and became a key element of the institutional mission when full university status was achieved in 2007. UiA has recognised expertise in the technical field of mechatronics (based in Grimstad campus), of relevance to local industries. It also has world class expertise in the fields of mathematics education and disaster management. UiA's latest strategic plan sets out the importance of working with external partners to its own institutional mission. "UiA seeks to be an open and inclusive university that is characterized by a culture of cooperation. Knowledge is successfully co-created when staff, students and the larger community challenge each other" (UiA, 2016).

Less than 10% of the local working population is involved with knowledge intensive industries, defined in terms of those industries which are typically highly intensive in their inputs of human capital and technology. The inputs for knowledge intensive industries in Agder are relatively weak. The levels of tertiary education attainment (particularly long term, i.e. more than 3 years) are below the national average (c. 35% of employees in Agder have a university education compared with 48% in Trondheim and 55% in the greater Oslo) (SSB, 2016). R&D investments per capita are likewise relatively low, 4,300 NOK per inhabitant in 2015, compared with 18,000 NOK for Oslo and 14,500 NOK for the Trondheim region (Gunnes, Sandven, & Spilling, 2015). At the same time, the region hosts a number of globally competitive firms operating in key niche markets. Earlier studies have shown that local small and medium sized firms (many of them family owned) largely rely on customer interaction and experiential knowledge as the basis for innovation (Aslesen, Isaksen, & Karlsen, 2012). The region has become increasingly dependent on the oil and gas industry as a customer for its technology; the recent decline in oil prices has reduced investments by the oil and gas sector and that has impacted heavily on Agder's offshore sector. As a result, regional unemployment, including amongst high skilled workers (engineers), has increased considerably and remains well above the national average despite a degree of stabilisation in the oil prices.

The regional labour market faces a number of challenges in adapting to contemporary circumstances, which come together to create a discouragement for highly skilled individuals to move to the Agder region. The regional culture, which is rather conservative in nature (particularly its western part), has been more resistant to gender equity in the labour market than other Norwegian regions, with a female employment rate of 61% (many of whom are on a part-time basis) compared to the national average of 65%. In addition, there are relatively high drop-out rates in upper secondary schooling and high levels of psychiatric disorders amongst young adults. Despite the presence of many foreign workers (many of whom possess high levels of higher education), the region has not been able to develop a distinct international profile. Agder is not seen as an attractive region for talented individuals, including ambitious youth from within the region who tend to migrate to the larger and more cosmo politan urban areas like Bergen, Trondheim, and Oslo. These various elements combine together to create a discouragement effect for the regional labour market, and which ultimately serve to decrease the amount of human capital available for the region to develop and upgrade its knowledge intensive activities.

This chapter therefore focuses specifically on the human capital problem of Agder, and in particular, the extent to which the local university is capable of providing knowledge, skills, and competencies that will enable the region to diversify economically. One important role for universities emerging from evolutionary economic geography is in helping to cross-fertilise existing industries with new skills that can help with the emergence of new industries by assisting with the provision of related variety (Neffke, Henning, & Boschma,

2011). By driving diversity in the industrial base, the economy as a whole is less vulnerable to particular shocks, such as the recent decline in global oil prices, and thus becomes more resilient to external events and circumstances (Martin, 2012). This chapter therefore seeks to look at the role played by the University of Agder in attracting and retaining highly talented individuals for the regional labour market. The chapter specifically focuses on the challenges (referred to here as tensions and dilemmas) that it has raised for the university in seeking to position itself as a more globally oriented university rather than a traditional locally embedded vocational college.

To address the overarching research question, our study adopts a case study research design (Yin, 2009), focusing on the interface between the case university and its surrounding region. Our data gathered approach is multi-method (Morse, 2003), based on semi-structured interviews (undertaken in late 2015 and early 2016) with selected university actors (unit and central levels) and regional stakeholders, following a purposive sampling and snowball approach, in the context of regional engagement and development. In addition, a desk-top analysis of official statistics and policy reports was undertaken, complemented by key insights from earlier studies on the topic, many of which the author of this chapter was directly involved with (Hauge, Wærdahl, Pinheiro, Kathrine, & Zyzak, 2013; Hauge, Pinheiro, & Zyzak, 2016; Johnsen, Normann, & Pinheiro, 2017; Karlsen, Flåten, Isaksen, Pinheiro, & Zyzak, 2013; Pinheiro, Normann, & Johnsen, 2017). Both the selection of interviewees and the interview guide used were developed in the scope of an international comparative project investigating the developmental role of universities in peripheral regions in Norway and the Czech Republic.[1]

Tensions and dilemmas facing the local university

The University of Agder (UiA) became a fully fledged university in 2007, and in the Norwegian context is a mid-sized university (2017) enrolling about 12,000 students (70% of whom emanate from the region) and employing close to 1,200 staff members, 57% of whom are involved with core teaching and research activities. UiA has seven core units[2] and its core activities are spread across two separate campuses (about 40 km from each other). Given the funding base for Norwegian higher education, and as is the case of most mid-size institutions in Norway, the strategic focus in the last decade has been two-fold, driven by output based funding measures introduced in Norway since 2004. The first has been in securing and sustaining growth in student numbers and graduation rates. The second has been on fostering the scientific profile of the university, and more specifically in increasing the number of scientific publications in the context of publication based financing in Norway. UiA has been highly successful on both fronts, increasing the number of enrolled students by 60% and its publication output by 300% in the last decade. These urgent demands on the university have led to the emergence of a number of tensions and dilemmas for it. As most mid-size universities in Norway and elsewhere (Pinheiro, 2012;

Pinheiro *et al.*, 2012c), UiA is facing a major dilemma on how best to articulate its regional mandate in ways that are supportive of, and directly contribute towards, its core functions and overall institutional profile whilst simultaneously enhancing its national and global competitiveness (Benneworth, 2012; Pinheiro, 2013).

The first dilemma relates to the difficulties that exist in coming up with a singular vision and structure for engagement in a university that faces very divergent pressures for change. UiA's teaching profile is strongly oriented towards professional and higher vocational courses, with the bulk of students being enrolled at the undergraduate level. The research profile has seen some pockets of research excellence emerge around a number of high profile individuals and research groups in fields like mechatronics, wind energy, math education, crisis management, etc. However, and despite the transformation of its publication outcomes, UiA still has a reputation as a relatively weak research institution when compared to the more established domestic universities, notably the Universities of Oslo and Bergen and the Norwegian University of Science and Technology at Trondheim. When it comes to regional engagement (the third mission), the data suggest that there is a general willingness by academics at all departments to collaborate with external actors across the public and private sectors; around 5% of the total university income is derived from external income (Sima, Beseda, Benneworth, & Pinheiro, 2017). At the same time, there has been a relatively low level of institutionalisation of this engagement.

Certainly there is an almost total absence of incentives (whether provided nationally or at the university level) for academics to engage with regional actors, with Sima *et al.* estimating that around 10 full-time equivalents (FTEs) in the entire university are allocated towards managing the business of regional engagement and partner relationships. The interviews revealed that there was confusion amongst UiA academics on what precisely 'engagement' was supposed to mean and regarding the expectations from management in this regard. One particular area of confusion was that the linkages (coupling) between teaching and research activities and third mission endeavours were largely weak or non-existent, with engagement occurring in a rather ad-hoc and unco-ordinated manner. That engagement was also heavily individualised, based on informal networks and short term initiatives rather than any comprehensive long term strategic plan or framework.[3]

Secondly, these internal challenges are also affected by the fast changing domestic and international higher education and science landscapes, which place a stronger emphasis on teaching quality, research excellence, and global competitiveness (Kehm & Stensaker, 2009). On the policy front, the Ministry of Education has recently developed a long term strategic plan (2015–2025) for the sector, focusing on three key goals:

- to strengthen competitiveness and innovation capacity;
- to solve major challenges to society;
- to develop high-quality research groups (Ministry of Education, 2015).

As is the case in other countries (Hazelkorn, 2009), the quest for world class status (scientific excellence) is driving policy developments in the realms of research funding. National policy developments in recent years have put an emphasis on the concentration of resources through mergers involving universities and university colleges (Pinheiro, Geschwind, & Aarrevaara, 2016). In 2013, following a staff referendum and opposition from a local business representative organisation as well as students, UiA's board decided not to merge with a university college from the neighbouring Telemark region. This, in turn, has created an additional tension for UiA's management as domestic institutions consolidate into larger, more robust and resourceful academic environments. It also meant that, more than before, strategic thinking is paramount, with UiA expected to articulate, both to the Ministry of Education and other external stakeholders, how its goals are to be successfully achieved in the absence of a new structure (resulting from a merger process).

A third challenge is coming to terms with its institutional legacy and in particular the fact that UiA was created as a merger of communities of teachers with very different backgrounds and behavioural norms. A 2009 OECD analysis on the regional innovation and entrepreneurial ecosystems pointed out that the two campus model adopted by UiA did not address these existing cleavages (OECD, 2009). Indeed, as the university has developed and taken on new tasks these cleavages have been recreated in new ways. One example of this is that disciplinary fragmentation between teaching units has undermined the development of interdisciplinary collaboration for research. The interviews with external actors also confirmed this persistent problem of internal fragmentation, with complaints emerging around lack of internal coordination for engagement and synergies within UiA; at the same time it was also reported that there had been some improvements in recent years.

Respondents also noted that they found that UiA also had a very low profile with respect to its main campus located in the city of Kristiansand, the largest urban area in the region and its de facto capital. In contrast, the much smaller Grimstad campus (34% of total enrolments), where the bulk of engineering training takes place, is regarded by many (external and internal stakeholders alike) as very engaged with the local community and being much more visible locally. The interviews we undertook confirmed an issue identified in previous studies that, in Agder, regional knowledge creation processes involving UiA have a tendency for directly involving students (Pinheiro *et al.*, 2017). Indeed, Karlsen (2007) described this as being a dominant conception of 'knowledge creation' based on clientelistic relationships (producing knowledge *for* someone) rather than co-generative (together *with* someone) (Karlsen, 2007).

A final challenge relates to the relatively unbalanced nature of the regional demand side, and its mismatch with the much broader set of teaching and research activities in the region. UiA has had to face a challenging situation in attempting to carve itself a distinct profile in domestic and international markets while facing increasing domestic competition for students and research funding. Certainly, when compared to other industrial and knowledge based regions, UiA has faced a regional industry that not only faces major challenges but also ranks relatively low in absorptive capacity and was unable to create a high volume of demand for knowledge emerging from UiA (Isaksen & Karlsen, 2010). This has in turn reduced the incentive for UiA to systematically undertake engagement activities because there has been a low and declining level of resources coming from regional activities into the university.

From tensions to a more strategic alignment

At the heart of the regional problem, seen from UiA's perspective, is the challenge of finding constructive ways to strengthen its core activities and institutional profile in ways that simultaneously enhance both its local relevance and global competitiveness or excellence. Conversely, the region of Agder faces the key challenge of diversifying its economic/industrial base, thereby reducing its dependency on a limited number of existing industries, some of which, like oil and gas, face major challenges. In the absence of large, generous investors, it is hard to find organisations that are willing to bear the risks of developing local partnership arrangements in new technology areas that can be profitable in terms of both academic excellence as well as international economic competitiveness. An exception to this role is the case of the recently established Centre for Research-based Innovation for offshore mechatronics, in the form of a partnership composed of UiA and multiple industry and academics partners both in and outside the region. The challenge, however, is a longer term one, how to hold partners together with a longer term shared interest but short term divergences to collectively progress towards the milestones on the road to excellence and competitiveness, particularly when national and regional funding instruments are not adequate. Understanding how this steady co-evolution has taken place provides some insights into how these tensions play out in practice and hence potential lessons that can be learned.

Despite these underlying tensions, both UiA and Agder have assets that can clearly contribute to building shared assets that help to create new promising sectors and research activities. The sheer number of UiA academics engaging despite the absence of incentives and the lack of clarity with respect to engagement is highly encouraging (for details see Johnsen *et al.*, 2017; Pinheiro *et al.*, 2017). This suggests that, as an *institution*, i.e. a collection of relatively enduring formal and informal rules and organised practices (Olsen, 2007), UiA's local values, informal norms, and belief systems are conducive to regional engagement. At the same time, these informal efforts are insufficiently aligned with or taken into account by (coupling) the university (sub-unit)'s strategic platforms (goals and ambitions) from faculty to department to research centres and groups. Despite their diversity, there are a number of important similarities amongst UiA's disciplinary units. For example, for the most part, they all share a commitment towards professional training and the linkages with the world of work. Similarly, they all, in different ways and degrees, are actively involved with regional actors (i.e. have developed trust networks), more often than not through student related activities like internships and thesis writing. Yet, UiA's central leadership has yet to develop a broad and inclusive 'regional engagement vision' that takes into account the characteristics of the already regional engaged sub-units and knowledge domains within the university.[4]

A second area where there is considerable engagement, albeit underappreciated, is the role of students in helping to align interests (Pinheiro, Langa, & Pausits, 2015). The data categorically show that students play a critical role in acting as *brokers* or mediators between UiA and regional actors. However, although widespread, these activities are not strategically coupled to the university. The student induction devotes very little time to explaining this regional brokerage role to students or indeed introducing them to the range of regional actors they might expect to encounter in the course of their courses. There is indeed more generally very little visibility of regional partners on the campus, and formal university activities tend to be limited to the two campus locations, emphasising an idea that the campus, and the student community, is something distinct from the city/region. This has a slightly self-reinforcing effect of reducing the demand from regional partners for students because they are simply unaware of the opportunities that exist to work with students at various levels.

UiA's geographic proximity to the city of Kristiansand (about 80,000 inhabitants), the economic and cultural engine of the region, should be an asset rather than a liability. There are attempts under way within the two campuses to address this gap between the engagement that exists, and the profile and awareness of that engagement amongst regional partners more generally. In 2013, a regional coalition comprising university, students, and local/central government actors, began developing a strategic plan to promote Kristiansand as a university city (Juul, 2014). The plan, based on a future vision for the year 2040, emphasised the physical infrastructure (pathways) to better connect the city with UiA's main campus, located 5 km from the city centre. The strategy articulated also for the first time explicitly a need for UiA and the city to better co-ordinate their urban planning activities, as well as the duty of UiA to be neighbourly in terms of opening itself up to cultural activities such as public debates and exhibitions, student-centred activities, showcasing ongoing joint activities with regional actors, etc.

The data suggest that UiA's national profile has been enhanced in the last couple of years, largely as a result of the change in status from a university college to a fully fledged university and its success in developing research activities as demonstrated by its publication points. This profile shift can itself benefit the region as well, addressing the issue that Agder is not a strong knowledge economy region and certainly not a hotspot for high technology jobs. This is a potentially valuable contribution given that in a global knowledge economy, regions compete with one another (both nationally and internationally) for talent, firms, and financial investments (OECD, 2005). But those research strengths have, for the most part, been developed with little consideration for the region, or rather, with little input from regional actors, with the result that there is a gap between the knowledge profile of UiA and Agder's regional economic structure. There is clearly a need to start to link or bridge the research agendas of the various research groups and individual researchers with aspects of relevance to the future development of the region.

In the absence of proper incentive systems, there are few signs that UiA's academic communities will adjust their behaviour in the light of the needs of the surrounding region and its various stakeholders. There appear to be two issues which will affect UiA's capacity to contribute regionally in the future. The first is the challenge of scale, i.e. building robust and sustainable academic groups and teaching programmes around these core research areas. The second is associated with the need to develop scientific synergies across disciplinary domains and areas of specialisation. Although UiA's profile is rather distinct from that of the established 'classic' universities (like Oslo and Bergen), there remains very strong disciplinary divisions that may undermine future inter- and trans- disciplinary collaborations. These are not simple challenges to address – the cultural split is in part underscored by the two-campus arrangement, with each campus having its own profile and stakeholder set (and with the Kristiansand campus being far closer to the public sector bodies developing the economic development strategies with which UiA seeks to fit). More importantly perhaps, both UiA and regional actors have yet to begin a systematic discussion on the types of (transdisciplinary) collaborative research areas that are worth investing in because of their likelihood for producing benefits to academic groups/UiA as a whole and the region alike. One exception is the recently established centre for e-health, which aims at establishing links with multiple academic groups and teaching programmes.

Conclusion and implications

This chapter sought to provide insights into how peripherality may undermine university-regional co-operation between universities and regional actors. The first research question asked was what were the main challenges and tensions that the local university and region faced on account of their peripherality, highlighting four main issues. The first were the difficulties that emerged for the university in seeking to develop a singular strategic response to regional engagement, specifically around a shared vision and an internal structure, given the complexity of pressures it faced. These internal pressures were, secondly, only exacerbated by the fast-changing external environment, particular the pressures towards mergers and an increasing emphasis on research 'excellence' rather narrowly defined. Thirdly, despite being a relatively young university, history cast a long shadow over UiA, with the 1990s mergers producing an institution of disparate communities made concrete in the two campuses with very different profiles. Finally, a major tension pertains to the lack of a strongly sophisticated regional demand-side for university activities able to quickly agree the kinds of activities that may contribute to building related variety and ultimately path-switching.

The second question was the extent to which these tensions determined the nature of the strategic interface, and the simple answer was that these tensions proved more of a problem for the strategic management level than for the many actively engaged academics. These tensions certainly hindered the central strategic management from developing a common articulation of what the vision was and thereby 'coupling' the university to the region. Clearly, one area where there was a strong regional interaction came through students, but there was a lack of activities to make the students and regional organisations more mutually aware and to create a sense that regional engagement was a more general expectation of the UiA student experience. The lack of strategic interface also undermined two other contributions to supporting the development of Agder as a knowledge region, in terms of creating employment opportunities for the highly skilled graduates emerging from UiA, and in contributing to the liveability and vibrancy of the locality in terms of its estates and university activities.

The case study provides a useful reminder and illustration of the fact that universities and their surrounding regions are both independent entities yet their internal dynamics influence one another, and that transformational changes are problematic as a result of institutionalised norms and traditions and existing assets. The region of Agder has been searching for a robust and resilient university, and UiA recognises that its future depends at least partly on Agder's future development, not least in terms of its attractiveness to students. UiA's main challenge is to develop an institutional profile and competence set (across teaching and research portfolios) that will enable it to survive and prosper in an increasingly national and international competitive landscape. Agder's core challenge pertains to economic diversification, which, in the context of an increasingly globalised knowledge based society, is a function of knowledge assets and competencies as well as global networks. As global pipelines, universities play a vital role in connecting peripheral regions, like Agder, to the world economy (Benneworth & Hospers, 2007). Yet, their ability to undertake this critical task depends on the ways in which universities are able to address the multiple demands posed by them by an increasingly complex and volatile environment (Enders & Boer, 2009). The case of Agder is a good illustration of a particular pathway chosen by young, mid-size universities searching for a distinct identity and market profile. The case highlights how such universities are particularly sensitive to these dimensions in the context of a national, Nordic, and supranational (EU) policy environment that puts a premium on world class excellence and global competitiveness. There is therefore a strong case for future research to consider how the idea of a world class university can fit with the notion of a regionally relevant university, particularly in those local environments where research traditions are weakly institutionalised, resources are scarce, and regional actors have limited absorptive capacity, as is the case of peripheral geographies.

Policy makers, particularly those at the national level, should critically assess the notion of 'one size fits all' (Benneworth, Pinheiro, & Sánchez-Barrioluengo,

2016) often associated with ideas such as research concentration and world class universities. Universities located in peripheral regions, often characterised as low knowledge intensive and facing multiple challenges, should face a policy framework that is specifically tailored to the local contexts in which they are embedded. From a policy perspective, this entails devising new governance mechanisms and co-ordinative frameworks that support, rather than constrain, universities' ambitions to meaningfully contribute to their localities (relevance) whilst nurturing world class research environments (excellence) that are more global in nature. Likewise, institutional leaders should be keenly aware that devising new strategies and structures alone is not likely to produce change in academic behaviour, partly due to the decoupling nature of academic work (Pinheiro & Stensaker, 2014), but also as a function of the absence of proper incentive mechanisms, including those associated with the nature of the academic profession (Kehm & Teichler, 2013). In the context of universities located in peripheral regions, future research inquiries (preferably longitudinal and using mixed methods) could, for example, shed critical light on the complex interplay between national policy frameworks, institutional strategies, academic/departmental cultures and regional characteristics and dynamics, and the extent through which they impact (positively or negatively) one another.

Acknowledgement

The research leading to these results has received funding from the Norwegian Financial Mechanism 2009–2014 and the Ministry of Education, Youth and Sports under Project Contract No. MSMT-5397/2015. Thank you to Paul Benneworth for constructive editorial comments on an earlier version of the chapter. Any remaining errors are the author's own responsibility.

Notes

1 More information at: www.perifproject.eu/.
2 For more information visit: www.uia.no/en/about-uia.
3 At the time of writing, UiA's new leadership (2016–2020) is currently devising a new strategic platform in which societal engagement features more centrally. However, our analysis is retrospective thus not taking into account the new efforts, still to be implemented from 2017 onwards.
4 This is starting to change as a result of the newly established strategic framework (2016–2020) centred on the vision of knowledge co-creation, currently being implemented (UiA, 2016).

References

Aslesen, H. W., Isaksen, A., & Karlsen, J. (2012). Modes of innovation and differentiated responses to globalisation: A case study of innovation modes in the Agder Region, Norway. *Journal of the Knowledge Economy, 3*(4), 389–405. doi:10.1007/s13132-011-0060-9.

Benneworth, P. (2012). The relationship of regional engagement to universities' core purposes: Reflections from engagement efforts with socially excluded communities. In R. Pinheiro, P. Benneworth, & G. A. Jones (Eds), *Universities and regional development: A critical assessment of tensions and contradictions*. Milton Park and New York: Routledge.

Benneworth, P., & Hospers, G. J. (2007). The new economic geography of old industrial regions: Universities as global–local pipelines. *Environment and Planning C: Government and Policy, 25*(6), 779–802.

Benneworth, P., Pinheiro, R., & Sánchez-Barrioluengo, M. (2016). One size does not fit all! New perspectives on the university in the social knowledge economy. *Science and Public Policy, 43*(6), 731–735. doi:10.1093/scipol/scw018.

Breznitz, S., & Feldman, M. (2012). The engaged university. *The Journal of Technology Transfer, 37*(2), 139–157. doi:10.1007/s10961-010-9183-6.

Charles, D. (2001). Universities and territorial development: Reshaping the regional role of UK universities. *Local Economy, 18*(1), 7–20.

Chatterton, P., & Goddard, J. (2000). The response of higher education institutions to regional needs. *European Journal of Education, 35*(4), 475–496. doi:10.1111/1467-3435.00041.

Clark, B. R. (1998). *Creating entrepreneurial universities: Organizational pathways of transformation*. New York: Pergamon.

Crespo, J., Suire, R., & Vicente, J. (2014). Lock-in or lock-out? How structural properties of knowledge networks affect regional resilience. *Journal of Economic Geography, 14*(1), 199–219.

Dahllöf, U., & Selander, S. (1994). *Expanding colleges and new universities: Selected case studies from non-metropolitan areas in Australia, Scotland, and Scandinavia*. Dept. of Education, Uppsala University.

Enders, J., & Boer, H. (2009). The mission impossible of the European university: Institutional confusion and institutional diversity. In A. Amaral, G. Neave, C. Musselin, & P. Maassen (Eds), *European integration and the governance of higher education and research* (pp. 159–178). Dordrecht: Springer Netherlands.

Goddard, J. (1997). Managing the university/regional interface. *Higher Education Management, 9*(3), 7–28.

Goddard, J., & Vallance, P. (2013). *The university and the city*. London: Routledge.

Gunasekara, C. (2006). Leading the horses to water. *Journal of Sociology, 42*(2), 145–163. doi:10.1177/1440783306064950.

Gunnes, R., Sandven, T., & Spilling, O. (2015). *Regional comparisons of R&D and innovation*. Report on science and technology indicators for Norway. Retrieved 24 April 2018, from www.forskningsradet.no/servlet/Satellite?cid=1253991139642&pagename=VedleggPointer&target=_blank.

Hauge, E. S., Pinheiro, R. M., & Zyzak, B. (2016). Knowledge bases and regional development: Collaborations between higher education and cultural creative industries. *International Journal of Cultural Policy*, 1–19. doi:10.1080/10286632.2016.1218858.

Hauge, E., Wærdahl, R., Pinheiro, R., Kathrine, B., & Zyzak, B. (2013). *Kompetansutfordringer på Agder: Forprosjekt om mulige forbindelseslinjer mellom velferd, kompetanse og arbeids- og næringsliv*. FoU rapport 7/2013. Kristiansand: Agderforskning. Retrieved 24 April 2018, from http://agderf.sitegen.no/customers/agder/reports/rff-final_januar_2014.pdf.

Hazelkorn, H. (2009). Rankings and the battle for world-class excellence: Institutional strategies and policy choice. *Higher Education Management and Policy, 21*(1), 1–22.

Isaksen, A., & Karlsen, J. (2010). Different modes of innovation and the challenge of connecting universities and industry: Case studies of two regional industries in Norway. *European Planning Studies, 18*(12), 1993–2008. doi:10.1080/09654313.2010.516523.

Johnsen, H. C., Normann, R., & Pinheiro, R. (2017). Universities' external relations. In H. C. Johnsen, E. Hauge, M. L. Magnusen, & R. Ennals (Eds), *Applied social science research in a regional knowledge system: Balancing validity, meaning and convenience* (pp. 274–286). London and New York: Routledge.

Juul, H. (2014). *Universitetsbyen Kristiansand: Utviklingsplan 2040.* Retrieved 17 April 2018, from www.statsbygg.no/files/publikasjoner/strategierPlaner/campusutviklingsplan-UiA.pdf.

Karlsen, J. (2007). *The regional role of the university: A study of knowledge creation in the agora between Agder University College and regional actors in Agder, Norway* (thesis). Norwegian University of Science and Technology.

Karlsen, J. E., Flåten, B. J., Isaksen, A., Pinheiro, R., & Zyzak, B. (2013). Kunnskap og innovasjon i Agder [Knowledge and innovation in the Agder region]. In K. Wallevik & G. Jørgensen (Eds), *Krise, omstilling og vekst -en regionanalyse av sørlandet* [Crisis, restructuring and growth: A regional analysis of Southern Norway] (Vol. FoU-rapport 1/2013 pp. 97–116). Kristiansand: Agderforskning.

Kehm, B. M., & Stensaker, B. (2009). *University rankings, diversity, and the new landscape of higher education.* Rotterdam: Sense Publishers.

Kehm, B. M., & Teichler, U. (2013). *The academic profession in Europe: New tasks and new challenges.* Dordrecht: Springer.

Lagendijk, A., & Lorentzen, A. (2007). Proximity, knowledge and innovation in peripheral regions: On the intersection between geographical and organizational proximity. *European Planning Studies, 15*(4), 457–466.

Lambooy, J. G., & Boschma, R. A. (2001). Evolutionary economics and regional policy. *The Annals of Regional Science, 35*(1), 113–131.

Martin, R. (2012). Regional economic resilience, hysteresis and recessionary shocks. *Journal of Economic Geography, 12*(1), 1–32.

Ministry of Education and Research. (2015). *Long-term plan for research and higher education.* Retrieved 17 April 2018, from www.regjeringen.no/en/topics/research/innsiktsartikler/langtidsplan-for-forsking-og-hogare-utdanning/id2353317/.

Morse, J. M. (2003). Principles of mixed methods and multimethod research design. In C. Teddlie & A. Tashakkori (Eds), *Handbook of mixed methods in social and behavioral research* (pp. 189–208). Thousand Oaks, CA: Sage.

Neffke, F., Henning, M., & Boschma, R. (2011). How do regions diversify over time? Industry relatedness and the development of new growth paths in regions. *Economic Geography, 87*(3), 237–265.

OECD. (2005). *Building competitive regions: Strategies and governance.* Paris. Organisation for Economic Co-operation and Development.

OECD. (2007). *Higher education and regions: Globally competitive, locally engaged.* Paris: Organisation for Economic Co-operation and Development.

OECD. (2009). *Entrepreneurship and the innovation system of the Agder Region, Norway.* Retrieved 17 April 2018, from www.oecd.org/cfe/leed/44542425.pdf.

Oleksiyenko, A. (2012). Resource asymmetries and cumulative advantages in regional knowledge systems: Exploring a university's growth/share strategy. In R. Pinheiro, P. Benneworth, & G. A. Jones (Eds), *Universities and regional development: A critical assessment of tensions and contradictions.* Milton Park and New York: Routledge.

Olsen, J. P. (2007). The institutional dynamics of the European university. In P. Maassen & J. P. Olsen (Eds), *University dynamics and European integration* (pp. 25–54). Dordrecht: Springer.

Perry, B. (2012). Excellence, relevance and the construction of regional science policy: Science frictions and fictions in the North West of England. In R. Pinheiro,

P. Benneworth, & G. A. Jones (Eds), *Universities and regional development: A critical assessment of tensions and contradictions* (pp. 105–123). Milton Park and New York: Routledge.

Pinheiro, R. (2012). *In the region, for the region? A comparative study of the institutionalisation of the regional mission of universities* (PhD dissertation). University of Oslo.

Pinheiro, R. (2013). Bridging the local with the global: Building a new university on the fringes of Europe. *Tertiary Education and Management, 19*(2), 144–160. doi:10.1080/13583883.2013.782063.

Pinheiro, R., Benneworth, P., & Jones, G. A. (2012a). Understanding regions and the institutionalization of universities. In R. Pinheiro, P. Benneworth, & G. A. Jones (Eds), *Universities and regional development: An assessment of tensions and contradictions* (pp. 11–32). Milton Park and New York: Routledge.

Pinheiro, R., Benneworth, P., & Jones, G. A. (2012b). What next? Steps towards a recategorization of universities' regional missions. In R. Pinheiro, P. Benneworth, & G. A. Jones (Eds), *Universities and regional development: A critical assessment of tensions and contradictions* (pp. 241–255). Milton Park and New York: Routledge.

Pinheiro, R., Benneworth, P., & Jones, G. A. (Eds). (2012c). *Universities and regional development: A critical assessment of tensions and contradictions*. Milton Park and New York: Routledge.

Pinheiro, R., Benneworth, P., & Jones, G. A. (2015). Beyond the obvious: Tensions and volitions surrounding the contributions of universities to regional development. In L. Farinha, J. Ferreira, H. Lawton-Smith, & S. Bagchi-Sen (Eds), *Handbook of research on global competitive advantage through innovation and entrepreneurship* (pp. 150–172). Hershey, PA: IGI.

Pinheiro, R., Geschwind, L., & Aarrevaara, T. (Eds). (2016). *Mergers in higher education: The experiences from Northern Europe*. Dordrecht: Springer.

Pinheiro, R., Langa, P., & Pausits, A. (2015). One and two equals three? The third mission of higher education institutions. *European Journal of Higher Education, 5*(3), 233–249. doi:10.1080/21568235.2015.1044552.

Pinheiro, R., Normann, R., & Johnsen, H. C. G. (2017). External engagement and the academic heartland: The case of a regionally-embedded university. *Science and Public Policy, 43*(6). doi:10.1093/scipol/scw020.

Pinheiro, R., & Stensaker, B. (2014). Strategic actor-hood and internal transformation: The rise of the quadruple-helix university? In J. Brankovik, M. Klemencik, P. Lazetic, & P. Zgaga (Eds), *Global challenges, local responses in higher education: The contemporary issues in national and comparative perspective* (pp. 171–189). Rotterdam: Sense.

Sima, K., Beseda, J., Benneworth, P., & Pinheiro, R. (2017). What are the cultural preconditions of universities' regional engagement? Towards a multi-dimensional model of university-region interfaces. *Higher Education Policy, 30*, 517–532.

Smith, H. L., Glasson, J., & Chadwick, A. (2005). The geography of talent: Entrepreneurship and local economic development in Oxfordshire. *Entrepreneurship & Regional Development: An International Journal, 17*(6), 449–478.

SSB. (2016). *Statistics Norway*. Retrieved 17 April 2018, from www.kommuneprofilen.no/Profil/Sysselsetting/DinRegion/syss_utd_region.aspx.

UiA. (2016). *Strategy 2016–2020*. Retrieved 17 April 2018, from www.uia.no/en/about-uia/organisation/strategy-2016-2020.

Yin, R. K. (2009). *Case study research: Design and methods*. London: Sage.

4 University roles in a peripheral Southern European region

Between traditional and 'engaged' roles through the provision of knowledge intensive business services

Hugo Pinto, Elvira Uyarra and
Manuel Fernández-Esquinas

Introduction

The roles that universities play in peripheral regions are complex and multifaceted (see e.g. Pinheiro *et al.*, 2012). Their strategic positions make them not just sources and providers of public knowledge and training, but also animators of regional innovation systems (RISs), strategic leaders for regional regeneration (Fernández-Esquinas and Pinto, 2014; Benneworth *et al.*, 2017) and local-distant connectors (Benneworth and Dassen, 2011). In peripheral regions, there may be a relative absence of other knowledge 'connectors', with universities being called upon to alleviate problems of peripherality and critical mass by increasing the inflow of external knowledge to the region and diffusing the benefits of such knowledge, thus stimulating 'local buzz'. This chapter will explore these multiple and conflicting roles using the case of the Algarve (Portugal) to illustrate the multiplicity of mechanisms through which the universities contribute to regional development. This provides a basis to reflect upon the tensions and challenges faced between the pursuit of traditional missions/global excellence and contributing to upgrading the local business knowledge base.

The Algarve is peripheral both within Portugal and the European Union. Its economic structure is relatively unbalanced, comprising a higher proportion of SMEs working within less knowledge intensive sectors, and with an important economic role for tourism. For the last decades the Algarve has undergone a development process that can be summarized as '*tertiarization without industrialization*', yielding a service economy that is far from knowledge intensive. In parallel with its overspecialisation in tourism, the region has a path-dependency problem that is not easily overcome (Cruz, 2014). Regional strategies have for 20 years underlined tourism diversification, but only recently has a broader consensus emerged regarding a need to develop other productive sectors as well as activities that benefit from synergies with tourism.

A public university was created in Algarve to raise education levels and catalyse regional development. Although long an actor of regional modernisation and social change, it has only very recently been expected to play an important role in innovation processes, economic restructuring and connecting the region to the knowledge economy. The university has been crucial in the recent wave of innovation policies around Research and Innovation Strategy for Smart Specialisation (RIS3), creating new industrial capabilities and the human capital to drive those industries. But this also drove a decoupling of the university from existing firms' needs, triggering a conflict between these innovation policies' new goals and the university's expected contribution. The role of universities in that process depends largely on its capacity for internal restructuring while maintaining its original strength.

This chapter firstly asks the question what roles can universities play in driving smart specialisation processes in peripheral regions. The chapter then sets out the case study region, and then turns to chart the innovation policy development in the region and the university's role in that process. The chapter highlights some of the conflicts in the region, identifies potential resolutions of those conflicts, concluding with a discussion of the key issues for science, policy and practice.

The regional development problem and the ubiquitous role of universities

Regional development in peripheral regions

Evolutionary economic geography literature indicates that diversified economies tend to be more resilient and adaptable, with industrial development unfolding as a branching process triggered by endogenous structural change. 'Related variety' research within evolutionary economic geography demonstrated that countries and regions tend to diversify or 'branch out' into technologically related industries (Frenken *et al.*, 2007; Neffke *et al.*, 2011) through local mechanisms of knowledge transfer from old to new sectors, including spin-off processes, firm diversification, mobility of employees or the formation of innovation networks (Boschma and Frenken, 2011). Economic activities evolve through exploring 'adjacent possibilities'; and the presence of a diversified economic structure increases possibilities for countries and regions to move into new, complex activities.

Evolutionary processes produce differentiated evolutionary trajectories for technologies, industries and regional economies; this may involve upgrading of mature paths, diversification through exploiting synergies between an existing path and a new one, or new path creation. Different regions may be differently positioned to achieve these developments, suggesting that a one size fits all approach is inapplicable to different regional types (Tödtling and Trippl, 2005). New path creation through evolutionary branching from established paths may be more likely in regions with a variety of generic competences, while other regions may only be able to transition to more value added activities via upgrading a mature path.

Peripheral regions are characterised by institutional and organisational thinness, and lack of critical mass and absorptive capacity (Tödtling and Trippl, 2005), undermining their capacity to capture value and diversify. Fragmentation, institutional thinness and a weak absorptive capacity undermine their capacity to invest in much needed innovation related activities (Oughton *et al.*, (2002). Many European regions, notably in the south, missed out on 'industrial revolutions', shifting abruptly from a very traditional economy and social structure, to a fully service economy, without the intermediate phases of industry-based development. These peripheral regions lack the initial agglomeration of core industrial areas, producing specialisation in low-knowledge-intensity service sectors.

The economic structure of these regions as late as the 1980s, was primarily mostly agriculture-based involving the transformation of agro-food products, some low-tech manufacturing, and traditional services. The dominant manufacturing industries were mostly 'enclave' industries outsourced from other countries because of labour costs and infrastructures. The social structure reflected economic activity, with few employees having secondary education or higher degrees, and a scarcity of the 'new middle classes' formed by technicians, professionals, entrepreneurs, and other qualified workers. However, these regions in the south of Europe underwent since then one of the most rapid processes of social and economic change ever seen in Europe. This produced service-based economies and raised living standards to the European average level, with some characteristics shaped by economic policies and the endogenous opportunities of the territory. These regions' economic structures were typically dominated by service firms, mostly SMEs, usually oriented to local markets, with low financial and technological capacities. The precise configuration varied to reflect local conditions; in many localities, this may be tourism-led; other areas were based around agriculture, branch-plant manufacturing or even the public sector. What these activities had in common was a lack of agglomeration economies and the absence of a knowledge economy, with local investment often concentrated on low-knowledge-intensive services, physical infrastructure and construction.

The public sector has often been important in these places, both as a host to the majority of knowledge capacities, but also because of their dependence on central policies for economic development and latterly innovation. Early innovation policies and their associated strategies were viewed as part of a modernisation strategy, including locating universities and research organisations in these regions as tools to drive development. More recently, regional and EU policies have greatly influenced the emergence of knowledge activities in these regions, again often linked to universities and other R&D and innovation actors.

Universities in peripheral regions

There has been an increasing interest of late on the potential for universities to overcome problems of peripherality and fragmentation (Benneworth and Charles, 2005; Coenen, 2007; Pinto *et al.*, 2015). Universities are a key actor influencing economic trajectories, through their impact on knowledge creation, human capital development, transfer of existing know-how, research-led technological innovation, capital investment, regional leadership, impact on the regional milieu and support to knowledge infrastructure. Universities' roles in peripheral regions often differ from the traditional technology transfer role involving licensing and contract R&D, and are instead expected to be more 'developmental' and engaged across all their activities such as human capital formation, associative governance and culture. This 'engaged university' model envisages a greater focus on capturing value for the region through their missions (Chatterton and Goddard, 2000; Charles and Benneworth, 2001; Gunasekara, 2006; Benneworth and Hospers, 2007; Uyarra, 2010).

In peripheral economies, universities can act as local-distant connectors (Benneworth and Hospers, 2007; Benneworth and Dassen, 2011), linking the region with external sources of knowledge. Given the relative absence of other regional knowledge 'connectors', universities may serve as knowledge-intensive business service (KIBS) providers to regional SMEs. Delivered via consultancy, technical services, use of facilities, among other mechanisms (Pinto *et al.*, 2015), these activities can potentially upgrade regional business environments and facilitate regional value capture processes. But universities' regional roles may be limited by a number of factors including:

1. Funding for regional activities tends to be extremely limited in relation to university funding for R&D, science and teaching.
2. Universities' regional roles are also threatened by public expenditure cuts arising from post-crisis austerity budgets in the wake of the economic crisis.
3. The increasing ubiquity of 'success metrics' for higher education forcing universities to conform to a one-size-fits-all model (emphasising publication and commercialisation).
4. Structural reforms taking place in many countries triggering mergers and reducing the diversity of higher education systems (Pinheiro *et al.*, 2015).

This creates three fault lines for universities engaging in peripheral regions. First, there is not enough financial support for the growing variety of tasks that universities are expected to perform at regional level, and indeed, there have been austerity cuts that have reduced available funding. Second, there is an ongoing incongruence between organisational goals, with peripheral universities expected to contribute to regional engagement and at the same time to compete in the global R&D race. Third, regional engagement policies are not consistent with the organisational and legal reforms universities face, and the weakness of the industrial environments around these universities mean they cannot replace falling governmental funding with firm-based financing as is common in more central universities.

This has implications for universities' urban and regional engagement. Structural reform in Higher Education may lead to more centralised structures and prioritisation of efficiency over external engagement, and of scientific excellence above regional relevance (Benneworth *et al.*, 2017). University mergers may shift the balance of power of actors in regions and cities toward dominant research-intensive universities, to the detriment of other universities more connected with local activities (Perry, 2008). Finally, universities in peripheral regions are disadvantaged by a lack of local funding emerging from lower levels of industrial R&D and with cuts to regional programmes (Charles *et al.*, 2014).

Universities and smart specialisation

Universities' role in supporting regional growth and diversification has been recognised by the European Commission's so-called 'smart specialisation' agenda, now a formal condition for receipt of EU cohesion funds. The smart specialisation concept emerged to improve regional innovation strategy development by preventing regions following an all too prevalent copycat strategy of building clusters in fashionable industries such as biotechnology. The main conceptual novelties of the smart specialisation agenda lie in a much stronger focus on selectivity and prioritisation, the idea of entrepreneurial discovery process as a mechanism for bottom-up diversification, and greater connectivity not only within but also and across regions (outward orientation). The entrepreneurial discovery concept, inspired by Hausmann and Rodrik's (2003) entrepreneurial self-discovery process, seeks to harness the collective knowledge and creativity of regional innovators.

However, the concept of smart specialisation is still in its infancy and has been critiqued for a failure "to explain concretely how the concept could provide a common political rationale for a socio-economically and territorially diverse set of regions and nations facing different place-based challenges and different innovation modes" (Capello and Kroll, 2016: 1396).

For peripheral regions, smart specialisation offers an opportunity for diversification in international market segments, although their potential to benefit from smart specialisation is constrained by lack of critical mass, low levels of entrepreneurship and insufficient institutional capacity. As Radosevic (2017) notes, Southern European regions have been particularly challenged in relation to identifying specific sources of new technological opportunities. Institutional weakness and other challenges related to understanding the concept and an absence of methodological frameworks for decision making has prevented regions from making difficult choices in relation to which activities and policies to prioritise. Consequently, 'specialisation' in Southern European regions has often been defined very widely, with many broad priorities (defined at one- or two-digit NACE codes) that are an unsuitable basis for supporting productive transformation through industrial diversification (Komninos *et al.*, 2014). Several observers similarly noted a tendency to continue strategies along previous paths rather than encouraging entrepreneurial discovery of new innovation and development paths (see e.g. Pugh, 2014).

The business-led 'entrepreneurial discovery process' approach also faces key obstacles relating to administrative and political barriers to involving business leaders alongside a more general resistance to experimentation (Radosevic, 2017). In many peripheral regions, strategies are often drafted by consultants involving only a limited group of stakeholders (Komninos *et al.*, 2014). Finally, despite the outward-looking orientation of smart specialisation, in terms of promoting international benchmarking of regions within global value chains and cross-regional projects and networks, strategies are too often inward oriented, particularly in peripheral regions (Tsipouri, 2017).

On the other hand, universities may play a number of roles in smart specialisation (Kempton *et al.*, 2013; Goddard *et al.*, 2013). As Kempton *et al.* (2013) note:

> Universities can … play a key role in defining a regional smart specialization strategy by contributing to a rigorous assessment of the region's knowledge assets, capabilities and competencies, including those embedded in the university's own departments as well as local businesses.
>
> (p. 4)

Universities may assist regions in understanding and assessing regional knowledge assets and competences (including those of universities). Universities can also potentially contribute to diversification by better matching industrial and research capabilities, and also playing a key role in entrepreneurial discovery processes drawing on their existing third mission roles of connecting economic and societal ('quadruple helix') actors. They may help to build capacity for the delivery of regional strategies for smart specialisation through training, consultancy services and supplying graduates in the field of economic development. Entrepreneurial processes and capacity-building on the demand side may be supported through universities' student enterprise programmes and graduate placements. Universities can function as global knowledge connectors helping establish whether a region has sufficient assets for specialising in particular areas, and identify societal challenges with both local and global dimensions. Finally, they can contribute with institutional leadership and governance. As mentioned earlier, in institutionally thin/fragmented regions, universities can act as key RIS anchor organisations and boundary spanners, a prerequisite for drafting and implementing RIS3 (Kempton *et al.*, 2013). Mobilising academic strengths for economic development may obviously appeal to peripheral regions given their limited public and private R&D capacities (Goddard *et al.*, 2013). The diversity in terms of scientific areas found in universities may contribute to a regional economy's long-term adaptability, avoiding pitfalls including overspecialisation and lock-in.

Nevertheless, the contribution of universities to smart specialisation is fraught with difficulties (Goddard *et al.*, 2013). Firstly, universities' participation in regional governance structures may be undermined by a poor alignment of policies at multiple levels, limits to leadership within universities, or by limited capacity and incentives for universities to get involved in regional strategies.

Tensions may also arise from a potential mismatch between universities' current academic profiles and the regional industrial assets that are the focus of smart specialisation. Priority areas may not correspond with university scientific strength and may therefore undermine the university's interest in RIS3. Alternatively, the chosen specialisations may relate to academic expertise across a range of departments and centres that are not easily mobilised coherently for regional partners (Goddard *et al.*, 2013). Finally, a key risk associated with the strong involvement of universities in regions lacking absorptive capacity on the demand side is that funds may be locked in science silos rather than used for innovation (Marques and Morgan, 2018).

Overview of the Algarve region

The Algarve is located in the extreme south of Portugal, distinct from other Portuguese regions, owing its character to a strong regional sense of belonging rooted in a common identity. This derives from the region's historical building process – the territory remains the same since the birth of the Portuguese nation in the early thirteenth century – and is also grounded on the peripheral character of the Algarve relative to the rest of the country. The Algarve is a small-sized region in relation to national and European regional average, with a territory, GDP and population around 5 per cent of the national total. However, the region revealed attractiveness in the last decade, being the region in Portugal with the highest population growth. The Algarve is internationally renowned for its 'sun and sand' tourism, the main economic driver, accounting for nearly two-thirds of GDP and employment, stimulating other activities as construction or real estate, essential to the development of the region, in terms of employment and wealth creation. This particularly productive specialisation has driven its transformation from a region considered poor within Europe to one of the most developed within Portugal (Guerreiro, 2008). Indeed, the region lost its 'convergence status' for European cohesion funds in the period of 2007–13, with a GDP now above 75 per cent of the European level, and despite the crisis, has retained this status, being designated a 'region in transition' for 2014–20. This loss of status has seen an overall reduction in the inflow of cohesion funds to the Algarve since 2007. The focus on tourism has constrained innovation and the diversification of the regional economy (Romão *et al.*, 2016).

The decentralised levels of governance coincide with the Algarve's spatial boundaries, something rather uncommon in Portugal. The district level coincides with NUTS II and NUTS III, and the area of influence of the Coordination Commission of Regional Development of the Algarve (CCDR) with the one of the association of municipalities and other agencies, such as decentralised ministry boards, regional tourism entities or sectors' associations. More information on the Algarve is presented in Table 4.1, showing the region's structural weaknesses, with levels of R&D far below Portuguese and European levels, low competitiveness and high growth firms, educational attainment, and high regional specialisation in the tourism sector.

Figure 4.1 Map of the Algarve
Source: Authors' own elaboration.

Today the Algarve is already steadily recovering from the crisis, but the negative impacts of the 2007/08 international crisis foregrounded the Algarve's limited socio-economic resilience. There is a need for a structural change to address the significant economic downturn and a rise in regional unemployment. This was a consequence of economic turmoil coupled with the over-specialisation of the regional economic structure in tourism, the lack of public instruments to stimulate the economy, substantial reduction of EU funds, and austerity measures affecting the public and private systems.

Innovation planning in the Algarve and the role of the public university

The University of Algarve

Successive regional strategies in the Algarve have sought to address overspecialization of the regional economic structure through encouraging diversification (Barreira, 2009). This can be seen for example in the attention given by the Regional Strategy 2007–13 (CCDR Algarve, 2006) or the Regional Innovation Plan (UAlg, 2007a), or more recently the RIS3 Algarve (CCDR Algarve, 2014). These documents all respectively assume the challenge of transforming the Algarve into a knowledge-based region, with the University of Algarve (UAlg) central to this transformation (Pinto *et al.*, 2012). UAlg is the only

Table 4.1 Key variables of Algarve, Portugal and Europe

	Algarve	Portuguese regional average	European regional average
Change of gross domestic product (GDP) per inhabitant, in purchasing power standard (PPS), by NUTS level 2 region, 2008–13	−4.80	−1.60	−0.46
Gross domestic product (GDP) per inhabitant, in purchasing power standard (PPS), by NUTS level 2 region, 2013	78.67	76.47	98.07
Change in unemployment rate, persons aged 15–74, by NUTS level 2 region, 2009–14	4.10	5.40	1.14
Unemployment rate, persons aged 15–74, by NUTS level 2 region, 2014	14.50	14.34	9.96
Gross domestic expenditure on R&D (GERD), by NUTS level 2 region, 2012	0.42	0.90	1.51
Change in gross domestic expenditure on R&D (GERD), by NUTS level 2 region, 2007–12	0.09	0.15	0.19
Regional Competitiveness Index – RCI 2013, 2013	−0.60	−0.54	0.06
High-tech patent applications to the European patent office (EPO) by priority year by NUTS 2 regions	1,108	2,206	1,854
Regional business concentration, by NUTS level 2 region, 2012	57.50	47.03	42.95
Density of high-growth enterprises in the business economy, by NUTS level 2 region, 2010	32.30	35.66	33.73
Employment in foreign firms, 2010 (%)	1.18	4.11	9.97
Nights spent in tourist accommodation establishments, by NUTS 2 regions, 2014	18.30	7.90	2.68
Population aged 25–64 with tertiary education, 2013 (%)	18.00	17.57	27.98

Source: Authors' own calculation, based on Eurostat data.

public higher education institution in the region, created in 1979, and recently it assumed a role not only as a centre of qualification of human capital but also as the most important regional research institution. In 1988, the Faro Polytechnic Institute was merged by a central government decree into the University of Algarve for the purposes of common management of the two institutions.

The student population was 7,900 in 2014 from more than 60 countries with around 800 teaching and research staff, making it a relatively small university even by Portuguese standards. It has three faculties at university level (Economics, Sciences & Technology, Human & Social Sciences) and four schools at Polytechnic level (Education & Communication, Management, Hospitality & Tourism, Institute of Engineering, and the School of Health), offering a range of undergraduate and postgraduate degrees. A relative decrease in Portuguese students has been compensated for by the attraction of non-regular and foreign students. This last group represents around 15 per cent of total students. More recently, in 2008 the Department of Biomedical Sciences and Medicine was created. An evaluation of UAlg performance in R&D and cooperation in services between 2000 and 2006 (Cruz & Pinto, 2008) highlighted that the expertise is concentrated in natural sciences, particularly in marine sciences, where the university has a critical mass in terms of excellence centres, training of human resources and market linkages. This specialisation as measured by international scientific publications has increased in recent years (UAlg, 2017).

The coexistence of the university and polytechnic subsystems in the same institution has also been identified as important for the strong relationship with the region (UAlg, 2007b). This can be read as positive as the university and the polytechnic subsystems are integrated, but could also have negative aspects, forcing a change of culture towards a more traditional focus upon scientific excellence in a polytechnic subsystem that was traditionally closer to industry. However, this regional 'monopoly' has helped develop relationships in recent years with regional firms seeking to invest in knowledge and innovation.

University's regional engagement structures

In 2003, the UAlg created for the first time an (informal) knowledge transfer office (KTO), the Regional Centre for Innovation of the Algarve (CRIA) to consolidate university-industry relations, while supporting and promoting the use of mechanisms for protecting intellectual property. It was an initiative within the ERDF-funded Inovalgarve. The university then extended the office beyond its original project life, using the same human resources, to ensure the university continued participating in various thematic networks at the national level for knowledge transfer and valorisation, namely the offices for industrial property promotion (GAPI) and the technology transfer and knowledge offices (OTIC), financed by public programmes. In the absence of specialist intermediaries, with a low density of regional innovators, and supported by its university status, this 'informal KTO' assumed a central role in the connectivity of the entire regional innovation system (CCDR Algarve, 2006; Pinto, 2012).

In January 2010, following the creation of new Statutes of the University of Algarve[1] to respond to the new legal framework of higher education institutions in Portugal, UAlg absorbed CRIA as a formal division of the university, the Division of Entrepreneurship and Technology Transfer within the Support Unit of the Scientific Research and Postgraduate Training UAIC.[2] UAIC coordinates the development and preparation of interdisciplinary research activities and assists research groups in developing major collaborative initiatives. Its tasks include communicating funding opportunities, intermediating with funding agencies, giving strategic advice about new research directions and aiding in proposal writing and coordination of large and complex grant and contract proposal efforts (see Pinto, 2017 for more information).

CRIA's mission is knowledge transfer via four channels: the implementation of initiatives to increase the levels of entrepreneurship inside the academia; direct support to business consolidation based on scientific knowledge; the establishment of partnerships with firms; and support for researchers seeking to transfer R&D results to industry. Since its creation, CRIA has supported the launching of 86 new spin-offs with a survival rate of 74 per cent, 150 requests of patents, 7 licensing contracts and more than a thousand requests of trademarks and logotypes. It helped the creation of more than 120 university-industry projects. It attracted around €18 million for university-industry consortia, €16 million innovation and entrepreneurship subsidies and €6 million for territorial cooperation (UAlg, 2017).

The creation of CRIA had a positive regional effect but it has become perhaps excessively central in the regional innovation network given the sparseness of other innovation intermediaries. A recent study (Pinto, 2016) looking at the network of innovation projects supported by the Regional Operational Programme 2007–13 highlighted the centrality of CRIA in the regional innovation ecosystem. CRIA is the crucial entity for the network connectivity, with 110 linkages, more than 10 per cent of the total number of connections in the network. Most actors had a low number of relationships, with only 21 actors having more than 10 connections. The analysis thus reveals that innovation networks are disproportionally concentrated with the university and its knowledge transfer office.

Role of UAlg in RIS3: an opportunity for diversification?

As the economic crisis peaked, European regions began developing their RIS3. The Algarve is currently implementing its smart specialisation strategy, following a number of innovation-focused regional strategies.[3] The previous strategy, PRIAlgarve, anticipated many of the ideas later introduced in RIS3, particularly identifying key regional development priorities. PRIAlgarve prioritised in particular the need to diversify the tourism offer, use its potential to catalyse research-based sectors, and explore other explicit and latent regional potentials.

The RIS3 development began at the end of 2011 and today still continues its implementation[4] with the University of Algarve involved since the outset. The process of development of the RIS3 in the Algarve generally followed the steps suggested in the RIS3 guidelines. In close cooperation with the CCDR, a group of university researchers were primarily responsible for collecting the evidence base and drafting the strategy documents, and CRIA prepared the entrepreneurial discovery process organising around a dozen workshops with regional stakeholders. This leadership role was accepted by other stakeholders and not contested. Six priorities were selected, based upon socio-economic analysis and several entrepreneurial discovery sessions with regional stakeholders. These highlighted both existing capacity and the latent potential of economic and scientific sectors in the region: (1) Tourism and Leisure, (2) Life Sciences, Health and Recovery, (3) Agro-food, (4) Renewable Energy, (5) New ICT, Multimedia and Intelligent Systems, and (6) Sea. Unlike many of the tourist regions identified by Bellini *et al.* (2017), which adopted a modernisation strategy for within an unchanged regional economic structure, the Algarve regards tourist innovation as a means to enhance the regional system's ability to move forward to a renewed economic structure. In the Algarve, the strategy explores connections between tourism and renewable energies/energy efficiency sectors, along with agri-food, by boosting value chains integrated with the tourism system.

Nevertheless, despite the prioritisation process following the RIS3 guidelines, and the effort of collecting a solid base of evidence, the 'domains' selected reproduced those in the 2006 innovation plan. Although there was a solid knowledge base for the definition of priorities, that base was considered somewhat top-down and the selected domains were excessively large – avoiding the true selection and compromise that are supposed to lead all RIS3 processes (Forte *et al.*, 2016). Policy-makers were wary of tensions with regional stakeholders and avoided committing to a more limited number of priorities. Priorities were also stated as sectors and/or domains, meaning that the effort to find real specific 'priority-activities' was not completely achieved. The official Algarve RIS3 suggests some specific key activities but they are mainly of a horizontal nature.

This failure in identifying relevant priorities for action is symptomatic of several system weaknesses. First, the strategy drafting and priority identification was led by a reduced number of actors; the relatively low heterogeneity of inputs to the process encouraged a more conservative approach of continuing with pre-existing priorities. Second, the actual university-led mobilisation of regional industry through entrepreneurial discovery was rather weak, limiting the identification of new innovation and development paths. These difficulties of making hard choices are also symptomatic of the lack of leadership by regional policy-makers.

The central role of the university in the process may have also limited the potential of the process to properly engage industry. Although the university was well placed to undertake technical assessment of the evidence base, defining indicators and developing monitoring system, the actual university's administrative barriers and lack of incentive structures limited how far its researchers could act as boundary spanners between academia, business and civic society. Further, the more applied orientation that a polytechnic university could have brought to the table was limited by the increasingly dominant logic towards scientific excellence.

Conflicts and tensions in universities' smart specialisation strategy roles

An important part of the framing of the discussion of tensions of the Algarve must be the fact that the regional university system has not been 'designed' to meet the current purposes of innovation policies. Although universities in peripheral Portuguese regions have been seen frequently as tools of modernisation, their orientation was led by other governmental levels, and in close cooperation with local elite interests. This meant that universities were effectively 'transplanted' from the core to the periphery. The resulting university institutions were not designed to promote R&D and innovation in specific sectors of the knowledge economy simply because the industrial fabric needed for this purpose did not exist. Higher education was shaped and designed by central governments and scientific communities, and then adapted to the periphery, without taking into account these places' specific needs or structure.

Another important component of the regional university system is the institutional configuration. Since universities are public bodies and the professors are public servants, once universities are established, their reorientation become difficult if local economic needs are not readily aligned with academic incentives. Curricular alignment has been closely related to the needs of particular professions, such as doctors, lawyers and teachers, demanded by public services, and also by general technical needs of the economic sectors, rather than particular strategic economic sectors' demands. In addition, the universities are also shaped by the expectations of the social milieu. The new middle classes usually find more opportunities in public administration employment (and some traditional economic sectors) than in risky and narrow labour markets for highly trained graduates in manufacturing and knowledge-intensive business sectors. These arrangements also produce an effect in university orientation, especially in curricula, and planning of research and innovation activities. It contributes to the emergence of general universities with low specialisation related to the local environment's economic sectors.

Pathways towards more constructive university contributions

Universities play a crucial role in regional development, particularly in peripheral regions. But are peripheral universities well equipped to contribute to structural change through economic diversification (dependent upon deviating from the *status quo*)? The answer seems negative not only because of limited public funding but also because of internal governance and institutional arrangements. It is evident that sometimes too much is asked from universities. Without appropriate proper institutional reforms these goals are not readily achievable because international excellence and the local industrial engagement represent conflicting forces. What is needed are specific institutional regional models for peripheral universities, re-aligning their mission and objectives with its structures. The requirement appears to be to avoid copying institutional models for core universities, and in particular, the institutional drag that centrally driven administration and bureaucracy can impose for regional engagement. In order for universities to act as anchor organisations to stimulate their localised comparative advantages, active efforts are required to align curricula and research lines with industrial demands – crossing existing and potential opportunities in the markets with capabilities in knowledge production. Here the notion of entrepreneurial discovery is relevant. Universities need to support the definition of a regional vision for the region towards structural change. Universities need to stimulate their collaboration within the region, creating trust and proximity benefits with geographically proximate actors but also act to connect with external networks and global value chains.

The industrial structure commonly acts as a restriction in the search for collaboration and innovation. In the case of the Algarve, even if crucial for its historical catching-up with more developed regions, overspecialisation in tourism created path dependencies, but left the region doubly exposed to the crisis after 2007 when expenditure on tourism fell, and the region was left exposed. Algarve was the Portuguese region where unemployment rose most rapidly, to the highest levels, and with the highest GDP contraction. After the crisis Algarve is steadily recovering but with minor signs of institutional learning from the crisis; although the RIS3 process was an opportunity to guide structural change it has to date been at best marginally successful.

Regional development policies, including S&T and innovation policies, require a huge and combined effort, involving actors within and outside the system, institutional reforms, and public and private funding. These problems cannot be solved or addressed by a single institution such as a university in peripheral regions, particularly where that university has to fit within a national framework derived from the needs of core regions. We here point to the inconsistency of many public policies and arrangements (financial incentives, institutional reforms and industrial policies) with the expected role of universities in peripheral regions. But given that universities concentrate a disproportionate amount of regional human capital resources and R&D capabilities, they automatically become strategic actors in the process. This internal strength gives influence and power to universities in shaping the implementation of regional development policies.

Universities can be an important partner in developing new policies and solutions for peripheral regions. But there is a risk of the universities becoming part of the problem, reproducing ineffectiveness and the *status quo*. The case of the Algarve illustrates precisely what happens when universities become incorporated into implementing a strategy that implicitly carries a linear model of innovation. Universities may work to ensure that their internal capabilities are prioritised over existing industrial demand and, if the changes proposed in the RIS3 conflict with universities' interests, they may show a strong resistance to development.

Innovation strategies, and specifically RIS3, are newly framed policies that are implemented within previous institutional developments and economic structures. These policies need to learn how to create a strong system and develop a balanced system in terms of density and connectedness in peripheral regions. Without a degree of flexibility from participants, policies can serve to stimulate reinforcing trends that replicate the strengths and weaknesses of the system, amplifying power relations and the *status quo* of particular actors in the system. As we have seen in this case, this can work to benefit the public universities, not out of any bad faith behaviour but in the absence of other institutional partners and capacity.

Acknowledgement

Hugo Pinto gratefully acknowledges financial support from FCT – *Fundação para a Ciência e a Tecnologia* for his post-doctoral research (SFRH/BPD/84038/2012).

Notes

1 Approved by *Despacho Normativo n.º 65/2008, 11 de Dezembro*, published in *Diário da República, 2.ª série, n.º 246, 22 de Dezembro de 2008*.
2 Regulation n.º 57/2010.
3 We here point to in particular the efforts associated with ETTIRSE (Regional Innovation Strategy Algarve-Huelva concluded in 2001, www.ccdr-alg.pt/site/sites/ ccdr-alg.pt/files/publicacoes/ettirse_pt.pdf), Inovalgarve (Innovative actions project concluded in 2004, www.ccdr-alg.pt/site/sites/ccdr-alg.pt/files/publicacoes/ inovalgarve_ideias.pdf) and PRIALgarv (Regional innovation plan concluded in 2007, www.cria.pt/estudos-e-projetos/plano-regional-de-inovacao-do-algarve-prialgarve/).
4 See RIS3 Algarve here: http://poalgarve21.ccdr-alg.pt/site/sites/poalgarve21.ccdr-alg.pt/files/2014–2020/ris3_algarve_2014-2020_pt_v10.5_8_2_2015_verfinal.pdf.

References

Barreira, A.P. (2009). O perfil regional do Algarve na inovação. *Spatial and Organizational Dynamics Discussion Papers*, Issue 0, 58–75. Available from: www.cieo.pt/discussion papers/discussionpapers0.pdf (accessed 24 April 2018).

Bellini, N., Grillo, F., Lazzeri, G. and Pasquinelli, C. (2017). Tourism and regional economic resilience from a policy perspective: Lessons from smart specialization strategies in Europe. *European Planning Studies* 25, 140–153. doi:10.1080/ 09654313.2016.1273323.

Benneworth, P. and Charles, D. (2005). University spin-off policies and economic development in less successful regions: Learning from two decades of policy practice. *European Planning Studies* 13(4), 537–557.

Benneworth, P. and Dassen, A. (2011). *Strengthening Global-Local Connectivity in Regional Innovation Strategies: Implications for Regional Innovation Policy*. OECD Regional Development Working Paper, OECD Publishing. Available from: http://ideas.repec. org/p/oec/govaab/2011-1-en.html (accessed 2 March 2014).

Benneworth, P. and Hospers, G. (2007). The new economic geography of old industrial regions: Universities as global-local pipelines. *Environment and Planning C: Government & Policy* 25, 779–802.

Benneworth, P., Pinheiro, R. and Karlsen, J. (2017). Strategic agency and institutional change: Investigating the role of universities in regional innovation systems (RISs). *Regional Studies*, 51(2), 235–248.

Boschma, R. and Frenken, K. (2011). Technological relatedness, related variety and economic geography. In P. Cooke, B.T. Asheim, R. Boschma, R. Martin, D. Schwartz and F. Tödtling (eds), *Handbook of Regional Innovation and Growth*. Cheltenham, UK: Edward Elgar Publishing, pp. 187–197.

Capello, R. and Kroll, H. (2016). From theory to practice in smart specialization strategy: Emerging limits and possible future trajectories. *European Planning Studies* 24, 1393–1406. doi:10.1080/09654313.2016.1156058.

56   *Hugo Pinto et al.*

CCDR Algarve (2006). *Estratégia de Desenvolvimento Regional 2007–13 Algarve.* Comissão de Coordenação e Desenvolvimento Regional do Algarve, Faro.

CCDR Algarve (2014). *Estratégia de Especialização Inteligente RIS3 Algarve.* Comissão de Coordenação e Desenvolvimento Regional do Algarve, Faro.

Chatterton, P. and Goddard, J. (2000). The response of higher education institutions to regional needs. *European Journal of Education* 35, 475–496.

Charles, D. and Benneworth, P. (2001). The Regional Mission: The Regional Contribution of Higher Education: National Report, Universities UK/HEFCE, London (published with nine regional reports).

Charles, D., Kitagawa, F. and Uyarra, E. (2014). Universities in crisis? New challenges and strategies in two English city-regions. *Cambridge Journal of Regions, Economy and Society* 7(2), 327–348. doi:10.1093/cjres/rst029.

Coenen, L. (2007). The role of universities in the regional innovation systems of the North East of England and Scania, Sweden: Providing missing links? *Environment and Planning C: Government and Policy* 25: 803–821.

Cruz, A. R. (2014). Tourism, creativity and talent: Breaking Algarve's tourism lock-in. *Regional Studies, Regional Science* 1(1), 138–144, doi:10.1080/21681376.2014.939529.

Cruz, A. R. and Pinto, H. (2008). As Redes de Investigação Científica: o Caso da Universidade do Algarve em Portugal. *Gestão Contemporânea* 5(5). https://mpra.ub.uni-muenchen.de/13511/.

Fernández-Esquinas, M. and Pinto, H. (2014). The role of universities in urban regeneration: Reframing the analytical approach. *European Planning Studies* 22(7), 1462–1483.

Forte, I.P., Marinelli, E. and Foray, D. (2016). The Entrepreneurial Discovery Process (EDP) cycle: From priority selection to strategy implementation. In C. Gianelle, D. Kyriakou, C. Cohen and M. Przeor (eds), *Implementing Smart Specialisation Strategies: A Handbook.* Brussels: European Commission, pp. 14–35.

Frenken, K., Van Oort, F. and Verburg, T. (2007). Related variety, unrelated variety and regional economic growth. *Regional Studies* 41, 685–697. doi:10.1080/00343400601120296.

Goddard, J., Kempton, L. and Vallance, P. (2013). Universities and smart specialisation: Challenges, tensions and opportunities for the innovation strategies of European regions. *Ekonomiaz: Revista Vasca de Economía* 82–101.

Guerreiro, J. (2008). *Caracterização da Estrutura Económica do Algarve.* NERA: Loulé.

Gunasekara, C. (2006). The generative and developmental roles of universities in regional innovation systems. *Science and Public Policy* 33, 137.

Hausmann, R. and Rodrik, D. (2003). Economic development as self-discovery. *Journal of Development Economics* 72, 603–633. doi:10.1016/S0304-3878(03)00124-X.

Kempton, L., Goddard, J., Edwards, J., Hegyi, F. B. and Elena-Pérez, S. (2013). *Universities and smart specialisation.* s3 policy brief series no. 03/2013.

Komninos, N., Musyck, B. and Reid, A. I. (2014). Smart specialisation strategies in south Europe during crisis. *European Journal of Innovation Management* 17, 448–471. doi:10.1108/EJIM-11-2013-0118.

Marques, P. and Morgan, K. (2018). The heroic assumptions of smart specialisation: A sympathetic critique of regional innovation policy. In Arne Isaksen, Roman Martin and Michaela Trippl (eds), *New Avenues for Regional Innovation Systems: Theoretical Advances, Empirical Cases and Policy Lessons.* New York: Springer.

Neffke, F., Henning, M. and Boschma, R. (2011). How do regions diversify over time? Industry relatedness and the development of new growth paths in regions. *Economic Geography* 87, 237–265. doi:10.1111/j.1944-8287.2011.01121.x.

Oughton, C., Landabaso, M. and Morgan, K. (2002). The regional innovation paradox: Innovation policy and industrial policy. *The Journal of Technology Transfer* 27, 97–110. doi:10.1023/A:1013104805703.

Perry, B. (2008). Academic knowledge and urban development: Theory, policy and practice. In T. Yigitcanlar, K. Velibeyoglu and S. Baum (eds), *Knowledge-based Urban Development: Planning and Applications in the Information Era*. Hershey, PA: IGI Global, pp. 21–41.

Pinheiro, R., Benneworth, P. and Jones, G. A. (2012). *Universities and Regional Development: A Critical Assessment of Tensions and Contradictions*. London and New York: Routledge.

Pinheiro, R., Geschwind, L. and Aarrevaara, T. (2015). *Mergers in Higher Education: The Experience from Northern Europe*. Dordrecht: Springer.

Pinto, H. (2012). *Transferência do conhecimento em Portugal. Mudança e institucionalização das relações universidade-empresa*. Tese de doutoramento. http://hdl.handle.net/10316/21366.

Pinto, H. (2016). Resiliência da inovação e desenvolvimento regional: Uma análise de redes de colaboração no Algarve. *Actas do IX Congresso Português de Sociologia 'Portugal: Território de Territórios'*.

Pinto, H. (2017). Actor-network creation and the institutionalization of knowledge transfer offices: Consolidation of the 'triple helix' consensus space within the Portuguese university. *Triple Helix: A Journal of University-Industry-Government Innovation & Entrepreneurship* – special issue on Institutions, Intermediation and Triple Helix Relationships. Springer.

Pinto, H., Fernandez-Esquinas, M. and Uyarra, E. (2015). Universities and knowledge-intensive business services (KIBS) as sources of knowledge for innovative firms in peripheral regions. *Regional Studies* 49(11), 1873–1891.

Pinto, H., Guerreiro, J. and Uyarra, E. (2012). Diversidades de sistemas de inovação e implicações nas políticas regionais: Comparação das regiões do Algarve e da Andaluzia. *Revista Portuguesa de Estudos Regionais*, 29, 3–14.

Pugh, R. E. (2014). 'Old wine in new bottles'? Smart specialisation in Wales. *Regional Studies, Regional Science* 1, 152–157. doi:10.1080/21681376.2014.944209.

Radosevic, S. (2017). Advances in understanding smart specialization: Overview and conclusions. in S. Radosevic, A. Curaj, R. Gheorghiou, L. Andreescu and I. Wade (eds), *Advances in the Theory and Practice of Smart Specialization*. Amsterdam: Elsevier.

Romão, J., Guerreiro, J. and Rodrigues, P. M. M. (2016). Tourism growth and regional resilience: The 'beach disease' and the consequences of the global crisis of 2007. *Tourism Economics* 22, 699–714.

Tödtling, F. and Trippl, M. (2005). One size fits all?: Towards a differentiated regional innovation policy approach. *Research Policy* 34(8), 1203–1219.

Tsipouri, L. (2017). Innovation policy for EU South. In S. Radosevic, A. Curaj, R. Gheorghiou, L. Andreescu and I. Wade (eds), *Advances in the Theory and Practice of Smart Specialization*. Amsterdam: Elsevier.

UAlg (2007a). *Plano Regional de Inovação do Algarve*. Universidade do Algarve, Faro.

UAlg (2007b). *Horizonte 2010, Princípios Estratégicos para a Universidade do Algarve*. Universidade do Algarve, Faro.

UAlg (2017). I&D investigação e desenvolvimento Made In Algarve. *UAlgzine* n° 10 – Abril 2017, Universidade do Algarve, Faro. Available from: www.ualg.pt/pt/content/revista-ualgzine (accessed 18 April 2018).

Uyarra, E. (2010). Conceptualizing the regional roles of universities: Implications and contradictions. *European Planning Studies* 18, 1227–1246.

5 'Strange bird'

A peripheral university college in a complex, peripheral region

James Karlsen

Introduction

> Outside, on the campus in Alta, there is a sculpture with the name Strange Bird. The name made sense for the institution. The institution was at that time a strange element.
>
> (Former rector Finnmark University College)

The above quotation relates to the first period after the establishment of the university college in a complex, peripheral region. Finnmark University College was established in 1973 in Alta in Finnmark County, and this chapter discusses the establishment of a higher education institution in a complex, peripheral region. Finnmark is Norway's most northern region, bordering Finland, Russia and the Barents Sea, and its geographical location makes it peripheral in Norway and ultra-peripheral in Europe. It is also Norway's biggest region with a surface area of 48,631 km^2 (the same size as Denmark) but the smallest in terms of population (about 75,800 inhabitants) making Finnmark one of Europe's most sparsely populated areas (1.6 inhabitants/km^2). As with many other peripheral regions, Finnmark faces challenges of low population growth, unemployment, lack of knowledge-intensive industries and a low rate of innovation, an ageing population, gender issues, low education, an uneven distribution of the population in the region, and lack of creation of new industrial development paths.

But it is a set of other factors that make Finnmark a complex region. First, its geopolitical location gives it a border with Russia, a global superpower, and for Norway, a small NATO (North Atlantic Treaty Organization) member, neighbourly relations with Russia demand a kid glove treatment. Second, its Barents sea location gives it access to rich natural resources both on land and at sea (fish, and oil and gas), and to add to this complexity, fish resources are jointly governed with Russia. Third, it is the Sami people's homeland, Norway's indigenous people, who historically were suppressed by the Norwegian government.

Finnmark has been strategically important to Norway during its history, with different policy approaches being used to maintain its population levels, giving it a state-driven developmental model. One of the most important policy initiatives was the 1990s establishment of an action zone for Finnmark and northern Troms, offering specific policy tools and subsidies to develop an attractive region for settlement, work, commerce and industry (St.meld. nr. 32, 1989–90). This chapter considers one specific regional development policy tool, namely the establishment of Finnmark University College, as part of the establishment of Norway's regional university college system in the early 1970s. This new college system sought to enhance local and regional access; to prevent mass migration of young people from peripheral areas into urban centres; and to stimulate regional economic development by providing the regions with a cadre of professionals for both the public and private sectors (Kyvik, 1981). In this chapter, I consider the research question: *how can a small, peripheral university college contribute to improve regional development in such a complex state-driven peripheral region?* The chapter presents a case study of the Finnmark regional college from its foundation in the 1970s to its merger with University of Tromsø – The Arctic University of Norway, in 2013. The chapter explores the ways in which three kinds of HEI practices, namely educational, research and regional mission intersect with and shape three kinds of regional economic development practices, namely educational level and skills, industrial structure and innovation and regional and local development. Through an analytic focus on the interactions and tensions between the HEI and the region, the chapter notes that the expectations to what a university college can achieve in such a region are relatively limited, and are primarily local rather than truly regional in their scope.

Theoretical framework

In this chapter, I explore the ways in which a higher education college in a region with a strongly state-driven developmental model can contribute to regional growth. I place this in terms of the emergence of a knowledge society, with Daniel Bell in his book *The Coming of the Post-Industrial Society*, arguing that more than 40 years ago theoretical (codified) knowledge had acquired a central place in modern societies, something not previously the case.

> What has become decisive for the organization of decisions and the direction of change is the centrality of theoretical knowledge – the primacy of theory over empiricism and the codification of knowledge into abstract systems of symbols that, as in any axiomatic system, can be used to illustrate many different and varied areas of experience.
>
> (Bell, 1999: 20)

Today, it is difficult to think of an organisation that does not make systematic use of theoretical knowledge. Higher education institutions, HEIs, are important producers of theoretical knowledge, which has resulted in an increase in the role of HEIs in advancing economic development at a national, regional and local level (Dunning, 2002; OECD, 2009). The literature on the role of HEIs in regional development has been expanding in recent years. A more normative discourse argues that HEIs have a duty to engage in regional development efforts in peripheral regions because they are the main actors and drivers for economic and regional development. However, evidence regarding HEIs' roles in fostering economic development is inconclusive, with more evidence required regarding HEIs' actual practices in driving regional development (Benneworth *et al.*, 2009; Drucker and Goldstein, 2007; OECD, 2007). Practice is organised human activities regulated by goals and standards (Schatzki, 2001).

Institutions are constituted in, and maintained through social practice, institutions here being defined as:

> patterns both of and for particular types of social practices, namely those that are distributed across time and space, routinized and taken-for-granted, 'objectivated' as existing apart from and beyond the people who embody them and legitimated in terms of an overarching institutional logic (Barley, 2008; Berger and Luckmann, 1991).
>
> (Lok and de Rond, 2013: 186)

HEIs are institutions producing theoretical knowledge. One approach argues that theoretical knowledge exists in opposition to practice; that it mistrusts intuition, ad hoc practices and personal commitment, by favouring objectivity, detachment and explicit assertions (Tsoukas, 2005). However, another position is that the production of theoretical knowledge is also practice, so the two are not in opposition, but that place- and context-specific practice is an integrated part of theoretical knowledge production (Tsoukas, 2005). There are different fields of practice; one is the practice of the institution, of the knowledge-producing unit, whilst another is the production of knowledge, such as research and teaching. Each field has different types of knowledge production, and in this chapter I consider the field of institution with its goals and practice.

The practices are education, research and the third mission, encompassing aspects around HEIs' wider societal contributions. This practice is also connected to the regions when named the *regional mission*, implying a direct engagement with socio-economic, political and cultural aspects of regional relevance to the region. The regional mission is defined as the purposive formal and informal efforts to address dimensions of relevance to various regional actors (Pinheiro *et al.*, 2015). One challenge in studying HEI practice is that HEIs have a complex internal architecture that is critical to their knowledge production with the resultant problem that: "Regional development perspectives assume all too easily that HEIs are simple organizations, with hierarchical decision-making and interest-representation structures, overlooking entirely universities organizational complexity" (Pinheiro *et al.*, 2012b: 4).

Chatterton and Goddard (2000) argued that HEIs and regions are involved in activities that have a potential for mutual benefit, and there is a *strategic management interface* between university managers and regional policy-makers, necessary for maximising mutual benefits. Each set of an HEI's teaching, research and regional engagement practice can be directly linked to critical regional practice of skills, innovation, and culture and learning, and aligning them is necessary to realise this mutual benefit. Their model was criticised by Pinheiro *et al.* (2012a) for ignoring the tensions that may emerge in this interface between university and regional actors, which *may* shape the development of both HEIs and regions. By addressing explicitly such tensions one can better understand both the HEI internal logic alongside the external logic regarding why specific practices and path-development trajectories are produced.

An overview of the regional economic development problem

Finnmark occupies a strategic geopolitical position in the far north-east of Norway. In the thirteenth century, this position led to the building of a fortress in Vardø, an island, on Finnmark's eastern coast, for defensive purposes. In the Second World War Hitler acknowledged Finnmark's position by using Kirkenes in eastern Finnmark as a military base for preparing for the attack on the Soviet Union, ultimately leading to Hitler's first defeat on the Eastern Front, in Litza in the Soviet Union, some kilometres from the Norwegian border (Jacobsen, 2014). The Germans withdrew from Finnmark in 1944 with scorched earth tactics, most buildings and infrastructure in the whole region were destroyed, and the establishment of HEIs in Finnmark is a part of its reconstruction as a modern, industrialised region.

Natural resource exploitation (fishing and related activities, mining, agriculture and reindeer farming) has led to cyclical economic development in Finnmark through booms and busts. Even in 2015 Finnmark had a higher share of employment within fishing and agriculture (6.3 per cent) than the Norway average (2.3 per cent). A series of specific public policy measures have been implemented to compensate for employment loss in resource-based industries (Eikeland, 2010), and to stimulate development of new knowledge-intensive industries. The de-industrialisation process resulted in a lower share of industrial employment (7.4 per cent) than Norway's average (9.6 per cent). The growth in knowledge-intensive industries has been low, with Finnmark having a much lower share of employment within knowledge-intensive services (11 per cent) than the Norwegian average (16.7 per cent). The public sector has grown strongly in the region, with almost 43 per cent of the workforce employed within this sector (35 per cent for Norway).

In many regional economic indicators Finnmark scores low. One of these indicators is completion from secondary school, seen as a minimum level of educational attainment for successful participation in further work and study (Lamb and Markussen, 2011). Compared with other Norwegian counties the relative number of secondary school drop-outs is much higher in Finnmark than any other county, with only 51 per cent completing secondary school in Finnmark after 5 years (data from 2005), the second worst being Troms county,

Finnmark
Finnmárkku

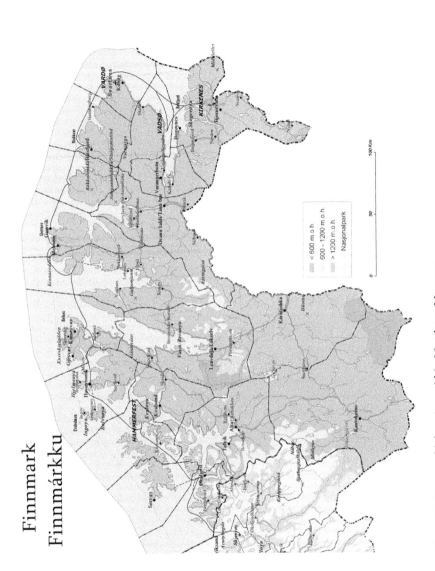

Figure 5.1 Finnmark's location within Northern Norway

Source: Wikipedia, reproduced under creative commons licence, by Jensens.

Finnmark's southern neighbour (63 per cent completion).[1] The county with the lowest rate is another peripheral region, Sogn og Fjordane, with 75 per cent completion (Markussen *et al.*, 2012). Population growth is another indicator of regional economic development. Compared with the population growth in Norway in the period from 1950 to 2016, the population growth in Finnmark has been weak (see Table 5.1). Population growth in this period in Norway was 59 per cent while it was only 17.5 per cent in Finnmark; Finnmark population growth increased from 1950 to 1980, then it decreased to 2000, and then stabilised. The recent increase results from foreign immigration from abroad, with both net migration to other regions in Norway and the natural growth rate (births–deaths) being negative.

The establishment of teacher education in 1973 and the establishment of economic administrative education some years later in Alta represents the introduction of HEIs and the knowledge society in a broader approach in Finnmark. Already established was a nursery education college in Hammerfest dating to 1960. The three institutions were merged within a wider Norwegian merger process in the 1990s under the new name Finnmark University College (HiF) in 1994. In 2007 a campus (Barents International School) was established in Sør-Varanger (Kirkenes), and as a result of a new wave of mergers HiF in turn merged with University of Tromsø in 2013. Before the merger, HiF was a mid-sized university college with about 2,000 students, 240 employees, and about 60 different courses and programmes mostly at the bachelor level.

One region, but different sub-regional development challenges

Finnmark's geographical size means there are many different development challenges split across the various sub-regions and centrally.[2] The central places are the municipalities Vadsø, where the county administration is located, Sør-Varanger, Alta and Hammerfest and the sub-regions are Coastal Finnmark and Inland Finnmark.

Alta and Hammerfest in the western part of the region, and Kirkenes (Sør-Varanger), close to the Russian border increased in population due to governmental policy. Alta's growth was driven by public infrastructure, education and service industries. Hammerfest is resource based experiencing in recent years an extremely positive development from the establishment of a gas processing terminal for the Barents Sea, the *Snøhvit* (Snow White) field; without this development Hammerfest would also likely be languishing. Sør-Varanger grew extensively due to recent increasing interaction with Russia, and a temporary fillip from an ore mine that reopened in 2009 only to go bankrupt.

Coastal Finnmark consists of ten coastal municipalities, and is the region experiencing the greatest population loss (a decrease of 38 per cent from 1950 to 2016) resulting from the declining fishing industry relating to the Barents Sea, a rich fishing resource. The industry grew from 1950 until 1990, since then numbers have fallen due to rising competition, falling transport costs

Table 5.1 Population development in sub-regions in Finnmark and Norway from 1950 to 2016

	1950	1960	1970	1980	1990	2001	2011	2016	Change 1950–2016 in %
Vadso	4,428	4,708	5,535	6,068	5,993	6,149	6,128	6,160	39.1
Alta	8,955	9,655	11,159	13,378	15,170	17,156	19,249	20,097	124.4
Hammerfest	6,175	8,038	9,188	9,642	9,248	9,066	9,927	10,455	69.3
Sor-Varanger	8,916	10,159	10,443	10,485	9,671	9,623	9,851	10,227	14.7
Inland Finnmark	11,118	12,349	13,188	14,487	14,463	14,288	13,421	13,483	21.3
Coastal Finnmark	24,884	25,197	24,511	22,586	18,608	16,562	14,117	15,336	−38.4
Finnmark	64,476	70,106	74,024	76,646	73,153	72,844	72,693	75,758	17.5
Norway	**3,278,546**	**3,591,234**	**3,874,133**	**4,091,132**	**4,247,546**	**4,520,947**	**4,979,955**	**5,213,985**	**59.0**

Source: Statistics Norway.

and technological changes, driving a fall in population, increasing unemployment and long-term sickness, and an outmigration of economically active residents. Investment in industries such as fish farming and tourism have not compensated for the loss, with a possible exception in Nordkapp, where the famous North Cape is located, which attracts more than 200,000 tourists each year; Nordkapp is also one of the few municipalities where the fishing industry remains wellfunctioning.

Inland Finnmark consists of five inland municipalities, the strongholds of the Sami people in Norway. Before national borders were established, the Sami people used to live in the northern parts of Norway, Russia, Finland and Sweden, but as national state systems were established the Sami people slowly settled into their then-host nation. Finnmark's twentieth-century modernisation drove firstly the loss of the Sea Sami (resident at the coast and fjords) people's language and traditional lifestyle. Sami reindeer herders were able to preserve their language and culture better than the Sea Samis because of their nomadic lifestyle. A conflict between the Norwegian government and the Sami people in the 1980s concerning the building of a hydro power plant escalated to the point where the Norwegian government found it necessary to approve the establishment of a Sami parliament. This parliament has been important for the Sami people and for the respect of the rights of Norway's Indigenous people. Since the Sami parliament was created, several Sami institutions have been created in Inland Finnmark, including the Sami Regional College in 1989. These new institutions have been important for preserving the population, employment and the Sami culture; the current challenge remains creating new industries to compensate for the loss of traditional industries, such as agriculture and reindeer herding. Table 5.2 summarises the main local and sub-regional challenges for regional economic development within Finnmark.

Method, data and analysis

This study is designed as a qualitative case study (Yin, 2013) reflecting the blurry borders between the object of study (HiF) and the region resulting from their interaction. The case study was theoretically informed, making theoretical assumptions explicit. In case studies as much information as possible should be generated using different methods. HiF was selected because it is located in a peripheral region which historically faced a number of economic, social and cultural changes. HiF's history begins with Finnmark's modernisation and the subsequent emergence of the knowledge economy, with it being integral to Finnmark's development since the 1970s. The study started with a review of secondary data sources, such as policy documents, research reports, HEI official documents and strategies, and statistical data from Statistics Norway and Database for Statistics on Higher Education. This provided an overview of Finnmark's long-term development. A book covering the first 30 years of the history of HiF (Berg, 2006) provided an overview of HiF, later supplemented with ten qualitative interviews, seven from HiF that represented academic and

Table 5.2 Summary of main regional development challenges of the sub-regions of Finnmark

Vadsø	Stagnation in population. Vadsø, which is an administrative centre in Finnmark, has over the last years lost many of its former centre functions. The challenge is how to develop new industries and service functions that can compensate for the loss of jobs.
Alta	Growth centre in Finnmark where the main campus of HiF is located. Even if Alta is a growth centre, Alta needs to handle the growth on the one hand and on the other hand secure further growth.
Hammerfest	Growth centre in Finnmark where a campus of HiF is located. The growth is mainly a result of the establishment of the gas terminal.
Sør-Varanger	A former mining town, now a centre for the commerce with North Russia. HiF has a small campus located in Kirkenes.
Inland Finnmark	The core area of the Sami people in Norway. Many new Sami institutions have been located in the region but there is a lack of new industries.
Coastal Finnmark	Path destruction of the fishing industry and no new paths have been developed to compensate for the loss of employment in the fishing industry. The effects of path destruction have been outmigration, high rate of unemployment and dropouts from secondary school.

Source: Author's own design.

administrative staff at different levels (rectors, vice-rectors, heads of departments, administrators, academics), and three respondents representing different private and public organisations. All interviews were recorded and later transcribed.

The analytic starting point was writing an overview of Finnmark's economic development, which highlighted Finnmark's extreme regional sub-differences, justifying a choice for considering sub-regions and central places, which made the analysis more nuanced but also more complex to handle. The case study covers the period from HiF's creation in the 1970s to the merger with University of Tromsø in 2013. The unit of analysis is the HEI as a knowledge-producing unit. For the simplicity of the analysis, I will use the name HiF, although the HEI changed names several times in the 1970s and 1980s and in a period even had two rectors due to internal tensions between staff from teacher education and economic and administrative education (Berg, 2006).

The strength with a long time period is in permitting the identification of specific development paths, although simultaneously reducing the depth of analysis. The analysis began considering how the establishment of HiF with its mission of education in business and administration, affected regional and local practices in Finnmark, highlighting the tensions and contradictions illustrating both different logics and motives between the HEI and Finnmark, along with highlighting those practices which were important for HiF's long-term development. An analysis of data is a sorting exercise (Wolcott, 1994), a search

Table 5.3 Operationalising the HEI – regional tensions

Type of tension	Key questions
Education and development of skills	When and how have different types of regional relevant studies developed and how has the regional demand developed?
Development of regional relevant research	When and how have different types of regional relevant studies developed and how has the regional demand developed?
Regional mission and local and regional development	What kind of regional and local consequences can be identified as a result of the establishment and development of HiF?

Source: Author's own design.

for patterns giving meaning to the problem statement (Mills, 1959). There are many different ways of sorting and ordering any data set, but they must relate to the chosen problem statement and theoretical framework. Table 5.3 shows the type of tensions and key questions used for the analysis, which provided the basis of our construction of three analytical stories, each story sharing the same historical starting point, namely the establishment of HiF.

HiF practices of education, research and regional mission

A new institution meets local practices about the need for education

The establishment of a system of district colleges in Norway in the late 1960s and early 1970s was a reform seeking to create a new type of education not covered by the existing universities. The arguments for the new system included the need for a shorter and faster education than offered by universities, and that universities' theoretical studies did not satisfy industry and commerce's need for more practical and vocational knowledge (Kyvik, 1983). The type of education launched was economic administrative education, said to represent the future knowledge necessary for industrial to be competitive and for the public sector to offer services of good quality. It took some time before the new HEI could fulfil its goal of offering education with administration and business because of challenges of recruiting qualified academic staff; the first business and administration studies degree was offered in 1981 supplemented in 1984 with information technology. A half-year fisheries study had been established already in 1978, and whilst clearly of regional relevance for the then-dominant fishery industry, poor recruitment led to its closure in 1985.

As these studies became established HiF soon realised that Finnmark's prospective students did not share the national educational discourse; resource-based industries were not founded on knowledge workers, and most local industry had small management (often a single person) and administration teams. Industrial demand at that time was for more hands, not theoretical knowledge, with necessary knowledge provided on-the-job, rarely demanding education beyond primary level. This created a clear mismatch between HiF's knowledge offer and the knowledge demanded by industry. As a former rector formulated it:

> When the institution was recently established, we felt that higher educa-tion did not fit into the dominating industry structure in Finnmark. It was a mismatch between higher education and the dominating industry. We felt that there were not many that were interested in us.
>
> (Former rector at HiF)

Whilst Finnmark's population understood the need for educating teachers and nurses, given the huge shortages, it was harder to convey why education was necessary for industrial employment. *Why use time sitting in the school, when you instead could start earning money just after primary school?* This attitude was a shared practice not only among young people but in general across Finnmark wher-ever resource-based industries were dominant. Gradually, however, Finnmark's industry became more knowledge intensive:

> This happened in the 1990s, late 1980, early 1990s. It was a marked shift that we were wanted and that we were wanted in every nook and cranny of the county.
>
> (Former rector)

As a consequence of this shift recruitment began to rise: in 1980 there were 90 students studying economy and business administration increasing to 595 students (1990) and 767 (1992), making it the most popular study at HiF (Berg, 2006). Finnmark's resource-based industry began declining in the 1990s, with a falling number of firms producing fish, the closure of mines in Inland Finnmark and Sør-Varanger, and high barriers to entry within agriculture and rein-deer herding. Employment opportunities did exist for people with economic administrative education from a growing knowledge-based industry located in Finnmark's central places (notably Alta, Hammerfest and Vadsø) along with an expanding public sector. At the time of writing, in 2017, the idea that you don't need education remained dominant in some parts of Finnmark, notably Inland Finnmark, especially within reindeer herding and on the fishing vessels in Coastal Finnmark. But the overall number of jobs in these communities and industries which do not demand a secondary education fell from 1970 to 2017. What accounted for the persistence of the practice were a few success stories of individuals who were lucky and able to earn a lot of money without having any education (Markussen *et al.*, 2012). There has been a time lag of 50 years between the arguments regarding establishing a university college system and today's realities in Finnmark. Even if HiF is acknowledged as an important insti-tution for education, and that almost all industries now need qualified persons, the practice is still alive in some parts of Finnmark that the maximum education level demanded is primary school, and HiF's establishment did not make acceptance of the need for higher education ubiquitous.

Another reason for a low rate of completion is the location of regional secondary schools in the central places of Finnmark, such as Alta, Hammerfest, Vadsø and Sør-Varanger. Young people living in Finnmark's periphery must move from home to a dorm at the age of 16, and for some this can be hard leading to non-completion of secondary school (Markussen *et al.*, 2012). For the others that continue to a HEI, this can mean saying farewell to their home, because of limited work possibilities for persons with higher education. The emergence of the knowledge economy has seen a regional divide emerge between Finnmark's central places, with their more knowledge-intensive industry, and small coastal municipalities, still struggling with fishery's secular decline, and with limited purchase of HiF in these places, there seem to be few opportunities for HiF to help these remote communities create new development trajectories.

Research of regional relevance

Before the 1980s little research was undertaken outside Norway's university cities (Kyvik, 1983). Research is an important part of the knowledge discourse, and also policy-makers in Finnmark were inspired to establish regionally based research institutions. In 1981, NIBR, a national research organisation within urban and regional development, established a department in Alta. Finnmark County also collaborated with HiF to establish a regional research organisation able to undertake research of regional relevance, with Finnmarksforskning (Finnmark Research) being established in Alta in 1988. The new research organisation aimed to initiate, conduct and disseminate research related to Finnmark's opportunities and problems around research topics such as fisheries, tourism, information management, business and community analysis, whilst also being of national and international interest. This created a division of labour between HIF and the research organisations in Finnmark, with HiF largely performing teaching and training while the research institutes were responsible for producing regional relevant knowledge.

Regional policy-makers' ambitions of research of regional relevance quickly encountered the lack of demand within the region for that research (just as there was little demand for many high-level qualifications). Finnmarksforskning found itself in competition with regional consultancy firms and after a number of years struggling merged with NORUT, a research organisation in Tromsø, in 2001, to create NORUT Finnmark, located in Alta. In 2003, NIBR and NORUT Finnmark merged to leave just one small applied research organisation alongside HiF serving Finnmark. The regionally relevant research was not an issue for HiF, which was not engaged with questions of the restructuring of the fishing industry or of reindeer herding in Inland Finnmark. The one area where HiF did build up research of regional relevance was around tourism research, related to the development of its nationally ground-breaking courses in tourism, which were established in 1988. In 1999, HiF became the first of the regional colleges to be permitted to award master's degrees in tourism, with the education drawing on these regionally relevant research strengths (Berg, 2006). This establishment was a result of a bottom-up initiative from a newly recruited associate professor.

> We had a couple of academic entrepreneurs who worked with the establishment … And this education was a mirror of the region. Tourism is important in this region.
>
> (Former rector of HiF)

What distinguished the tourism sector from the resource-based industries was that there was a regional demand for research within tourism among regional stakeholders, and over time, this research emerged from being a topic of regional relevance to become a field of national and international interest. The regional focus is still present in HiF's research, but now under the name of *winter adventure* tourism. The aim of the research is connected to comprehensive and complex changes regarding technology, knowledge, risk assessment and accessibility, which shape the development of core products of Arctic winter tourism.[3] Although regional policy-makers had high ambitions regarding the potential of regionally relevant research to drive regional development and create new trajectories, the results were meagre, with little concrete resulting in Finnmark beyond this emergent research around winter adventure tourism.

Local versus regional consequences

When HiF was located in Alta in the 1970s Alta's population numbered just 11,000 inhabitants, passing the 20,000 mark by 2017. There have clearly been positive benefits for Alta from the presence of HiF with a secondary set of effects around Hammerfest where the nursery education is present although rather small in size.[4] The local economic and cultural effects of both students and staff are considerable for a small city such as Alta; Alta represents not just a place to study but also a place to live and work after students have completed their education. It is also an attractive place for the location of new firms, certainly more so than elsewhere in Finnmark. The share of people with higher education is therefore much higher in Alta than in Finnmark in general. "Students preferably settle in the same place as they studied, since they know the place well. Secondly, they choose the other administrative municipalities, and finally the small coastal municipalities" (Berg, 2006: 171).

This implies that the students from the coast that choose to study in Alta also take an implicit choice about their future residence, because the chances that they will return home to work are small because of the absence of jobs for highly educated people, particularly for families where both parents have higher education and want relevant jobs. Alta municipality's growth strategy since the 1960s resulted in creating new knowledge organizations in addition to the HEIs, including the aforementioned research organisations, but also a knowledge park and a knowledge park for culture. A number of public organisations have found it attractive to be located in Alta, along with a number of knowledge-intensive firms, with more people working in this sector than the average for Finnmark. This growth of Alta alongside the parallel decline in surrounding coastal municipalities has created tensions.

> And when this happens, it is generally perceived by our neighbour municipalities, that Alta takes everything. Regardless of whether we have any fault in it or not. Sometimes we are to blame for it. Other times there are others who make decisions. However, Alta takes everything. This is how we experience it, but we must live with it.
>
> (Chief of Industrial development in Alta municipality)

HiF's management strategy was from the outset to build a strong institution, and being aware of the tensions between Alta and the other municipalities in the region therefore deliberately chose not to arrange official meetings with Alta municipality in the first years of the establishment. The official position was that HiF was neutral regarding this tension (Berg, 2006), but later HiF established regular meetings with Alta municipality. There have been tensions between HiF and other institutions, such as Finnmark County, located almost 500 km from Alta, and a very important regional actor. Many regional policy-makers also wanted a campus in eastern Finnmark, not just in the west (Berg, 2006), with serious attempts being made in the early 1980s to establish a campus in Vadsø, Finnmark's county capital, with 6,000 population at a time when Alta had 13,000 residents. "The arguments against a campus was that it would be better to strengthen the recently established campus in Alta than establishing a new campus in a relatively small city as Vadsø" (Berg, 2006: 89).

Another attempt from regional actors was to establish a course in aquaculture at Nordkapp, located at the coast, but this attempt also failed, with the course being located in Alta. HiF's practice was to build a strong institution in Alta; under pressure of demands for new campuses, HiF offered decentralised education (mainly within teacher education and nursery nursing) in Finnmark's smaller municipalities (Berg, 2006). To do that effectively demanded that they collaborate with local actors, such as industrial competence centres and development agencies. HiF's decentralised education has functioned well, and allowed many people that were not in a position to move to Alta the possibility to be educated in their place of residence. It was the third attempt to create a third campus in Finnmark that succeeded in 2007 with the localisation in Sør-Varanger although with fewer than 20 staff there it is a relatively small location. Prior to the University of Tromsø merger, three of Finnmark's four central places had a campus, with only the county capital Vadsø lacking a campus.

HiF's prime concern was building a strong institution, not explicitly in promoting regional engagement. Its history has nevertheless had regional effects in two main areas. Firstly, HiF has primarily been a local development institution for Alta's development, and to a lesser extent, through its nursery nursing education activities, of Hammerfest. Secondly, HiF has done little work with Inland Finnmark nor engaged with Sami issues since 1989 despite the fact that Sami education was among the first studies established in 1974 at the teacher college, something that was of a high regional relevance. In 1989 a Sami University of Applied Sciences was established in the Inland Finnmark village, Kautokeino, with 1,200 of the municipality's residents living in the village. HiF's Sami department, located at the teacher training college, was moved to this new institution and this created tensions between the Sami department and the management of the teacher education (Hætta, 2013). When the department moved, there was for many years' little communication and collaboration between the two institutions, creating a division of labour between the two HEIs. "For the Sami University it was important to build their own profile with Sami as the language of teaching and administration. Finnmark University College defined on the other hand all Sami matters outside their remit" (Hætta, 2013).

Finally, Coastal Finnmark and the central place Vadsø were effectively excluded from HiF's regional mission, and certainly from its wider regional contributions. This arose not out of any explicit strategy, but rather because the aim of constructing a solid HEI in Alta necessitated regional concentration and this regional concentration precluded the expansion of provision into Coastal Finnmark and Vadsø.

Discussion and concluding comments

This case study examined the institutionalised practice of the development of a district college in Alta in Finnmark, a complex peripheral region. The research question is: *how can a small, peripheral university college contribute to improve regional development in such a complex state-driven peripheral region?* The main finding is that the expectations of what a small university college can contribute to regional development in a complex, peripheral region, such as Finnmark, are limited. The biggest impact has come through education, particularly in supplying an expanding public sector with well-qualified candidates. This is a result of the wider regional policy of the establishment of regional colleges, and such colleges, and comparable results, have also been seen in other Norwegian regions (Kyvik, 1981). However, the relative share of the population with their highest education level being primary and secondary school is still today higher than the average of Norway, and the impact of regionally relevant research has been undoubtedly minor as a whole (albeit significant for the regional tourism industry).

When it comes to local development, the positive developmental contributions have been considerable for Alta, where the main campus is located. The effects are multidimensional, going further than the more traditional effects associated with teaching and research. Indeed, the overall effect of establishing an HEI has been to stimulate interactions which have had wider cultural and social effects, and for small places located in peripheral regions these kinds of effects are undoubtedly important. An HEI also creates an attractiveness effect on other public institutions and knowledge-intensive industry decisions, witnessed here in a number of their decisions to locate to Alta. Conversely, the regional effect is rather limited for the sub-regions of Finnmark outside the main towns. Coastal Finnmark has not yet managed the transition from an industrial economy to a knowledge-based industry economy, and new, knowledge-intensive industries have not emerged that could compensate for the path exhaustion effect of the fishing industry in the 1990s. There is a mismatch between the knowledge a HEI can offer and the knowledge the industry needs. As a final point, Vadsø, the county capital, has faced substantive challenges in transforming from a public service place to developing knowledge-intensive industries.

On this basis, the chapter seeks to make two wider theoretical contributions to contemporary debates about the roles of HEIs in peripheral regions. Firstly the establishment of a HEI does not necessarily produce regional effects in peripheral regions, even if the local effects are considerable. Geography matters, as Massey (1984) underlines, and with considerable physical distance between municipalities, specifically between Alta and other municipalities, these local effects quickly peter out. A HEI is an institution that produces theoretical knowledge, and its practice is connected to this. If there is mismatch between an HEI's knowledge and regional knowledge demand, then the industry structure and the challenges in the different regions are too complex for a small HEI institution to solve. At the same time, it is important here not to be too critical, noting that no other actors or policy tools have so far succeeded in solving Coastal Finnmark's challenges. But we here see in this case – HiF and the regional research organisations – of the limitations of such organisations to create positive regional development effects in complex, peripheral regions.

Building on this, the second contribution is to argue that the discussion about the effects of the practice of HEIs in peripheral regions should more clearly distinguish between local and regional effects. Such a distinction makes the discussion of HEI practices more nuanced. Within the regional innovation systems approach the concept of *region* is usually defined as an physical area between the national and the local (Cooke, 1998). In big physical regions with low population density, the impact of an HEI is restricted to the boundaries of the place. The chapter started with a quote about the sculpture *Strange bird* at the campus in Alta, and I will end the chapter by arguing that the mission of higher education and research still has a way to go. Not in Alta, but in the sub-regions of Finnmark. And as the baton of responsibility was picked up by the University of Tromsø through the 2013 merger it will be interesting to see the practice of the University of Tromsø in Finnmark as it unfolds into the future.

Acknowledgements

The research leading to these results has received funding from the Norwegian Financial Mechanism 2009–2014 and the Ministry of Education, Youth and Sports under Project Contract No. MSMT-5397/2015.

Notes

1 All statistical data in this paragraph is from Statistics Norway.
2 This distinction is inspired by Angell *et al.* (2012).
3 See https://uit.no/prosjekter/prosjektsub?p_document_id=345272&sub_id=345273 for more details (accessed 5 October 2017).
4 On average, the number of nursing students in Hammerfest was between 100 and 200 with around 20 staff.

References

Angell, E., Eikeland, S., Grünfeld, L. A., Lie, I., Myhr, S., Nygaard, V. and Pedersen, P. (2012). *Action Zone for Finnmark and Nord-Troms – Performance and review of policy incentives*. Norut Alta, Report 2.

Barley, S. R. (2008) Coalface institutionalism. In: Greenwood, R., Oliver, C., Sahlin, K,, *et al.* (eds) *The SAGE handbook of organizational institutionalism*, London: Sage, 491–518.

Bell, D. (1999) *The coming of post-industrial society: A venture in social forecasting*, New York: Basic Books.

Benneworth, P., Coenen, L., Moodysson, J., *et al.* (2009) Exploring the multiple roles of Lund University in strengthening Scania's regional innovation system: Towards institutional learning? *European Planning Studies* 17: 1645–1664.

Berg, K. (2006) *Fremmed fugl? Historien om Høgskolen i Finnmark [Strange bird? The story about Finnmark University College]*, Alta: Høgskolen i Finnmark.

Berger, P. L. and Luckmann, T. (1991) *The social construction of reality: A treatise on the sociology of knowledge*, London: Penguin.

Chatterton, P. and Goddard, J. (2000) The response of higher education institutions to regional needs. *European Journal of Education* 35: 475–496.

Cooke, P. (1998) Introduction: Origins of the concept. In: Braczyk, H-J., Cooke, P. and Heidenreich, M. (eds) *Regional innovation systems*, London: UCL Press, 2–25.

Drucker, J. and Goldstein, H. (2007) Assessing the regional economic development impacts of universities: A review of current approaches. *International Regional Science Review* 30: 20–46.

Dunning, J. H. (2002) *Regions, globalization, and the knowledge-based economy*, Oxford: Oxford University Press.

Eikeland, S. (2010) Frå stat til region - og tilbake? Nordnorske innovasjonssystemer under nordområdesatsinga [From state to region – and back. Northern Norwegian innovation system under the High North Strategy]. In: Angell, E., Eikeland, S. and Selle, P. (eds), *Nordområdepolitikken sett fra nord [North area policy seen from the north]*, Bergen: Fagbokforlaget.

Hætta, S. K. (2013) Dårlig samarbeid mellom høgskolene i Finnmark. *Samisk skolehistorie* 6. Available at: http://skuvla.info/skolehist/solveigh-n.htm (accessed 24 April 2018).

Jacobsen, A. R. (2014) *Miraklet ved Litza: Hitlers første nederlag på Østfronten*, Oslo: Vega.

Kyvik, S. (1981) The Norwegian regional colleges: A study of the establishment and implementation of a reform in higher education. *Studies in Research and Higher Education*. Oslo: Norwegian Research Council for Science and the Humanities, 134.

Kyvik, S. (1983) Decentralisation of higher education and research in Norway. *Comparative Education* 19: 21–29.

Lamb, S. and Markussen, E. (2011) School dropout and completion: An international perspective. In: Lamb, S., Markussen, E., Teese, R., *et al.* (eds) *School dropout and completion: International comparative studies in theory and policy*, Dordrecht: Springer, 1–18.

Lok, J. and de Rond, M. (2013) On the plasticity of institutions: Containing and restoring practice breakdowns at the Cambridge University Boat Club. *Academy of Management Journal* 56: 185–207.

Markussen, E., Lødding, B. and Holen, S. (2012) *De' hær e'kke nokka for mæ: Om bortvalg, gjennomføring og kompetanseoppnåelse i videregående skole i Finnmark skoleåret 2010–2011 [This is nothing for me: About dropout, implementation and competence achievement in high school in Finnmark school year 2010–2011].* Oslo: NIFU – Nordic Institute for Studies of Innovation, Research and Education.

Massey, D. (1984) *Spatial divisions of labour: Social structures and the geography of production*, London: Macmillan.

Mills, S. W. (1959) *The sociological imagination*, New York: Grove Press.

OECD. (2007) *Higher education and regions: globally competitive, locally engaged*, Paris: Organisation for Economic Co-operation and Development.

OECD. (2009) *OECD regions at a glance*, Paris: Organisation for Economic Co-operation and Development.

Pinheiro, R., Benneworth, P. and Jones, G. A. (2012a) Understanding regions and the institutionalization of universities. In: Pinheiro, R., Benneworth, P. and Jones, G.A. (eds) *Universities and regional development: A critical assessment of tensions and contradictions*, Milton Park and New York: Routledge, 11–32.

Pinheiro, R., Benneworth, P. and Jones, G. A. (2012b) What next? Steps towards a recategorization of universities' regional missions. In: Pinheiro, R., Benneworth, P. and Jones, G.A. (eds) *Universities and regional development: A critical assessment of tensions and contradictions*, Milton Park and New York: Routledge.

Pinheiro, R., Benneworth, P. and Jones, G.A. (2015) Beyond the obvious: Tensions and volitions surrounding the contributions of universities to regional development. In: Farinha, L., Ferreira, J., Lawton-Smith, H., et al. (eds) *Handbook of research on global competitive advantage through innovation and entrepreneurship*, Hershey, PA: IGI, 150–172.

Schatzki, T. R. (2001) Introduction: Practice theory. In: Schatzki, T. R., Knorr Cetina, K. and Von Savigny, E. (eds) *The practice turn in contemporary theory*, London: Routledge, 1–14.

St.meld. nr. 32 (1989–90) *Framtid i nord*. Levekår og framtidsutsikter i Nord-Troms og Finnmark. Kommunaldepartementet.

Tsoukas, H. (2005) Do we really understand tacit knowledge? In: Tsoukas, H. (ed.) *Complex knowledge: Studies in organizational epistemology*, Oxford: Oxford University Press, 152–160.

Wolcott, H. F. (1994) *Transforming qualitative data: Description, analysis, and interpretation*, Thousand Oaks, CA: Sage Publications.

Yin, R. K. (2013) *Case study research: Design and methods*, Thousand Oaks, CA: Sage Publications.

6 The case of the Telemark region and the university college of Telemark

Nina Kyllingstad

Introduction

The Telemark region is a county located in southeastern Norway, with a population of 171,953, and is one of Norway's most industrial counties, with the dominant regional sector being manufacturing, with 17.3% of the working population employed in this sector in 2004, the third highest of all Norwegian counties. At the centre of this sector lies Hydro-Porsgrunn Factories, a global aluminium company located in Porsgrunn, which is the centre of the processing industry in the county. Hydro deals with production, sales, and trading throughout the whole value chain from the generation of energy and the processing of alumina, through producing primary aluminium to the recycling of used aluminium. The region currently faces an unemployment problem: although its unemployment rate is not high (3.2% compared to the national average of 3.6%) since 2008 and the financial crisis, the region has lost over 3000 jobs in this sector, a disturbing trend when one considers how dependent Telemark is on this industry (PERIF, 2016b).

Related to this industrial inheritance and structure is the relatively low educational level of Telemark. Similar to the region of Finnmark in the previous chapter, the educational level of the population of Telemark is characterised by a higher number of low-educated people and a lower number of highly educated people than the Norwegian average. A total of 29.7% of the population have completed primary education and lower secondary education, 44.9% high school, 20.1% further education, and 5.3% higher education. This compares with figures for Norway as a whole of 26.9% (primary), 20.9% (high school), 25% (further), and 9.2% (higher). This means that young children who finish their primary education are not continuing their educational pathway, or at least do not continue their education in Telemark county, which is certainly a problem when the region is desperately in need of highly skilled employees (PERIF, 2016b).

The low volume of high skilled labour has long been a challenge for the region, as exemplified by the problems of recruiting qualified engineers. In 2014, the local newspaper *Varden* wrote of a local work fair where 40 firms gathered in order to find suitable candidates to recruit, seeking a total of 160 new employees. The newspaper reported that these firms were all struggling to find qualified labour and the firms needing qualified engineers commented on the situation saying that there are few people in the region who are able to do the work. This neatly highlights the regional problem of a shortage of regional engineers, although there has been a change in the last two years as a result of redundancies across Norway in the oil and gas sector of these highly skilled engineers as a result of the historically low oil prices (Knarrum Tollefsen, 2014). The low skill level is not the only problem for the region, with a high share of young adults with psychological problems and diagnosis (Folkehelseinstituttet, 2015), the problems that are caused by a demographic ageing in the region, as well as dealing with the environmental consequences of the pollution that has been caused by the regional process industry are also significant problems.

As part of a wider Norwegian policy to create university colleges, Telemark University College (TUC) was created in 1994 from the merger of four training colleges for teachers, engineers, professions allied to medicine, and social sciences and literature spread across the county. As with the other creation of regional colleges in Norway (see previous chapter), TUC was created to educate professional workers for the Telemark region and thereby contribute to raising the overall educational level as well as guaranteeing the quality of public service in the county. The Norwegian university colleges originally did not have a research remit, although over time they did develop regionally relevant research, and TUC became a regionally significant partner to try and break the low developmental state of the Telemark region. In this chapter, we specifically consider the role that the university college was able to play in Telemark by creating new developmental paths and contributing to breaking regional lock-in. We ask the overall research question of *What are the main challenges in the Telemark region and what initiatives do the university college of Telemark need to take in order to improve the current situation?* This provides a means of understanding the way that less research-intensive and more professionally oriented higher education institutions, such as the Norwegian university colleges, can contribute to stimulating regional economic development in the peripheral regions.

The role of a university college in challenging regional path dependency

This volume is concerned with the role played by universities and higher education institutes in contributing to development processes in peripheral regions. This chapter is concerned with a region that has become very strongly dependent on a single industry, in this case the aluminium industry, and around which there is a strong regional cluster of firms. The region had until recently a relatively stable labour market: Hydro-Porsgrunn Factories provided high-quality employment without necessarily demanding very high education levels. The region can be considered as having settled into what the OECD (2014) has referred to as a low-skills equilibrium commonly found in regions dependent on resource extractive and processing industries. The challenge for such regions is to create new development opportunities that build on the region's existing strengths, although it can be extremely challenging to persuade regional partners when things are performing well that the time has arrived to take decisive action to avert the decline.

This framework builds on ideas in evolutionary economic geography which seeks to explain the ways in which places evolve along particular evolutionary pathways (Martin, 2011). From this perspective, today's economic activity in a particular region is shaped by what has happened in the past, not only in terms of the existing industries and their interconnections, but also the policy frameworks, the support actors, and the related public sector actors that support those industries (Boschma & Frenken, 2006; Sydow, Schreyögg, & Koch, 2009). As sectors mature, these networks of partnerships can lose sight of the problems they face with partners assuming that just as things have gone well to date, they will continue to do so into the future (Martin, 2010). Policy frameworks and support activities therefore become increasingly oriented to solving the quotidian problems and challenges faced by the existing sectors rather than trying to invest in new future growth areas (Hassink, 2005). These type of regions are often vulnerable to economic disruptions (Martin, 2012). When dominant industries becomes deterministic in their nature because they follow the same patterns and the same paths, and vulnerable to risk then there can be a case to argue that a region is suffering from lock-in and the region is caught within processes of path dependence (Sydow *et al.*, 2009).

There are a range of different repertoires by which collections of regional actors can seek to collectively break path dependence. Where existing sectors offer substantive resources that can be productively redeployed to new varieties of these industrial sectors, then there can be processes of path extension (which characterises the example of Tampere presented in Chapter 11 as Nokia sought to reinvent itself as an ICT rather than mobile telephony company). Where there are opportunities to create new combinations between the existing sectors and new sectors to create new promising economic development potential areas, then there are processes of path renewal, with a cross-fertilisation between existing sectors creating new opportunities. Where there is a collection of knowledge assets that can be creatively combined to create entirely new sectors, activities, and development potentials, then there can be processes of path creation through constructing regional advantage or smart specialisation (Asheim, Boschma, & Cooke, 2011; McCann & Ortega-Argilés, 2013).

But there can be a challenge in regions dominated by declining industrial sectors that there are no regional animateurs who are able to persuade locked-in regional partners to break their existing ways of working, and shift from their declining paths into areas of new economic opportunity (Tödtling & Trippl, 2005). In these circumstances, universities may be able to play this role because of their connections in much wider technological and knowledge networks (Goddard, 2011). Alongside this is the fact that unlike other kinds of regional actors, universities do not have a single strategic interest that can become locked-in, with their regional innovation connections depending on the activities of their academics who each have their own regional and global connections related to their teaching and research activities (Benneworth, Pinheiro, & Karlsen, 2017). Universities therefore seem to offer an opportunity to break out of path dependency and to help build new industries that will create both a demand for, as well as a corresponding supply of, highly skilled jobs that in turn break the low-skill equilibrium.

From the perspective of this chapter, however, there is a lacuna in the literature on university regional contribution because of the particular ideal type of 'university' that features in these models. Goddard and Vallance's (2013) idea of a civic university seems to implicitly have internalised the notion of a large, research-intensive, urban university with many different faculties including a medical school. As with many of the other authors in this volume, our concern is with small, specialised, teaching-intensive institutions, which whilst having a research mission, see that mission as being quite distinct from, and less globally theoretically oriented (Lepori & Kyvik, 2010) than the university perhaps implicitly invoked when considering path-breaking activities. In their role of what Jongbloed (2010) calls 'regional knowledge providers', it might be expected that they would have links to existing sectors, and therefore be part of the locked-in network rather than having the autonomy and independence to break that lock-in and create new economic developmental paths. In this chapter, we therefore use our case of Telemark to understand how these regionally relevant higher education institutions can make a contribution to changing regional economic development trajectories.

Methodology

To explore this issue, we present a case study of Telemark University College, which existed as an independent university college in the period 1994–2016. This chapter is based on work conducted in a research project at Agderforskning in Kristiansand, Norway. The case region, Telemark, was one of three Norwegian case regions in a project between partners in Norway and the Czech Republic, called PERIF ('Higher Education in the Socio-Economic Development of Peripheral Regions'; see Acknowledgements). The overall focus of the research project was to focus on the collaboration between higher education institutions and peripheral regions, with the specific goal being to identify and assess the relationship between regions and higher education institutions in order to strengthen the basis for long-term collaboration to improve the region. The case study therefore reuses and repurposes data gathered within an existing research project, rather than being gathered specifically for the purposes of addressing the particular framework of this book. Particular care has therefore been taken in preparing this chapter that the case study material has been prepared and presented transparently to address this issue of a non-research-intensive university participation in contributing to breaking lock-in processes.

The method used on the PERIF-EU case study (applied in both this and the preceding chapter) was firstly to gather secondary data such as strategy plans for both the region and for TUC, along with other documents and plans relevant for explaining the development of the region and the role the university college has had throughout the years. There was a primary data gathering exercise in which the research team conducted a set of semi-structured interviews with relevant actors, in this case covering representatives from the county authority, the Norwegian Labour and Welfare Organisation (NAV), and the local businesses. In total, six interviews of up to one hour each were undertaken and subsequently transcribed. It is this secondary and primary data that forms the basis for the material in this chapter. It is important to note that TUC ceased to exist in 2016 in the sense that it underwent a merger with Buskerud and Vestfold University College (itself created as a merger from two university colleges in 2014) effective from January 2016 to create the University College of South East Norway. This university college will be the second largest university college in Norway with altogether 18,000 students and 1500 employees (USN, 2016). The work in this chapter primarily predates this merger process as the fieldwork and document gathering was largely completed before the merger took place.

Telemark region and Telemark University College (TUC)

This chapter focuses on both Telemark University College (TUC) and the Telemark county. To understand the economic development trajectory of the region it is necessary to understand both the region and the university college in their long-term historical development trajectory. In this section, we firstly set out to provide more detail on the county of Telemark and the particular challenges that it faces in trying to deal with de-industrialisation. We then set out the background and evolution of Telemark University College in order to provide an understanding of the resources that it has been able to offer to the region in its attempts to create new future developmental trajectories and to break its economic development pathways.

Telemark region

Telemark as a county has 171,953 inhabitants and a GDP of NOK 325,506 per capita in 2013 (approximately £33,900/€40,100 at contemporaneous exchange rates). The GDP per employee was NOK 723,662, slightly below but equivalent to the Oslo value of NOK 728,605. Regional population increased by 4.3% since 2000 at a time when the overall population of Norway increased by 15.9%, indicating that Telemark is not a strongly growing region. In terms of surface area, Telemark is the median county, being the 10th largest of Norway's 19 counties (with a surface area of 15,299 km²). When it comes to population, the county ranks at number 13. Telemark is a sparsely populated, rural region and with a negative natural population growth. Between 2010 and 2015, the population growth was 2.2%, while the whole county saw a 6.3% growth (5.8% when the dominant capital city of Oslo is excluded) (PERIF, 2016b) – almost all of this growth can be accounted for by net immigration to Norway, and despite this large increase in national population there has not been a comparable growth of population in Telemark.

The two largest cities in Telemark are Skien and Porsgrunn (after which Hydro-Porsgrunn Factories is named). They are relatively small cities (although large in the Norwegian context) having 53,745 and 35,755 inhabitants respectively; 12 out of Telemark's 18 municipalities in Telemark have fewer than 6000 inhabitants (the smallest is Nissedal with only 1375 inhabitants). Both Porsgrunn and Skien perform below the national average in terms of the number of employees working in the business sector (from 2001 to 2011) and this absence of a strong business services sector has been identified as one of the factors contributing to Telemark's relatively weak growth (Vareide & Nyborg, 2012). The strong focus on industries such as building and construction (and historically also the dominance of forestry) have created conditions for possible regional lock-in whilst undermining the potential for endogenous path-breaking activities.

The Telemark region has had a negative growth in terms of overall numbers of employment positions in recent years. During the period 2001–2011 the Telemark county had the weakest workplace growth in the whole country, and its growth was below national average for every year in this decade excepting 2008 when Telemark's employment growth equalled the national growth rate (Vareide & Nyborg, 2012). This is a function not only of employment in the private sector, but also in the public sector, and employment growth in the public sector in Telemark has been weaker than the rest of the country. Because of its strong oil and gas sector, Norway was less adversely affected by the global crisis, and was primarily affected by the more recent decline of oil prices, and the country as a whole experienced only a small downturn because of the crisis, recovering the positions lost during the crisis by 2009; conversely, Telemark has continued a period of decline throughout this period (Vareide & Nyborg, 2012), which might be seen as typical for a region with a few specialised industries.

When one looks at the location quotients of industries in Telemark, then the largest industries by LQ were the processing industry, trade and commerce, and building and construction (Vareide & Nyborg, 2012). At the same time, these were all industries that declined in both absolute and relative numbers in the period 2008–2012. The growth sectors for Norway in this period were oil and gas, scientific services, telecoms, and ICTs, and these are all sectors that are themselves underrepresented in Telemark. Table 6.1 shows the distribution of employees in different industries per fourth quarter 2015.

As well as these directly economic challenges related to high unemployment rates, concentration of employment in declining sectors, and the lack of a highly qualified workforce, there are also additional challenges tied to demographic and other social and environmental dimensions. Even though there has been a slight increase in inhabitants, Telemark is still struggling with a birth deficit and has a birth rate that is 15% lower than the national average. The reason why the population has grown despite this natural decrease rate is at least partly

Table 6.1 Distribution of employees by sector in Telemark, Q4 2015

Industry division	Employees
Agriculture, forestry, and fishing	1.9%
Mining and quarrying	2.1%
Manufacture	10.7%
Electricity, water supply, sewerage, waste management	1.9%
Construction	9.5%
Wholesale and retail trade: repair of motor vehicles and motorcycles	13.9%
Transportation and storage	4.4%
Accommodation and food service activities	2.7%
Information and communication	1.7%
Financial and insurance activities	1.1%
Real estate, professional, scientific, and technical activities	4.7%
Administrative and support service activities	4.2%
Public administration, defence, social security	5.5%
Education	8.0%
Human health and social work activities	23.0%
Other service activities	3.6%
Unspecified	1.0%
Total	100%

Source: Statistics Norway.

due to immigration. Most immigrants come from Asia (Iraq), followed by EU countries in Eastern Europe (e.g. Poland) and Africa (Somalia). In Telemark, currently one in ten of the population are immigrants or have parents who are immigrants, and this immigration flow has been seen as a way or a possibility to create new opportunities in the region and to compensate for the problems of demographic ageing that are hindered the development to a more dynamic economy (PERIF, 2016a).

There are other social problems facing the region, including the high share of persons between the age of 15 and 29 with psychological symptoms and diagnosis, a level above the national average and which has become in recent years something demanding policy attention. Telemark is also struggling with demographic ageing and according to prognoses, the number of persons over 67 years in the region will double by the year 2040; conversely, young adults (20–39 years old) comprise a lower share of the overall population base in Telemark compared to the national average.

The extent and the depth of these regional issues in the Norwegian context is something that demands a serious policy response. The decline of traditional and important industries, the high unemployment rate, and the relatively low skills levels are not problems that are easily solved or can be solved by individual partners and have demanded a response from all parties involved in regional development, most notably the municipalities, county authorities, local businesses as well as the university college. In terms of the overall strategic context for the county, it is worth noting that the Norwegian government requires every region to develop a plan that covers a number of critical elements, including climate and energy, nature, urban development, and value creation. Reflecting these challenges, the Telemark plan has added two additional areas that are seen by regional stakeholders as critical for creating new development pathways in the region, namely competence and education and culture experience.

Telemark University College

Telemark University College (TUC) was established in 1994 as part of a more general streamlining process by the Norwegian government of the tertiary education sector. In the post-war period there had been a proliferation of small vocational institutions, often very specifically focused on single educations or professions. The reform envisaged the creation of broader state colleges, and involved going from 98 vocationally oriented institutions to 26 public-run state colleges. The focus in these new institutions was on training of professionals in the region (PERIF, 2016a). TUC emerged out of this process as the result of a merger between Telemark district college (focusing on social sciences and the humanities) located in the city of Bø, Telemark teaching education college located in Notodden and Rauland, Telemark nursing education college located in Skien, and Telemark engineering college located in Porsgrunn. Table 6.2 shows the six locations comprising Telemark University College in 2013.

Table 6.2 The campus locations comprising TUC, c. 2013

Campus	Students (pr. 2013)	Main teaching profile	Faculty
Porsgrunn	2300	Engineering, nursing, teaching (child welfare, computer science, and business studies)	Faculty of Health and Social Studies, Faculty of Technology and Faculty of Art, Folk Culture, and Teacher Education
Notodden	1650	Teacher training	Faculty of Art, Folk Culture, and Teacher Education
Bø	1500	Sports, outdoor life, culture, the humanities, economics, information technology, nature, health and environment, and art professional writer studies	Faculty of Arts and Science
Rauland	1050	Education in folk culture	Faculty of Art, Folk Culture, and Teacher Education

Source: PERIF (2016a).

Table 6.3 Research groups at TUC

Telemark modelling and control centre	LEBE!
Practise, tradition, and technology	Culture and Sports politic
SMART	Energy and CO_2 capture
Welfare services for deferred groups	The occupations of the welfare state
Climate change and alpine ecosystems	Embodied making and learning
Municipal health services for elders	Body-movement-meaning
Water power and utility power	AQUA- HiT
Health & exercise – a life course perspective	Youth and education
Process security, combustion, and explosions	Qualitative methods in professional
Cultural heritage in use	practice
Political culture	Sustainable tourism

Source: PERIF (2016a, p. 55).

TUC consists of four faculties divided between four different campuses (with some overlap) located across the major towns of Telemark, with the exception of Skien (the former nurse training in Skien moved to Porsgrunn in 2000). The teaching profile of TUC includes 50 first-cycle bachelor-level programmes usually lasting 3 years, 16 2-year master-degree programmes, and 3 doctoral programmes lasting 3–4 years. Because the university college was created to train professionals in the region, research has not been its main focus although there are three centres that have come out of this professional teaching profile, namely the centre for professionalisation, the centre for welfare work, and the centre for culture and sport studies. There are also 21 research groups, representing different focus areas of the region, e.g. welfare technology in smart buildings and cultural heritage projects (see Table 6.3).

TUC has gained over its 22-year life a number of regional campuses which reflect the region's strong identity with a rich and distinctive historical and cultural heritage. The Telemark region is known for different types of crafts-manship such as silver and wood carving, strong meat and fish traditions, and mushroom and berry harvesting. The famous author Henrik Ibsen comes from this region and it is also the location of a famous porcelain factory, Porsgrund. Tourists also often travel to this region for its mountains to ski or hike. These various regional strengths of Telemark are reflected in the educational courses offered by TUC. But the nature of these strengths meant that it was difficult for TUC to find ways to capitalise on these strengths to develop those regional activities which Norwegian policy-makers were seeing to encourage. TUC has performed relatively weakly in terms of the acquisition of EU funding, most recently having received just NOK 78,800 (£7500; €9600 – 2014) and NOK 125,000 (£10,100; €13,600 – 2015) having received no funding in the period 2011–2013 (DBH, 2016). TUC's grant and commissioned funding both increased from 2009 to 2015 which might suggest an increased focus on research programmes, however there is still a struggle to obtain funding from the Research Council of Norway as well as from the European Union (PERIF, 2016a). TUC has made improving its research performance a substantive priority, with one interviewee noting "People are often bought out of other work assignments in order to apply for regional, national or EU-funds."

Path-breaking initiatives undertaken within Telemark

Telemark County has undertaken a number of regional initiatives recently in order to address its problems, and more specifically to break the lock-in it currently faces and therefore to try to create new regional opportunities. In the previous section, we identified that there were four main issues that the region was addressing, and it is unsurprising that in each of these areas, initiatives have been taken to address them. These four areas are a high degree of sub-regional differentiation, the complex problem of demographic ageing, alongside high unemployment rates, and low education levels. Although TUC has undertaken initiatives in each of these four areas, there are no specific incentives given to TUC actors to encourage regional collaboration, and some respondents reported feeling that the county and local businesses were not interested in collaboration.

Being adjacent to East Agder it is perhaps unsurprising that the region, and its successful university collaboration (see Chapter 3 for more details) has become a reference point for identifying the shortcomings in these co-operative relationships. One interviewee noted that whilst in Agder there were perceived as being many more sources of regional funding for the university than in Telemark: "We have received NOK 10 million from the county authorities, after years of struggles. That's it." This situation is not helped by the fact that TUC only has a few public PhD students and no PhD students funded by industry; interviewees were united in sharing the belief that this will increase in the coming years. It is hard to see the extent to which this is just a perception (particularly given the relatively low level of regional income reported by the University of Agder), and this negative discourse has a positive value for TUC in reflecting a clear sense of institutional pride at TUC with regards to creating a lot of external activities despite the relatively low levels of financial and other support received by the region. One informant believes that this pride might be the reason why TUC is regularly regarded as one of the most effective institutions within this sector.

Decentralisation

Telemark University College is a decentralised university college with four campuses spread throughout the region, but this is according to TUC not a challenge because they view this structure as a strength and "this model makes it possible to be present in different parts of the region and thereby by an actor the society can rely on" (PERIF, 2016a, p. 63). At the same time, as an informant told us, the relationship between the different parts of the region and constituent colleges that are present in those locations varies, reflecting a varied sub-regional geography within Telemark region. The four original institutions pre 1994 came partly as a result of lobbying and strong political will as part of a more general decentralisation of public activities across Norway, and as exemplified by the Ottosen Committee implementation of the 1970s, creating the district colleges (Kyvik, 2008). Although this process was intended to be technocratic, with each region receiving one district college to be located in its main centre, this implementing group realised very quickly that this was a process prone to capture by lobbying interests. The college of Bø was the site of arguably the bitterest debate about the college location in the 1970s, between rural and urban districts, and the rural location was chosen (Bø) because it was a municipality where New Norwegian (*nynorsk*) was the prevailing language. TUC's contemporaneous campus configuration therefore reflects at least partly this historical patterning, but at the same time there has been some evolution in each of its campuses reflecting interaction with and input from local business communities in each part of the region.

During the last three years of the case study, TUC had several projects located both on the individual locations, but also involving collaboration between the different locations, and there has been important institutional learning about organising engagement processes. One informant explained some of the collaborative history at the Bø location, where a campus project seeks to include the municipality and other actors, for example, a hotel and Telemark Research (research centre), in defining campus locations to develop TUC as a knowledge company. This has necessitated the involvement of the municipality to ensure that local development and land use plans enable this development. One of the concrete plans promoted within this has been the knowledge part concept to better integrate the campus and produce a more creative zone. There has also been co-operation with the municipality to improve student facilities, including developing a kindergarten and a pub; these activities are typical of the larger and smaller projects by which the four campuses are building up their municipality co-operation. A second example of this kind of collaboration is at Porsgrund where TUC have become involved with an industry incubator company, Proventia, as both shareholder and board member, despite the fact that this is not related to teaching or research efforts – it is seen as being an investment to support more regional engagement by TUC.

The issue of the coming merger cast a long shadow over the later years of the TUC campuses, with the creation of the new University College of South East Norway creating one of Norway's largest HEIs with activities spread across eight locations in three Norwegian counties. Although the intention before the merger was to retain all eight campuses, there was a doubt about the degree to which this intention was realistic and possible. At the time of the research, immediately before the merger, questions were already starting to be raised and would probably continue to be raised as one of the informants explained: "Are we able to control the chaos this may cause? Are the students taken sufficiently care of?"

Ageing, unemployment, and the environment

One of the reasons behind the ageing population is that the younger generations are leaving Telemark, along with a negative natural population change (the birth rate being lower than the mortality rate). Telemark therefore faced the challenge of how to keep the younger generations in the region, most notably by ensuring that there are jobs available and preferably relevant, reflecting the close relationship between the two regional challenges of demographic ageing and unemployment. Some may also use the argument of identification with the region (its lack of a strong, distinctive regional identity) as a contributing factor for the younger people to leave. One way of improving this might be the work TUC was doing with regards to assignments tied to regional actors, e.g. students working at a local festival. Telemark has a festival called 'Slottsfjellfestivalen' where students can work and receive credits from TUC in fields such as marketing, cultural studies, and management.

The need for jobs is not just pressing for the younger generations, but also for the society as a whole; one of the results of this ageing population is an increasing demand for health services and it is clear that in Telemark at the time of writing there were not enough people employed in health care to meet regional demand levels. One more positive note was provided through immigration, which was contributing to an overall positive population growth rate, and many of the immigrants had suitable qualifications to be working in the health care sector, although it is not clear whether this is a sustainable development to provide Telemark's long-term social care needs. One response from TUC in this was the development of a PhD programme in health promotion at TUC as a collaboration between three TUC departments and building on the longer-standing competencies within TUC in professions allied to medicine.

A final element of the regional challenge is adapting to the environmental challenges of de-industrialisation in a region in which heavy industry has left a significant footprint, and being a long-term source of regional pollution. When environmental standards changed considerably in 1975, there was a substantial improvement in air quality, but increasing numbers of road vehicles, and particularly local transport in Telemark means that some localities still suffer extensively from air pollution. This challenge is met by TUC with a goal in their strategy stating that TUC has a goal of improving the environmental profile in all segments, both in terms of their teaching/research activities but also in terms of their own institutional practices.

Low educational levels

Low educational levels in a region are often tied to the quality and offers at the local educational institutions, and because of TUC's position as the dominant HEI provider for the Telemark region, Telemark depends on TUC to raise its education levels; one of the main ambitions of TUC in recent years has been to become a fully fledged university, which in the case of Norway means meeting particular quality criteria, and for TUC one of the most critical criterion to meet reflects the quality and volume of research undertaken in the college. The various changes to the law of higher education have facilitated TUC as with the HEIs in Agder and Finnmark to upgrade their overall research profile and to change as an institution from purely educating professionals to becoming more research-intensive, and in particular in using their research to inform their education. One additional dimension of this in Norway is the perception that an important indicator of research quality is the acquisition of external funding for research, and clearly for Telemark, with its low access to Research Council of Norway and EU funding, working with local businesses and research organisations on projects with regional benefits can be a way to attract those external resources and thereby to improve their research profile.

There is also a concern that this undue focus on research might bring a number of costs for TUC, and in particular a neglect of those areas within TUC that are already strong, and also those that have evolved to reflect the relatively sparse funding environment. One interviewee noted their fears that an increase in infrastructure investments and structured research policies would create a more one-size-fits-all perspective on the kind of research that TUC should be undertaking. There was a particular fear that a structure forcing all disciplines to collaborate in particular ways with their external environments might downplay or work against the distinctive character of each discipline, as well as undermining research that was necessary but which did not have an immediate regional connection.

One area where TUC have been advanced is in developing e-learning facilities, as part of dealing with the challenge of managing education across four campuses, an experience that has left them as a leader in e-learning in Norway (PERIF, 2016a). The e-learning infrastructure they have is part of a wider set of efforts to ensure that people across the county, and most particularly those most remote from the four campuses, are able to attend the university college by not requiring them to travel to or move to one of the campuses. The intention is therefore to lower the barrier to access to higher education for those living in communities with no immediate physical access to the university college, and thereby to contribute to an overall increase in the region's education level.

Even though there are examples of collaboration and a positive trend in funding received from external sources, the whole issue of collaboration between TUC and regional actors remains thorny. An informant explained some of the attitudes and perceptions they as TUC are met with by regional actors: "we have to educate great candidates. And I also think they [private and public actors] expect us to contribute to research and development projects. But I think they sometimes expect us to contribute for free."

This is a specific problem for Telemark because what generates research funding for the university college is the Norwegian research funding system in which universities are awarded a block grant based on 'publication points' that are awarded for various different kinds of publication (e.g. journal articles or books) and which therefore does not reflect collaborative engagement projects, including those with local actors. One of the ways TUC do collaborate with their regional business partners are through the masters students who undertake placements as part of their thesis writing, and interviews noted that there were examples of these students being a useful resource for supporting regional projects, as well as being interesting for the students in providing an opportunity to get to work on contemporary challenges and issues.

Both the region and TUC partook in establishing a knowledge centre called 'Du Verden'. This was created in order to increase children's interest in science, but also in history and hopefully improve their sense of belonging in Telemark (USN, 2016). There is also a collaboration between the local actors to continue the 'Trainee Telemark' programme where newly graduated students can work different places in the region and hopefully make their work placements permanent afterwards. TUC have organised similar collaborations with a number of other significant regional employers including the Norcem cement factory, NAV (Norwegian Labour and Welfare Organisation), and the regional hospital.

The role of a university college in challenging regional lock-in

University colleges in ordinary industrial regions could do more to challenge regional lock-in. In this case it starts with TUC's strategies that are aimed at both improving the university college and meeting the societal challenges of the region. "TUC shall expand and strengthen co-operation and contact with society and business, for example, through its decentralized structure the college will rise up in the region as a naturally strategic partner" (PERIF, 2016a, p. 59). One way of improving the collaboration is to facilitate the faculty members with incentives. However, to say that incentives should be made available for faculty who collaborate with regional actors might be easier said than done. Since TUC's merger with another university college in January 2016, the incentives might be needed for something entirely different.

One of the most important strategic goals of the new university college is to become a fully fledged university. In order to achieve that, the research production has to increase. As mentioned, the lack of external funding from the Research Council of Norway and the EU might make it attractive to try to get external funding through collaboration with regional actors. However, it is still too early to say where their focus will be in terms of acquiring research funding. Ideally, both the regional actors and the university college should make an effort to improve and increase their collaboration in order to meet both the research demands, but also to meet the societal challenges such as increasing the number of people in health care services and increasing work possibilities for the unemployed including both those who are highly educated and those with less formal education.

An important benefit an industrial region might have from collaborating with regional actors is highlighted by an informant, stating that the biggest security measure TUC can take is to show the regional actors that it is useful to have campuses locally. By maintaining the local campuses, TUC are also able to provide each part of the region with specific education and research matching the local needs which in turn might challenge the regional lock-in. The decentralisation might however have the opposite effect, where a continuing focus on the local engagement and specialised research simply leads to further lock-in as opposed to a new or changed path that might come from broader constellations and larger groupings of students and faculty. Thus, the balance between meeting local needs and staying relevant has been important for TUC and will be increasingly important in the new constellation where there are eight campuses in three counties.

One way that this university college has worked to keep the balance is to further the e-learning initiatives that TUC are already specialising in. This way, the uniqueness of the separate locations might be preserved while at the same time making teaching possible for larger bodies of students. Examples of this are the use of flipped classrooms, where students can follow seminars in real-time regardless of where they are situated, or asynchronous e-learning where students attend lectures when they have time. This way of using technology can therefore be a way of maintaining the decentralised structure which is important for local collaboration partners while at the same time increasing the educational level in the region. This is because it enables higher education for people living elsewhere in the region and for persons who must work during the day.

TUC has been through a merger before. The time for mergers is once again present in the Norwegian educational sector and probably in several other countries. During such processes it is important to have clear strategic goals which can be communicated well to all parts of the university colleges. TUC is, in addition to merging with another university college, working on becoming a fully fledged university. For this to happen, the research must increase which in turn entails applying for funding. The issue of balancing mergers, becoming a university, and external funding is not unique for TUC. However, the way they have previously dealt with mergers and the effort they have put into infrastructure such as e-learning to maintain the decentralised campus structure might serve as an example for other university colleges. This said, the societal challenges facing Telemark should be even closer connected to the university college. This is especially important to keep in mind, to avoid e.g. increasing number of unemployed, ageing in the region, etc. A good university college needs regional support and vice versa.

Acknowledgements

The research leading to these results has received funding from the Norwegian Financial Mechanism 2009–2014 and the Ministry of Education, Youth, and Sports under Project Contract No. MSMT-5397/2015.

References

Asheim, B. T., Boschma, R., & Cooke, P. (2011). Constructing regional advantage: Platform policies based on related variety and differentiated knowledge bases. *Regional Studies, 45*(7), 893–904.

Benneworth, P. S., Pinheiro, R., & Karlsen, J. (2017). Strategic agency and institutional change: Investigating the role of universities in regional innovation systems (RISs). *Regional Studies, 51*(2), 235–248. doi:10.1080/00343404.2016.1215599.

Boschma, R. A., & Frenken, K. (2006). Why is economic geography not an evolutionary science? Towards an evolutionary economic geography. *Journal of Economic Geography, 6*(3), 273–302. doi:10.1093/jeg/lbi022.

DBH. (2016). *Database for higher education statistics in Norway*. Bergen: Norwegian Social Sciences Data Service.

Folkehelseinstituttet. (2015). *Folkehelseprofilen 2015 Telemark*. Retrieved 11 October 2017, from http://khp.fhi.no/PDFVindu.aspx?Nr=08&sp=1&PDFAar=2015.

Goddard, J. B. (2011). *Connecting universities to regional growth: A practical guide*. Brussels: DG REGIO.

Goddard, J., & Vallance, P. (2013). *The university and the city*. London: Routledge.

Hassink, R. (2005). How to unlock regional economies from path dependency? From learning region to learning cluster. *European Planning Studies, 13*(4), 521–535.

Jongbloed, B. (2010). The regional relevance of research in universities of applied sciences. In S. Kyvik & B. Lepori (Eds), *The research mission of higher education institutions outside the university sector*. Dordrecht: Springer.

Knarrum Tollefsen, T. (2014). 160 nye jobber å søke. *Varden*. Retrieved 18 April 2018, from www.varden.no/nyheter/160-nye-jobber-a-soke-1.1063120.

Kyvik, S. (2008). *The dynamics of change in higher education: Expansion and contraction in an organisational field* (Vol. 27). Dordrecht: Springer Science & Business Media.

Lepori, B., & Kyvik, S. (2010). The research mission of universities of applied sciences and the future configuration of higher education systems in Europe. *Higher Education Policy, 23*(3), 295–316.

McCann, P., & Ortega-Argilés, R. (2013). Modern regional innovation policy. *Cambridge Journal of Regions, Economy and Society, 6*(2), 187–216. doi:10.1093/cjres/rst007.

Martin, R. (2010). Roepke Lecture in Economic Geography – Rethinking regional path dependence: Beyond lock-in to evolution. *Economic Geography, 86*(1), 1–27. doi:10.1111/j.1944-8287.2009.01056.x.

Martin, R. (2011). Regional economies as path-dependent systems: Some issues and implications. In P. Cooke, B. Asheim, R. Boschma, R. Martin, D. Schwartz, & F. Tödtling (Eds), *Handbook of regional innovation and growth*. Cheltenham, UK: Edward Elgar.

Martin, R. (2012). *Knowledge bases and the geography of innovation*. Lund: Lund University Press.

OECD. (2014). *Job creation and local economic development*. Retrieved 18 April 2018, from www.oecd-ilibrary.org/industry-and-services/job-creation-and-local-economic-development_9789264215009-en.

PERIF. (2016a). *Case university report: Telemark University College*. Retrieved 18 April 2018, from www.perifproject.eu/wp-content/uploads/2015/07/WP-2-_case_report_HiT_Telemark_final.pdf.

PERIF. (2016b). *Telemark Region, Norway*. Retrieved 18 April 2018, from www.perifproject.eu/wp-content/uploads/2015/07/WP1-case-report-Telemark_final.pdf.

Sydow, J., Schreyögg, G., & Koch, J. (2009). Organizational path dependence: Opening the black box. *Academy of Management Review, 34*(4), 689–709.

Tödtling, F., & Trippl, M. (2005). One size fits all? Towards a differentiated regional policy approach. *Research Policy, 34*(8), 1203–1219.

USN. (2016). 2016, from www.usn.no/om-hsn/.

Vareide, K., & Nyborg, H. (2012). *Regional analyse for Telemark* [Regional analysis for Telemark region] (Vol. TF-notat nr 87/2012). Bø, Telemarksforskning.

7 Vysočina region

From a remote rural region straight into the virtual world

Libor Prudký and Michaela Šmídová

Introduction

Much of the debate about regional peripherality and the contribution of universities has focused on the roles of universities in driving economic development, despite a rhetoric driven by European institutions emphasising the importance of driving social and sustainable development in parallel. Much of the consideration of how universities contribute to these activities has focused on universities becoming involved in particular kinds of social or sustainability activity. This runs the risk of creating a disconnect between the small-scale university activities, on the one hand, and the larger-scale regional economic development trajectories on the other. In this chapter, we seek to look at the roles that universities can play in promoting social and sustainable development in peripheral regions by considering the overall contribution that they make to the overall processes of regional change.

The reason for doing this is not just one of completeness, but because we can see that there is a particular class of region that can actually seek to use social and sustainable development processes to improve its overall socio-economic performance. There are regions which are underdeveloped and have therefore avoided many of the problems that are brought by industrialisation, with strong social and environmental infrastructures. At the same time, their economic infrastructures may be weak, and there is the risk that these regions choose to transform their structure by attracting inward investment (for example) that severely weakens their environmental and social structures without providing the robust basis for economic modernisation. There is a growing literature that stresses how remote rural regions can attract digital entrepreneurs who value the characteristics of underdevelopment (a high quality of life) and are yet not disadvantaged by this regional remoteness. And so our overall research question is how can a higher education institution contribute to these processes of socially and sustainability-driven development?

This chapter does this with reference to a single region, Vysočina in the Czech Republic (CR), which lags economically and has a weak economic structure. At the same time, the region ranks very highly in Czech terms in social and environmental aspects of life. Vysočina lags in terms of many of the popular developmental indicators such as economy, R&D development, innovations and level of education but it leads in quality of environment, cultural and historic heritage, civic participation, health, life satisfaction, social cohesion and regional identity.

Our analysis draws on concepts of quality of life, a concept that is complex, multidimensional and vague, with different definitions and measures being used in different policy concepts. In this chapter we define quality of life as a state of well-being which characterises regional (i.e. social and not individual) level of development structured into three pillars: environmental, social and economic. In the next section we propose a more detailed research methodology, followed by a description of Vysočina region structured according to our framework into three main parts complemented/accompanied by information about regional demography ('human capital'). In the fourth section we will present strategic aims and needs of the region with special attention paid to the collaboration with the local/regional HEI. Two examples will give detailed insight into the region–HEI collaboration. Finally we highlight potential contributions which universities can make to regional development processes in these remote rural regions, drawing lessons from the case of Vysočina, arguing that much more consideration needs to be given to the roles that universities can play in contributing to developing social capital as a source of socio-economic development for peripheral regions.

Applying the quality of life approach to the Czech context

In this chapter, we make a distinction between three pillars that contribute to the overall quality of life of a region, namely the economic, the environmental and the social. It must be emphasised that pillars are mutually connected, related and in close mutual interaction, together constituting the overall quality of life. This framework is also necessarily a static framework, which provides an explanation of the present situation, which in turn provides an expanded view of the region which enables the generation of an understanding of how past situations translated into the future, and then reflecting on how this might also affect the transformations into the future. The economic pillar is relatively well understood, it is the extent to which the current economic structure provides the basis for well-balanced and endogenously embedded regional economic development, with high levels of employment, low levels of employment, rising productivity and wage levels. The social reflects the overall social cohesion of the population directly indicated by the social networks and less directly through health and longevity indicators. The environmental pillar is the extent to which the regional environment provides both direct benefits to its residents through for example leisure activities, as well as indirectly by avoiding the imposition of additional health problems.

This framework is explored through the use of a case study of the Vysočina region in the Czech Republic. This case study, along with many of the other empirical chapters in this book, was derived from a much more extensive

1) Descriptive part (gathering of data – quantitative, qualitative)

2) Identification of needs/demands (based on regional strategies)

3) Identification of co-operation (and their actors)

4) Creation of matrix of needs and HEI reactions

5) Linking to quality of life within social, environmental and economic pillars of development

6) Formulation of challenges and potentials (in relation to given research questions)

Figure 7.1 General design of our research
Source: Authors' own elaboration.

research project, PERIF: 'The Contribution of Higher Education Institutions to Strengthen Socio-economic Development of Peripheral Regions in Norway and the Czech Republic'. The breadth of the research question necessitated a relatively broad research design (see Figure 7.1). The analysis focused primarily on identifying the needs/demands of the region and mapping of co-operation activities between regional actors and regional HEIs based on these identified regional needs.

The case study was developed from a mix of quantitative and qualitative analysis, including a selection of available statistical data, mainly from the Czech statistical office (CSO) which collects and processes demographic, economic and environmental data at a national as well as regional level. Analytic and strategic documents relating to both the region and the HEI were analysed for the period 2015–2020. Analytical or strategic documents are used which relate to both sides (i.e. region and HEI). In addition, we also conducted a secondary analysis of surveys where regional data were available (European Social Survey, 2014) which focused on identity and social cohesion. These data allowed a characterisation of the contours of regional problems, development and activities. Semi-structured interviews with ten regional stakeholders from administration, private and public spheres and HEI were undertaken to complement the analysis of statistics. The aim was to enrich mainly quantitative and 'strategic' data and to obtain another support for analysis. The analysis involved creating a matrix matched to the region and university needs to allow comparison, focusing on these developmental pillars. HEI data focused on structures (policy, strategy, resource allocation), activities (within teaching, research and third mission) and networks where formal, informal and regional coalitions are distinguished.

Quality of life in Vysočina following the three pillars

From the perspective of the framework the Vysočina region has typically strong social and environmental pillars of development and a weak economic pillar. The region is located entirely within the territory of the Czech Republic with

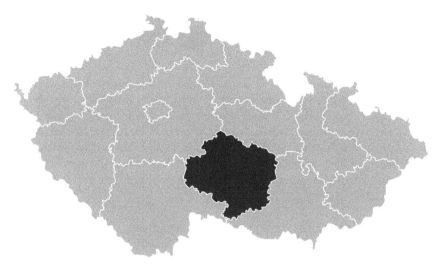

Figure 7.2 The location of Vysočina in the Czech Republic

Source: Reproduced from Wikipedia, author Miraceti under a CC 3.0 Sharealike Attribution licence.

no land borders, straddling the historical divide between Bohemia and Moravia. The region is the fifth largest of the Czech regions (6,800km²) with a relatively high average altitude (between 300m and 800m above sea level). It has a long-standing tradition of pastoral farming, crafting and other simple processing of forestry products in its many dispersed, remote villages.

Part of Vysočina's peripherality has been its long-term demographic stability, with its population remaining relatively stable in numbers and composition, without large migration waves, at a time when the overall Czech Republic population increased by 40 per cent (1869–present). Although there was displacement of population around the Second World War, there were no subsequent resettlement programmes. Even after 1990, although there has been a small migration deficit, it has been relatively limited in comparison to overall levels of Czech outmigration, and the regional population remains characterised by a high level of ethnic homogeneity and a low percentage of resident foreign-born population, with 2 per cent of long-term residents being foreign born in comparison to a national average oscillating between 4.5 per cent and 5 per cent.

Another key regional demographic challenge for Vysočina is demographic ageing, with the proportion of people aged above 65 increasing from 12.9 per cent to 18.22 per cent (1994–2014). Finally, Vysočina seems to be the most rural region in the Czech Republic; only one-third of residents live in urban regions, and the regional capital, Jihlava, has only 50,000 citizens. There is a very fragmented settlement structure, along with a very fragmented governance structure, reflecting the relatively harsh natural conditions. The region has 704 municipalities and half of those cover villages of fewer than 200 residents, with just 34 municipalities having the status of town. The provision of infrastructure and public services is very difficult under these circumstances. As one interviewee, a regional deputy, noted:

> One of the weak sides of Vysočina is residential fragmentation and sparse settlement. We have approximately 70 inhabitants/km². Not only do we have 704 municipalities but many of them are divided into separate units, so we have together 1300 individual residential units. And do you know where a disadvantage is? We have much higher costs on infrastructure. When you have to build a gas pipe for a village where 70 people live or to one apartment block where 70 people live. This is a real difference! Or roads…

The region's educational structure is quite problematic with still almost 19 per cent of the region's working age population having only primary or even unfinished primary education, and 9.5 per cent of the population not having attended at all (compared to a Czech average of 12.5 per cent (Census; CSO, 2011a)). Table 7.1 shows the educational structure of the region in comparison to the Czech Republic as a whole, showing that for lower educational levels, Vysočina has more than average numbers, and for higher education, below average numbers.

Focusing on the *economic pillar,* the business structure is dominated by metalworking (21%), engineering (16%) and automotive (11%) and food processing (11%) (CSO, 2013b). At the end of 2014 the statistical register of the Vysočina region counted 108,800 companies, meaning the Vysočina region occupied the second last place in the ranking of all the country's regions. Despite this ranking, the number of companies in the region grew by 225 per cent between 1994 and 2014. But even this apparently impressive trend lags the trends in the country as a whole. There are several large companies in the region: the largest measured by annual turnover are Bosch Diesel and PSI, two of the largest 100 companies in the Czech Republic in 2014. Zdarske Engineering is widely regarded as one of the most stable large companies in the country, whilst the Dalešice nuclear power station (in the Trebic district) is part of the Czech Republic's second largest company.

Investment (both national and foreign) in recent years has been mainly aimed at the traditional sectors and companies, with relatively little investment in ICT and with the lowest numbers of people working in research and development (R&D), 1077 in 2012 with just 21 in the state sector. This may also contribute to the region's below average position in relation to labour productivity and its indifferent average for household disposable incomes. But a more positive trend can be observed in increases of disposable income between 1995 and 2013. In 1995 Vysočina was one of two Czech regions with the lowest disposable income (national average 81,000 CZK and Vysočina average 72,000 CZK) while in 2013 it was the sixth highest of 14 regions

Table 7.1 Education of population of Vysočina region compared to Czech Republic

Region	No. of inhabitants older than 15 years	No. completed education %							
		Compulsory and unfinished	Secondary	Full secondary	Higher special	University	No education	Not known
Vysočina 2001	429,424	24.2	40.6	26.3	1.0	6.7	0.4	0.8
Vysočina 2011	431,767	0.4	18.5	37.5	27.1	4.0	9.5	3.0
CR 2001	8,571,710	23.0	38.0	27.1	1.3	8.9	0.4	1.3
CR 2011	8,947,632	0.5	17.6	33.0	27.1	4.1	12.5	5.3

Note: In the reporting period, there was a change in compulsory education for all children up to 15 years compared to the previous number of years of primary school.

Source: CSO (2003) and CSO (2011b).

with average 190,000 CZK. Although this is still below the national average of 195,000 CZK, this is a considerable convergence. Although unemployment has not been a significant regional problem, there were systematic labour market problems during the crisis, with an average of 33 people seeking each job offered in the region from 2008 to 2012. This indicates a structural fragility of a job market still primarily based upon low-technology, low-innovative potential manufacturing and services, with little opportunity to absorb highly skilled job-seekers.

If Vysočina is below average in terms of the quality of life in the economic pillar, Vysočina performs above average for the *social and environmental pillars*. According to sociological surveys of local and regional identity (ongoing research by CVVM – the Public Opinion Research Centre) or participation measured through electoral participation, these indicators are above the national average. As one interviewee related:

> If you say Vysočina everybody knows what it means. I think this is because of our strong sides and, in addition, there is people's identification with the region. If you look at Ústecký, Moravskoslezský or Liberecký regions, their people are not still 'natives' even if they live there for 70 years. But we have something like traditional families or family clans in our villages, they keep traditions. A local patriotism exists. We have also one of the lowest divorce rates here and high safety. From these perspectives this is a really great place to live.
>
> (Citation from interview, regional deputy)

There are a high number of social activities, and strong common cultural backgrounds across the whole region. Vysočina is also typical of a low share of post-material values and a high proportion of material values in Inglehart's terminology. It proves the conservative, traditional and less open value orientation approach of the inhabitants (authors' own calculations, European Social Survey, 2014). Conversely, Vysočina displays a very low share of accepted value orientations enhancing ego (i.e. strengthening self-confidence and individual drive), but together with higher concentration on the transcendental orientations. This is possibly related to the higher share of the region's religiosity among Czech regions which is reported by about one-third of the region's population according to the last Census (CSO, 2011a). Vysočina is rich in traditions and creative activities with many cultural festivals. In addition, it has the highest per capita concentration of cultural heritage, three monuments on the UNESCO list (a Jewish cemetery and Jewish town in Třebíč, St John Nepomucensis church in Žďár nad Sázavou, urban historical zone/area in Telč) as well as many other monuments of national importance.

The health of the Vysočina inhabitants is positive when measured against most indicators, despite a health service that has insufficient resources to secure field health and ambulatory care. The region has ten contributory (non-private) health premises, five of which are hospitals, along with four well-equipped first responder services. Median life expectancy was in 2012–2013 in Vysočina slightly above the national average: 75.88 years for men (Czech Republic expectancy 75.23 years) and 81.68 for women (Czech Republic expectancy 81.13 years), values which are nearly the highest among all the regions.

The distinctive feature of social coexistence in the region is high social cohesion within communities. It appears as significant self-reliance and neighbourly co-operation, independence, widespread civic initiatives as well as widespread respect for the traditions of rural life, including greater importance of religious roots and rhythm of life connected with nature. Compared to most regions in the Czech Republic, this region is characterised by substantially lower weight of anomic existence. On the other side high social cohesion means both closeness and conservativeness as well.

For the development of quality of life in the region high-quality *environment* is very important. It is not only associated with clean air, water, soil and nature, but also with the traditional spirituality of the landscape and its natural beauty. The region possesses essential resources for the development of tourism – biking, hiking and skiing. The existing tourism is similar to the overall characteristics of the region: it is lower cost and relatively simple. Environmental protection still lacks the means and capacities to complete some facilities such as sewage and sanitation, partly a result of large numbers of municipalities and fragmentation of sewage service purchase. Water management is being significantly improved, and the damage from recent floods has not been as severe as in most other regions, but even in Vysočina there have been pressures to

Table 7.2 Development of selected pollution and environmental expenditure in Vysočina

	2005	2010	2013
Solids t/km^2	0.70	0.51	0.51
SO$_2$	0.37	0.33	0.34
NOx	2.13	1.41	1.32
CO	6.00	4.83	4.69
Environmental investment (1000s CZK)	974,591	777,614	1,371,712
Non-investment environmental expenditure (1000s CZK)	520,382	1,022,298	1,112,013
Municipal waste/person	265.5	301.6	317.7
Dirty water waste/1000s metres^3	24,088	20,668	(2014) 18,782
No. of waste water treatment plants	172	156	(2014) 186
Share of cleaned waste water (%)	77.7	85.7	(2014) 87.6

Source: CSO (2013a).

improve the quality of flood defences. Although the population's health cannot be attributed directly and exclusively to a good environment, the Vysočina, thanks to its relatively unaffected nature, is considered as 'the healthiest' region of the Czech Republic. Moreover, during the last ten years there has been a decline of pollution with measured values significantly below national average, although there are persistent problems with the arranging of municipality waste collection and domestic sewage services.

Current co-operation strategies in Vysočina

The current regional strategy is entitled the 'Strategy of Vysočina region 2020' (promulgated in 2012 (Regional Office, 2013)) which identifies five main developmental areas reflecting the needs and problems previously identified. These main developmental areas are:

- Developing Vysočina as an attractive countryside, including improving functional regional centres; protecting the attractive countryside and the development of agriculture.
- People in Vysočina: with effective and targeted education, improving health services and adapting social services to the new challenges.
- Protection of natural wealth: including the use of water as an important landscape component along with effective forest management.
- Modern infrastructure: notably a quality regional road network; rail modernisation and improvement of personal transportation; installation of suitable energy sources and energy savings; effective waste solutions; and expanding ICT infrastructure.
- Competitive economics: with small and middle-size enterprises as the regional economic backbone; supporting e-services and e-safety; and harnessing touristic potential.

(Source: Strategy of Vysočina region 2020 (Regional Office, 2013))

Perhaps surprisingly, there is no role for higher education in this strategic document, although this reflects the fact that public HEIs do not fall under the responsibility/competences of regional administrations. But at the same time, the main regional HEI, the College of Polytechnics in Jihlava, was established as a 'regional project' thanks to the strong interest of the regional authority in having its own HEI located in the region. What then happens is that although there is not a strong formal relationship between the university and the regional authorities, there are relatively strong and informal ties, as will be demonstrated later. This tie was born with the regional reform in 2001 when a new administrative division was introduced and the Vysočina region was approved as one of the 14 units created under the Law on Regions No. 129/2000. This newly created regional authority sought its own regional structures, including its 'own' higher education institution, making the establishment of a new HEI a priority for the newly created regional administration:

> My duty [at the regional government] was education and human resources development, so support for establishing public HEIs had been seen as one of the most important needs.
>
> (Senior management of the College of Polytechnics)

Regional representatives started negotiations with the Czech Ministry of Education, Youth and Sports (MEYS) and relatively quickly (in 2004) received a positive reaction. The College of Polytechnics (VŠPJ) was practically/professionally focused from the very beginning of its existence because it was pragmatically formed out of a prior vocational school (providing short-cycle professionally focused higher education) in Jihlava. A strategic motivation to create an HEI in the region was to promote regional development as well as both attracting people to study as well as reducing the outmigration of highly skilled residents. Co-operation between the regional administration and representatives of the HEI (formerly the Vocational school) was close during the process of establishing the institution, with personal networks from that period still appearing important to the institution at the time of writing. The act of establishing VŠPJ is arguably the most intensive and successful effort in regional-HEI co-operation, with the HEI declaring that the focus of its study programmes would be related to the demands of regional employers, and its accredited study programmes being connected to regional strategic plans (see Table 7.3). Historically, there were some shifts in study programmes' focus from student numbers being concentrated in

Table 7.3 Focus of VŠPJ's study programmes and relation to developmental needs of Vysočina region

Study programmes	Degree programmes	Specific regional needs
Electrical Engineering and Informatics	1. Applied Computer Science 2. Computer Systems	Support of e-services and e-safety
Economics and Management	3. Travel and Tourism 4. Finance and Management	To develop touristic potential
Midwifery Health Care Clinical Social Work Specialization in Healthcare	5. Midwifery 6. General Nurse 7. Clinical Social Worker 8. Community Care in Midwifery (MA)	Demographic changes (ageing); increasing of provided health service; and adaptation of social services network on new challenges

Source: Modified by the authors according to annual report VŠPJ and Strategy of Vysočina Region.

Table 7.4 Applicants, students and graduates of VŠPJ

	2006	2008	2010	2011	2012	2013	2014
Number of applications	2092	2099	3265	2949	3099	3090	2421
Number of newly enrolled students	546	1070	1400	1347	1105	1578	1289
Total number of students	1091	2204	2997	3119	2793	3001	2651
Total number of graduates	–	99	341	398	719	549	542

Source: Annual reports of VŠPJ.

Table 7.5 Study fields and numbers of students

	IT	Economics (incl. tourism)	Health care and social work
2014	259	1842	560
2010	294	2461	266
2006	124	980	–

Source: Annual reports of VŠPJ.

economics to larger numbers of students in health care and social work alongside a relatively slow growth of student numbers in technical study programmes.

VŠPJ is a very young and non-university-type HEI, professionally and practically oriented, something that is not very common in Czech higher education, with only one similar non-university public HEI (in České Budějovice) alongside a number of private HEIs. This has created a slightly problematic situation for VŠPJ in the region:

> …because our HEI is special – there are only two HEIs of this type, and there was never previously this kind of HEI, people are not used to such type of institution. We are not a university; but despite that we are a public institution, a state HEI, without tuition fees. So, the first thing is to explain that we are a public HEI and what does it mean, because people can't imagine what that means. So, we are an HEI without tuition financed by government. The second thing is that we are a non-university institution, we have a different organisational structure [no division into faculties and no providing of PhD study programmes].
>
> (Middle management, academic employee)

There have been some attempts to establish long-term co-operation, but they have emerged as being rather partially based around mainly ad hoc activities. At the time of writing the University of the Third Age was being presented as a flagship of co-operation between the regional administration and VŠPJ. It has been very successful with respect to the numbers of participants, increasing gradually, as well as providing this education through several different cities of Vysočina, ensuring that education is being delivered close to the demand for it. Given the relatively poor quality of public transport and low levels of access to private transport for elderly residents in the region, this makes that distributed provision particularly important for the region. And clearly, providing higher education to ageing citizens comes some way to meet the challenges of demographic ageing that the region faces. At the same time, the reality was that this co-operation emerged as an accident rather than as a strategic goal. The regional administration was considering creating the University of the Third Age at Masaryk University in Brno (MUNI), the second largest HEI in the Czech Republic and without a location in Vysočina. But MUNI did not have sufficient capacities and so suggested to the region administration that they had their own regional HEI much closer to home.

Another activity which is no doubt original within the Czech higher education area is the establishment of a travel agency providing traineeships for tourism students as well as for regional promotion activities. In addition, VŠPJ organises a relatively rich programme of cultural and social activities such as presentations of scientists (not only from VŠPJ but also inviting well-known and popular Czech scientists from other regions), as well as the curation of special movie seasons. These activities are focused mainly on a broad public and have proven to be a relatively successful tool for improving the visibility and public understanding of a new and non-traditional higher educational institution.

Nevertheless, VŠPJ is still not considered as a natural partner for many regional actors probably due to its novelty, being an institution without a long tradition. As one respondent mentioned this is also exacerbated by the time cycle that emerges as a consequence of the political electoral cycle. Building trust between the universities and newly elected deputies and Ministers throws up a barrier to creating continuing, long-term co-operation between VŠPJ and region stakeholders:

> I see the problem rather in … – but this is the same everywhere – once the political elite changes, we must start again, again and again: To explain who we are, why we are here and what we could possibly be for them.
> (Middle management, academic employee)

There is one additional important role for VŠPJ in the region. According to a senior manager at VŠPJ, the presence of the HEI in Jihlava has motivated more of the regional population to study in a region that has traditionally had a relatively low level of educational aspirations, derived from the region's traditional dominance by agriculture and industry where people did not need to study at university; at the same time, the nearest HEIs were at Prague or Brno, and they seemed remote to the residents of small villages who typically did not continue in formal education after secondary school. The results of state evaluation tests of school children (15 years old) from the region were in the top third of the rating, but the number of secondary students who subsequently continued to university or other HEI study was one of the lowest in the Czech Republic.

Specific attempts to improve regional-university connections in Vysočina

VŠPJ's teaching role follows its mission of offering practically oriented study programmes to produce directly employable graduates, reflected in all its accredited eight study programmes offering at least a one-semester compulsory traineeship in firms/institutions. This is relatively rare in the Czech HE system and usually restricted to regulated professions such as medical doctors, nurses or social workers, whilst VŠPJ includes it for all programmes. Behind this principle lies a high reliance upon teachers' personal networks; the study programme 'clinical social worker' is a de facto regulated profession, and VŠPJ has recruited one practitioner with long-term experience to help organise accreditation. They used their own networks in local hospitals, social services and NGOs to help prepare this study programme within the legal framework. These (and similar partnerships) are important to long-term collaboration but lack systematic support and financing from the regional authority which leaves the university dependent on those institutions willing to provide managers and employees to tutor and mentor students. This situation also holds outside the regulated professions, where hosting placements is tax-deductible, but the time involved in supervision makes it effectively a voluntary activity for hosts.

In terms of a research role, VŠPJ has never had the ambition to pursue academic or even excellent research but originally sought to provide regionally relevant applied knowledge. Contacts with regional actors and VŠPJ have remained ad hoc, although without a simple single explanation. The largest regional employer (and largest investor in R&D) is Bosch Diesel, producing electrical automobile components, building on Vysočina traditions, especially Jihlava and its surroundings as former centres of engineering industry. Bosch was constituted as a foundation meaning that most earnings remain in the region, but there has been to date no stable and long-term co-operation between Bosch, VŠPJ and the regional government, partly because R&D in Vysočina is not a priority for Bosch. Nevertheless there has been some more systematic collaboration between Bosch, the VŠPJ and the region. This concrete example shows that Bosch's strategies do not include research as a priority in the Vysočina region, and its research centre is in another region.

> But they [Bosch] have their research centre in České Budějovice … When we offered some research co-operation and that we would like to be their partner, they actually told us it is not interesting for them and we can't help them anyhow.
>
> (Regional public administration official)

Secondly, the regional administration's efforts to build and define priorities connected with promoting research and innovative potential is recent and rather tentative, with the pilot project on 'innovative vouchers' beginning only in 2016. The hopes were high for these vouchers, to encourage firms to seek out regional universities or research centres, but demand was slow to build.

> We are at the beginning … we had actually two rounds and interest was not as high as we expected … We expected that firms which expressed some interest would appreciate the fact we offer some money, but finally interest is low, it is only the beginning … We can serve rather to [small and middle] firms than big ones. Those big firms are on a different and very professional level. They do not care about something new, what is not tried and tested. Small and middle firms have currently bigger potential, they even feel some responsibility to the region, and they share regional values.
>
> (Regional public administration official)

The tensions and barriers in promoting regional interaction

This chapter is concerned with the barriers that may inhibit a university in a peripheral region from trying to meaningfully contribute to a regional development strategy focused on promoting the quality of life in its broadest sense. In the course of the practical efforts to create a regionally relevant HEI that can make those contributions, a number of tensions have become evident. There is a regional strategy for innovation – 'Regional innovation strategy 2020' (Regional Office, 2015) – which seeks to provide a harmonised drive towards effective regional innovation. There are two main tensions, the relatively low implementation potential, along with a clash of competencies between different government structures.

The Vysočina regional authority has only recently introduced strategic planning in all fields, including for its co-operation with the university, and there are weaknesses both in development of those strategies, but more importantly in translating that into effective innovation. In the regional innovation strategy, there is a vague articulation of how policy will create innovation and research potential, and the role of VŠPJ is unclear. Much of the political capital that was developed in the course of mobilising the movement to create the university was associated with particular regional authority representatives, who because of political pressures have themselves moved on. These natural links with the regional authority have atrophied just at the point they would have been most valuable to the region, and now remain rather ad hoc.

The second tension arises because of segmentation between different government authorities. This is partly vertical, with the region being mainly concerned with activities with a directly regional footprint; primary and secondary education is an exclusively regional competence. But public higher education is subject to national criteria, and the region is unable to influence the funding, content, development and or specialisation of VŠPJ. At the same time, VŠPJ is a rather unusual institution, and does not fit well with the public law framework oriented towards basic research-focused universities, and so this framework does not accommodate regionally active universities who would 'naturally' engage with public authorities. Vertical segmentation is not the only problem, but the region also suffers from a degree of bureaucratic inefficiency, indicated by the fact that groups of municipalities have created their own Local Action Groups – in areas of business, social work and tourism. The close fit of these domains with areas of interest for VŠPJ demonstrate how the HEI is being pulled in multiple directions in its regional engagement without having a strong legal basis on which to make its choices.

There are a variety of ways in which VŠPJ's present activities in regional engagement, often ad hoc and based on personal relationships, could be expanded to create a stronger platform for regional development. VŠPJ has worked well to facilitate communications between different actors, and so expanding this to create a regional platform for cultural and social development activities could help to provide more visibility for the elements of the Vysočina developmental model. Likewise, there have been good examples where regional partners have on an ad hoc basis been able to participate in international research co-operations organised through VŠPJ, and there is clearly scope in expanding this to benefit local industrial and public administration more generally. The health services research centre, building on the school's expertise in professions allied to medicine, offers the opportunity to support the social pillar of the university. VŠPJ could also potentially expand study programmes most immediately relevant to the region and regional problems, potentially in co-operation with and for local companies, authorities and NGOs. Students offer arguably the most important influences that VŠPJ can offer, particularly in adding value to the traditional professional education route. One is in identifying ways that international students could be better embedded in the region, and another is in ensuring that student research (particularly for placements and graduation theses) is tightly aligned with practical problems emerging from regional partners.

Discussion

In this chapter we have asked the overall research question of how can a higher education institution contribute to these issues of socially and sustainability-driven regional development? We have specifically focused on the region of Vysočina because of its efforts to drive transformation through a balance of change in its economic, social and environmental pillars that contribute to a better quality of life. From the perspective of our analysis the region was a historical inner periphery, and there was a sense amongst regional partners that the factors that have served to underline and reinforce its backwardness are those that may in the future serve as sources of its development, providing a distinct advantage in the growth and sustainability of quality of life in the future. In this, we have also found a variety of ways in which the HEI was able to contribute to these processes, including through stimulating new businesses, building social cohesion, building understanding of civic needs and improving the quality of public administration.

One potential development trajectory for such regions is in the development of firms that are primarily involved in what can be considered as the fourth phase of modernisation, relating to information and communications technologies and the internet of things. This involves more homeworking as well as increasing importance of highly sophisticated technical work on decentralised networks linked between sites. There will be less construction investment and more reliance on the use of highly creative staff and teams, and this clearly offers a source of development potential for regions with their population dispersed into small settlements. At the same time, successfully implementing this development approach in these regions requires avoiding a more productionist bias (as seen more widely in the Czech Republic) where development is seen in terms of square metres developed, production volumes and absolute experts. Although higher education cannot act to create the conditions for such an industrial transition, what has happened in Vysočina highlights that universities can play a role at two levels. They can help to mobilise the talents and human assets necessary for the implementation of such strategies based on decentralised, self-managing teams. They can also work as strategic partners to encourage regional partners to engage more seriously with these issues and to embed them more into regional strategies that are subsequently more effectively implemented.

The second area where HEIs can make this contribution is in the support of the social pillar, and in particular increasing civic participation in policy-making, building trust and openness amongst people and institutions. Just as the absence of mass production industry becomes an advantage rather than a source of backwardness, the situation in Vysočina is one in which the absence of a strong regional state has allowed local collaborative activities to emerge, such as the LAGs. There are here clearly opportunities for higher education to participate in activities across regional partners that can support this civic life and participative activity. In particular, the particular strength of these more vocational HE colleges that nevertheless have a research thesis requirement in their curricula is that the volume of students can help many activities in parallel. In the absence of strong top-down mechanisms to articulate civic desires, interests and needs, student research can provide a means to place those very local interests on the wider regional agenda. In particular through the development of a wider regional platform, or platforms, for social, civic and collaboration activities, the HEI can serve to consolidate and develop an important source of strength and quality of life in the region, this high degree of social capital. The HEI in this case serves as a means of harnessing this strong social capital to the regional strategic agenda, and ensuring that the various regional strategies that are developed build on and augment the existing social capital and civic cohesion, to improve quality of life.

It is this dimension, the role of universities in contributing to social capital in peripheral regions, that we see has been insufficiently explored to date. Peripheral regions in the main may suffer from different kinds of problems with their social capital – old industrial regions may be locked in and lack the connections to break out of the dependency on old sectors. Remote island and mountainous regions may lack a depth to their social capital that prevents it serving as the basis for collective action to identify, mobilise to address and ultimately solve these social problems. More rural regions may have very strong social capital that remains internally fragmented and is unable to harness itself to regional authorities and strategic decision-making activities that ultimately see its potential strengths being overlooked. All of these various contributions may not be seen because of a predominance of the economic imperative in regional policy-making, with the result that although economic development is driven it does not raise quality of life and ultimately make peripheral regions better places to live. We therefore argue that more attention needs to be paid to these issues of the contribution of universities to social capital, and the immaterial social and environmental benefits that this can bring to regions, as well as the political and administrative constraints that can lead it to be overlooked.

Acknowledgements

This case study is a part of the project 'The Contribution of Higher Education Institutions to Strengthen Socio-Economic Development of Peripheral Regions in Norway and the Czech Republic' financed by the Czech-Norwegian Research Program through Norwegian financial mechanism 2009–2014 (PERIF project).

References

College of Polytechnics (2006–2014). *Výroční zprávy o činnosti VŠPJ (Annual Reports of VŠPJ)*, www.vspj.cz/skola/uredni-deska/vyrocni-zpravy-o-cinnosti, accessed 4 September 2017.

CSO (2003). *Úroveň vzdělání podle krajů a okresů (Level of education according to regions and counties)*, www.czso.cz/documents/10180/20537676/411303a4.pdf/d0902493-cab2-41df-837d-feff87cb6456?version=1.0, accessed 4 September 2017.

CSO (2011a). *Census – Sčítání lidu, domů a bytů 2011 (Census 2011)*, www.czso.cz/csu/sldb/home, accessed 4 September 2017.

CSO (2011b). *Vzdělanostní struktura obyvatelstva v kraji Vysočina (Educational structure of Vysočina population)*, www.czso.cz/csu/xj/vzdelanostni_struktura_obyvatelstva_v_kraji_vysocina, accessed 4 September 2017.

CSO (2013a). *Životní prostředí (Environmental Statistics)* 2005, 2010 and 2013, www.czso.cz/csu/czso/zivotni_prostredi_zem, accessed 4 September 2017.

CSO (2013b). *Databáze průmyslových podniků a jejich provozoven v kraji Vysočina (Database of industrial firms in Vysočina Region)*, www.czso.cz/csu/xj/ekonomicke_subjekty_v_kraji_vysocina, accessed 4 September 2017.

European Social Survey (2014). *ESS round 7. Data file edition 2.1. NSD – Norwegian Centre for Research Data.* Norway – Data Archive and distributor of ESS data for ESS ERIC.

Regional Office (2013). *Regionální inovační strategie kraje Vysočina (Regional Innovation Strategy),* www.kr-vysocina.cz/regionalni%2Dinovacni%2Dstrategie%2Dkraje%2Dvysocina/d-4053782/p1=61524, accessed 4 September 2017.

Regional Office (2015). *Strategie kraje Vysočina (Strategy of Vysočina Region).* Jihlava: Krajský úřad, www.kr-vysocina.cz/assets/File.ashx?id_org=450008&id_dokumenty=4052133, accessed 4 September 2017.

8 Usti region

Learning hard about industry modernisation

Inna Čábelková and Jan Kohoutek

Introduction

To an outside observer the Usti region should be destined to be one of the most prosperous regions in the Czech Republic. Its favourable geographic location in Central Europe on the transport axes between the capital city of Prague in the Czech Republic and Dresden in Germany creates conditions for Czech Republic transactions. Ústí nad Labem, a city with one of the largest railway junctions in the CR and the largest Elbe river port, presents an ideal point for logistics and transportation. Abundant natural resources including the largest national deposits of brown coal, high levels of urbanisation and industrialisation, good transportation, and easily available newly built industrial zones create a solid basis for industries. Fertile soils constituting half of the area enables agricultural production. Diversified natural conditions and protected landscape areas present attractive spots for tourism. One of the youngest populations compared to other regions offers prospects for long-term prosperity.

Yet, according to GDP per capita, average and median incomes, and unemployment rate the region scores as one of the poorest regions in the Czech Republic. Though the level of industrialisation is high, it lags behind in diversification and development of high value adding sectors. The Usti region reports one of the lowest levels of education – higher educated population constitutes only 7.8%, while the average for the country, though still small internationally, reaches 12.5%. The region suffers from environmental damage, higher rates of mortality, morbidity and crime, and a significantly large number of ill-adjusted inhabitants such as Roma minority. The low education, weak social structure, and concentration of production on heavy industries with high energy demands with low value added reduced the competitiveness of the region at the beginning of the 1990s and locked in the region as an old industrial area.

The low education levels and poor economic performance called upon a new regional university to be established. The University of Jan Evangelist Purkyne (UJEP) was founded in 1991. Since then the university has helped to increase the percentage of the higher educated population from 4% in 1991 to 7.8% in 2015, however its existence was not enough to reverse the overall trajectory of the regional development.

The aim of this chapter is to contribute to the debate on the regional role of the university by analysing the needs of the peripheral region and the possibilities for the regional university to fulfil the regional role in the old industrial area using the example of the Usti region in the Czech Republic. The research question is: to what extent can universities contribute to improving regional innovation ecosystems in peripheral regions that lack strong centres of gravity?

We employ the method of historical institutionalism relying on primary and secondary documents, available quantitative data, and qualitative field research based on interviews with relevant actors (15 interviews) and expert opinions.

The role of universities in driving industrial modernisation

This chapter is primarily concerned with the roles that universities can play in driving modernisation projects in old industrial regions. Much of Eastern Europe went through a substantial economic shock with the end of socialism and the later accession to the European Union and this had profound consequences for its economic base which came for the first time into competition with industries that had often enjoyed dominant market and technology positions. Those regions most dependent on traditional industries suffered extensively as firms were privatised often being acquired by foreign investors or failing. The main challenge for these regions in the first instance was in finding any kind of employment to replace those jobs lost through these radical restructurings. But the search for job creation often led to the creation of branch plant and assembly activities based on wage cost competition and which offered little potential for neo-endogenous regional growth. These regions can be considered as locked-in to their industrial activities lacking the actors able to take the initiative to start building new regional sectors. The notion of 'lock-in' usually describes the situation where a process (technology, industry, regional economy) has become stuck in a particular trajectory that has become inefficient in some way (Martin & Sunley, 2006). This position in economic geography is described as growing rigidification and the implied erosion of adaptability (Arthur, 1989). The nature of lock-in implies that the regions are not able to change their trajectories to a more efficient ones without external force.

In this chapter, we draw on the framework of Lester (2003, 2006) who identified four repertoires by which regions can break this technological lock-in and begin processes of transformation towards knowledge-based regional development.

1. To concentrate on creation of new technologies and industries from within the region.
2. To import new industries from elsewhere.
3. To diversify/transform existing local industries to employ better technologies.
4. To revitalise and upgrade the existing industries by developing new products, and infuse new technologies.

The first option is science driven, when the PhD-level scientists and engineers are supposed to develop the technologies in the universities and government labs and through collaboration with industry or entrepreneurial activities of the students commercialise the results (Lester, 2003, 2006). This option requires high levels of education and innovative capacities within the region and a strong research-oriented university. The second option of importing new high technological industries is also contingent upon a highly qualified workforce for adopting already existing technologies and collaboration with the university or governmental labs in order to develop them further (Lester, 2003, 2006). Diversification, revitalisation, and upgrade of existing industries (the third and the fourth option) are less sensitive for the education of the workforce, and are based on customer-driven innovation, continuous improvement, and 'best practices'. These options require masters-level engineers, faculty-student knowledge of industry practices, and business problems, internships, rotations (Lester, 2003, 2006).

These individual repertoires may all be more or less present in particular regions in terms of their transformational pathways. Universities may potentially have a range of roles in each of these shifts (OECD, 2007). The university may contribute through its teaching activities, providing highly skilled graduates to create and work new business sectors, and with the competences to ensure that they upgrade their skills as they progress through the labour market. The university may contribute through its research activities, working with regional firms and other partners to develop new knowledge in wider networks, thereby bringing new knowledge into the region and deploying that productively in new commercial settings. Finally, a university may also contribute through its collaboration activities with other partners, helping to improve their own activities, to create new collective activities that benefit the region, or ultimately improve the quality of strategic decision-making and policy in that particular region.

The methodology

Methodologically our empirical analysis resorts to historical institutionalism and qualitative field analysis based on expert interviews. Historical institutionalism is a method that studies path dependencies through a set of critical junctions.

> Outcomes at a 'critical juncture' trigger feedback mechanisms that reinforce the recurrence of a particular pattern into the future. Path dependent processes have very interesting characteristics. They can be highly influenced by relatively modest perturbations at early stages. Once actors have ventured far down a particular path, however, they are likely to find it very difficult to reverse course. Political alternatives that were once quite plausible may become irretrievably lost. Thus, events or processes occurring during and immediately following critical junctures emerge as crucial.
>
> (Pierson & Skocpol, 2002, pp. 699–700)

At each juncture a set of choices are possible and those options chosen close alternative options and create institutions that lead to self-reinforcing processes influencing the longer-term developmental path. Historical institutionalism is not exclusively an institutional approach; what is also relevant here are the decisions within institutions taken and executed by agents possessing relevant power (Battilana, 2006; Battilana *et al.*, 2009) and often interconnected via informal social networks. These networks serve to socialise and support information exchange between agents (Bathelt, Malmberg, & Maskell, 2004; Padgett & Powell, 2012; Powell, 1998). Most importantly, the networks are associated with higher trust levels among actors (Benneworth, Pinheiro, & Karlsen, 2014; Owen-Smith & Powell, 2008).

Appropriate methods for developing such analyses are case studies, with argumentation often based on counterfactuals (Capoccia & Kelemen, 2007). This chapter presents the case of the Usti region, which formed one of six case studies of PERIF projects (see acknowledgements) along with the Vysočina and Olomouc regions in the Czech Republic and the Telemark, Finnmark, and Agder regions in Norway. To create this case study, we firstly analysed primary/secondary documents, comparative analysis, expert opinions, qualitative field research in the regions and higher education institutions. After studying the relevant material we conducted 15 interviews with stakeholders in the region, along with an expert on the higher educational policy in the Czech Republic.

Usti region: setting the stage

The Usti region is by most standards a peripheral region in the Czech Republic. This was not so 100 years ago, when Usti was an exemplary success of early capitalism in Central and Eastern Europe, creating an industrial complex of technological-based enterprises run by new social elites formed from owners and managers of major companies (Koutský, 2011). This successful development trajectory was interrupted by World War II and forced expulsions of the German population followed by in-migration from other economically weaker Czech Republic regions. These historical events disrupted vital production chains with neighbouring Germany and significantly diminished regional economic diversification. The forced expulsions dislocated a settled population and caused deep-seated alienation, and those industrial sectors linked to German capital and markets (particularly textiles but also glass and wood processing) entered a secular decline, at least partly replaced with a significant absolute strengthening in mining, metal production, and the chemical industry (Koutský, 2011). By the fall of socialism, the region was heavily industrialised based on extractive resources (lignite mining, thermal power stations, inputs for production in the chemical industry), alongside a significant share of heavy industry producing basic components for more specialised manufacturing sectors located elsewhere. The economy was dominated by vertically organised companies characterised by over-employment of mostly unskilled labour, lacking flexibility to respond to economic conditions and the capital intensity to invest for the future. External

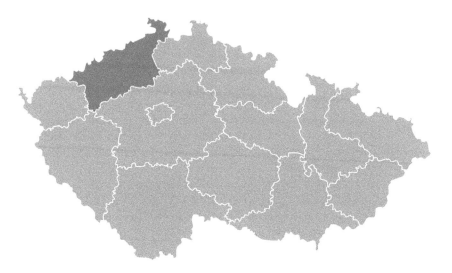

Figure 8.1 The location of Usti in the Czech Republic
Source: Reproduced from Wikipedia, author Miraceti under a CC 3.0 Sharealike
Attribution licence.

state control over strategic economic sectors (mining, chemistry) hampered the
development of local economic elites (Koutský, 2011).

Most of these economic structures failed in the 1990s when Usti was
exposed to market competition, and the region clearly lacked a knowledge base
necessary to diversify and modernise economic processes. Population education
levels were low (just 4% of residents had a university degree in 1993). The high
unemployment rate along with the government policy to support immigration
to the region drove down property prices which had a self-reinforcing effect.
Environmental damage that emerged from the socialist mining, heavy metal-
lurgy, and chemical industries negatively affected residents' health conditions.
This poor environment, low education levels, and the absence of well-paid
jobs served as a push factor for brain-drain whilst nearby Prague and German
cities exerted strong pull factors. The region became locked into a position of
a technologically old industrial region with an ageing infrastructure, a poorly
educated population, and low value adding production with little endogenous
ability to change its economic trajectory.

The efforts to address the regional problems

The government's first re-industrialisation strategy sought to attract FDI inflows
through offering favourable locations, newly built industrial zones, excellent
transport connectivity, low labour costs, and direct incentives, including that
from EU Structural Funds after the Czech Republic joined the EU in 2004.

Low local education levels meant that this restructuring favoured cost controls and price competition rather than competition on quality and innovation, what has elsewhere been called the 'low road strategy'. These efforts indeed succeeded in attracting foreign capital, with Czechinvest accounting for 185 of the investment projects launched in Usti region (1993–2010). Of these projects 90% were in the manufacturing industry, notably the automotive sector, with the vast majority of companies operating at the second to third level of hierarchy of production, performing relatively easy operations with few high technological processes. This approach locked Usti region even further into its position of low education, low innovation, and low value added industrial production. Highly educated people often emigrated because of a lack of local employment opportunities whilst firms resisted bringing innovation-intensive production because of a perception of a lowly educated labour market. Likewise, educated residents in other regions were unwilling to move to Usti region because of its image as an old industrial area with polluting enterprises, full of smog, and socially maladjusted groups of people (Piknová, 2014).

In an attempt to break this vicious circle, the region adopted the 'science and technology parks' strategy to attract high technology, high value added business, and raise the region's innovative capacity. This sought to stimulate regional development by developing new technologies and industries, and import technologically intensive industries from elsewhere and develop them further in the region. The rationale behind this approach was twofold, an attempt to import *both* the industry and the qualified labour force to the region. Firstly, the strategy sought to exploit the region's relative proximity to well-functioning high technological areas in nearby Germany and the advantageous geographic position on the axis between Prague and Germany to reduce the transaction and transportation costs of relocating businesses and commuting time for educated employees living elsewhere.[1,2] Secondly, compared to Germany, Usti was able to offer lower labour and rental costs and offer EU structural funds financial support.

The largest science and technology park (STP) project was NUPHARO, launched in 2015 as a technology park, business incubator, and innovation centre offering rental space for a diverse group of companies   from technological start-ups to large multinationals. The park sought to promote smart energy, direct current, and other innovative technologies. The overall investment was €27 million (Sujan, 2016), of which approximately €12 million was invested by the Ministry of Industry and Trade (MPO) using European subsidies from the Operational Program OPEI Prosperity (Cerny, 2016b). NUPHARO was located approximately 6km from the regional centres of Usti and Labem, and was close to the highway D8 connecting Prague to Germany. Originally, the park was intended to host divisions of CISCO, E.ON, Philips, IBM, and other large multinational firms (Vorlicek, 2013). However, these multinationals later withdrew their proposals for unknown reasons, although they would have been discouraged by the economic downturn and lack of a qualified workforce. Out of the 20 firms potentially accommodated, at the time of writing only 5 small firms were located on the park, mostly in production rather than research. In August 2016, the park was on the verge of bankruptcy, posting an operating loss of c. CZK 1.6 million rather than the intended profit (approximately €60,000 (Cerny, 2016a). Attempts to build science and technology parks and business incubators within the regional university were similarly unsuccessful, more often than not defaulting to renting space for local firms with little technological input. These centres were also focusing on short-term project-related seminars, training activities, and journal publishing, a far cry from the intended commodifiable research-driven innovations in hard science utilisable by regional industries.

The university and its regional roles

One of the main reasons emerging in the previous section for the lack of success of attempts to upgrade regional industry was a lack of qualified workforce, something which has driven the unfolding regional role of the local university. The University of Jan Evangelist Purkyne (UJEP) was founded in 1991 as a public regional university in a euphoria at the end of the communist regime, initially comprising three faculties, namely Education, Environment, and Social & Economic Studies.[3] Aside from UJEP, there are five branches of three other publicly funded universities in the region: Czech Technical University (an off-shoot of the Faculty of Transportation as well as a Faculty of Nuclear Sciences and Physical Engineering); University of Chemistry and Technology, Prague; a branch of the Czech University of Life Sciences, Prague (the Faculty of Environmental Science and the Faculty of Economics and Management), however, the numbers of students in these branches are rather small.

Though UJEP was vital to the region, its faculties and departments were established reflecting the university professors' personal possibilities and ambitions, accreditation requirements, and the basis of the prior educational institutions which had been merged to create UJEP. The only state authority able to guide the process from above, was the Ministry of Education, Youth and Sports Accreditation Commission. This Commission's mandate was primarily around input oriented quality assurance, and the regional contribution of graduates, whilst formally required, did not play a large role in the accreditation process. Despite this lack of co-ordination from above, the first three faculties addressed the three most pressing social needs of the region: education of teachers on various levels, improvement of the polluted environment, and addressing the population's economic and social needs. Although these were not oriented towards industrial reinvention, they fulfilled social expectations and became an important background for later changes. The second wave of faculties enabled the university to establish itself as a regular university with a number of different specialisations, including Commercial Art and Design (2000), Science (2005), Philosophy (2006), and Production Technology and Management (2006). The most recently created faculty Health Studies (2012) reflects regional health care needs and also the opportunity to offer health care services to residents from neighbouring Germany. In 2004 the University was granted, by the regional authorities, its own site in Usti nad Labem, which it transformed to a university campus.

The university's regional education role

UJEP clearly had an impact on the education level in Usti region, with the percentage of workforce with a degree rising from 4% of 7.8% (1991–2015) although this level is still significantly below the national average (12% in 2015). There are several factors limiting UJEP's regional educative role. First, many graduates do not work in professions they are trained for due to low wages (notably primary and secondary school teachers and social workers). So, despite the sufficient graduate numbers there remain staffing shortages in some public sector branches. Next, graduate outmigration to other regions reduces UJEP's regional impact; to address this 'brain drain', local government introduced graduate stipends for students staying in the region; this well-intended scheme was not effective as students proved willing to save and return the money if they were offered better-paid positions elsewhere. UJEP since sought to address this by providing a unified university system of graduate-tracking to provide comprehensive and more reliable information about UJEP students' graduation paths and study-related reflections. UJEP intended to use this information to feed back into programme design and course innovations, to help enhance their region-specific relevance.

UJEP's regional educational role was constrained by the limited numbers of faculties; while socially important professions (such as school teachers, and professions allied to medicine) are well covered by the university, graduates in technical professions are still in short supply, although most vital to change the region's overall industrial trajectory. Technical education in Usti is fragmented with several specialisations in UJEP and a number of other courses offered by regional branches of Prague technical universities. The strict accreditation procedures including professors' academic qualifications (including publications) also hindered universities' flexibilities to adapt to regional industry's demands, and to hire industrial staff as course teachers. Despite that, UJEP and its faculties were able to develop a number of creative co-operations to enhance graduates' relevance for regional employers. These included student internships, joint thesis supervision, a 'teenage university' promoting education and careers in science, faculty interactive workshops with school teachers, and special events such as career days. Our research, however, also points to several downsides associated with such activities, namely faculty fragmentation, co-ordination problems, and difficulties in impact evaluation. There has been an issue around surging intakes for technical specialisations and associated problems of massification, including high drop-out rates; to date discussion has centred on whether it is realistic to cap publically financed student numbers. UJEP's response has been to improve student recruitment and retention through long-term co-operation with selected secondary schools and tertiary professional schools.

These trends are not unique for Usti region, but have been more pronounced in the region given the population's weak socio-economic structure in terms of employment and education levels. UJEP has helped raise the regional education level, but has not proven sufficient nor decisive in shifting the region's economic development trajectory and breaking its lock-in as an old industrial region.

The university's regional research role

A university's second regional function is to participate in research and development, and in Usti region, seeking to shift towards a path of industry diversification and upgrading, what would be more useful to regional firms would be supporting customer-focused firm-led innovation than developing an internationally excellent science base. However, similarly to many other universities, UJEP's incentives to engage in firm level research are limited, with universities being pushed by rewards systems to produce internationally competitive publications, part of a more general trend of regional universities and teaching colleges striving to assert themselves as national or international research universities (Gonzales, 2012, 2013).

There are three reasons for this in the Czech Republic, namely: (i) performance-based funding, (ii) accreditation/habilitation requirements, and (iii) prestige. The Czech Republic's National Research and Development Methodology uses performance-based funded which rewards high-profile (Thomson-Reuters or Scopus-indexed) publications by renowned publishing houses. The methodology was roundly critiqued for its failure to support diverse institutional missions, and national priority areas, using arbitrary output indicators that impede developing long-term research strategies and creating science-industry links (Arnold, 2011; Linková & Stöckelová, 2012). Despite this criticism, the Government continued with this performance-based funding system with the effect that Czech HEIs with strong regional missions such as UJEP have been forced to orient themselves towards top-class international publications. Funding for the regional mission was intended to come from contractual research, commissioned analyses (expertise-drafting for Usti regional and municipal administration), revenues from licenses, consultancy, and also paid-for vocational training. However, in UJEP, regional-oriented consultancy activities comprised no more than 0.3% of UJEP's budget from 2010 to 2014. We contend that this minimal percentage speaks volumes as to UJEP's real contributions in commissioned research, analysis, and consultancy to regional stakeholders: despite a wealth of strategies and good-will intentions the actual demand for commercial research, analysis, and consultancy done by UJEP is very low as has been more true more generally with private sector R&D spending within Czech HEIs (Drahoš, 2012).[4]

Two other factors also affect universities' regional research roles. The national accreditation requirements for study programmes and career prospects of teaching staff impose significant demands on peer-reviewed internationally recognised publications. Without sufficient numbers of professors publishing internationally, the university is not able to acquire (re-)accreditation for teaching programmes. This has had a diversionary effect on teaching and research activities, encouraging international publication over firm level research, and also making it more fragmented and ad hoc within a few faculties that are able to tolerate it. Finally, facing the discouraging image of Usti region, UJEP sought to make itself more attractive to potential staff as an international researchbased university as that would bring better professors, better students, and more prestige, also reflecting that the Czech Republic has lacked a tradition of vocational or practical regional universities as in for example neighbouring Germany.

It is clear that the current system of financing and accrediting educational programmes and competition for students has created a strategic overload within UJEP and forced it to make a choice between its international profile and its regional relevance. The pressures have been such that it has had to systematically prioritise its international profile, and specifically publication in international journals for renowned publishers, over any kind of systematic or strategic regional engagement activities. This remains a significant problem for the Usti region, which is in desperate need of highly educated professionals as well as the provision of innovation and research support services to assist its firms with innovation upgrading processes.

The university's regional collaboration role

A final regional role for universities is in participating in regional development plans and strategies, with universities working systematically with regional officials and business representatives (see for example Etzkowitz & Leydesdorff, 2000; Leydesdorff & Etzkowitz, 1996). The reality in Usti is far from ideal, despite substantive efforts by regional representatives and UJEP employees to work together to create regionally embedded projects within the university. The key problem has been, as with regional collaboration in the other missions, that collaboration has lacked a systemic approach and has been heavily dependent on individuals. There have been several factors that have driven this fragmentation, relating to fundamental differences between regional authorities (particularly those responsible for regional development) and UJEP.

Firstly, although regional authorities have been represented in UJEP's governing bodies there has been a feeling that the university is alien to the region and that regional authorities have been unable to materially influence the university's course. The regional authority has not been able to influence the university through its own funding, and central government funding has not been dependent on engaging with regional authorities and actors, and the region has not even developed a strategy for co-operation with UJEP. UJEP has a relatively low regional profile amongst the population; many in the region, but also in Usti nad Labem city where the university is located, were unaware that there was a university in the region and certainly were not informed about its specific study programmes. In the absence of institutional co-operation, there has been a strong dependence on individual contacts, something vulnerable on both sides to the election cycles for regional and university authorities. Indeed it was reported that a number of promising projects for university-regional co-operation had been discontinued following the end of the term of electoral office of one of the individuals in those collaborations.

Conversely, collaboration with local authorities of Usti nad Labem city (not subject to electoral cycles) has been more promising, including collaboration with the city's Employment Office to strengthen graduate retention rates (although still dependent to a degree on personal relationships). The Usti nad Labem authorities gave the whole campus location to the University and partly financed reconstruction. Local and regional officials participated in UJEP's scientific council and in its board of trustees, albeit in a way that was described as passive by interviewees. There are several developmental projects that were successful: this is exemplified by the Faculty of Commercial Art and Design that has regularly created indoor and outdoor exhibitions of student creative activities, contributing to improving the environment of Usti nad Labem city.

One unavoidable element of the institutional fragmentation within Usti is that it is a consequence of lock-in, with various partners having their own interests in continuing elements of the locked-in situation, and therefore generating opposition to proposals for change. There have been many actors involved in these discussions, including the regional administration, the chamber of commerce, the innovation centre of Usti region, the representative of the government for innovations in Usti region, various panel and working groups that conduct seminars and conferences on the development of the region.[5] These discussions have this far often ended with broad statements that have been difficult to translate into concrete projects, and what projects have been created have often faltered due to a lack of funds, the absence of co-ordination, or simply because the projects were unsuitable for Usti.

Although there are very few recurrent university funding streams for regional development, UJEP does have an Institutional Development Programme (IDP) for which it receives an annual institutional subsidy from the Ministry of Education. IDP was designed as a block grant funding scheme to help foster Czech HEIs' strategic development (Kohoutek, 2011) and has been considered a good practice example also internationally (File, Weko, Hauptman, Kristensen, & Herlitschka, 2006). In UJEP, IDP funding (3% of the total annual budget, c. CZK 26 million), has been used to support some regional engagement activities including course innovations, student internships, and UJEP regional promotion. However, these activities are themselves rather fragmented, ad hoc, and have not developed recurrent linkages and relationships with other regional stakeholders.

The lack of use of national funding to drive regional priorities reflects a fragmentation of Ministry interest in Usti; the university IDP is funded by the Ministry of Education, whilst the regional development programmes are subsidised by the Ministry of Regional Development, and commercial enterprises fall under the Ministry of Trade and Industry. This encourages sectoral isolation, inducing a 'playing on one's own sectoral pitch attitude'. It is clearly unrealistic to expect a fragmentation that reflects divisions at the level of central government to be adequately compensated by co-ordination (the Economic and Social Board of Usti Region) or supervisory bodies (UJEP board of trustees) alone. At the time of writing the Czech Republic government had launched a new funding initiative to resolve this issue, entitled 'RE:START', facilitated by brokerage of a special governmental envoy, although it was not clear to what extent this sought to deliver a trans-formation of government policy in the regions or merely sought to create positive publicity for the government in the run-up to the Autumn 2017 general elections.

Solutions and tensions

In the previous sections we have seen that UJEP's regional engagement in teaching, research, and regional collaboration has been hampered by lack of co-ordination, political cycles, insufficient leadership, and lack of adequate financing. It is worth also making explicit that the relative youth of the uni-versity, and its recent transformation from colleges into a full-blown university have created a strategically focused environment where the focus lies primarily on ensuring that the university can justify its new-found status in terms of its international research performance and the international quality of its teaching staff. We have seen that UJEP's regional activities were obstructed by diffi-culties in accreditation processes, task overload in research, and alienation in third role activities. Given these conditions, UJEP has at least been successful in raising overall skill levels, particularly in social and environment professionals. However, educating these professionals is clearly not going to be sufficient to lead to path-switching processes in Usti, and there remains a need for a sub-stantive improvement in technical education and industrial co-operation. The question remains of where might there be possibilities within this externally dominated system that encourage higher levels of regional engagement by the universities.

Smilor, Dietrich, and Gibson identified as early as 1993 that external pressures could be positive in stimulating university regional engagement, but at the same time identified a number of locally specific factors that might encourage regional engagement by universities (see also Chakrabarti & Lester, 2002). One of these, namely the demand emerging from industry for employees for high-technology sectors has been difficult to realise in Usti, as has the desire by UJEP to increase its funding from external sources, again limited by weaknesses inherent in the Czech RIS. However, there is one pressure in their framework, namely new demands upon universities for accountability by regional leaders could potentially be present. At the time of writing, those pressures from regional authorities have tended to be piecemeal and not exerted in ways that might lead to a substantive behavioural change within the universities. But where there has been any kind of encouragement and expectation from authorities, clearly UJEP has sought as far as is possible within the constraints that it found itself, to deliver regionally and meet those regional expectations.

A key issue emerging here is that there is not a strongly science-led model of economic development; in Usti, what path-creation activity there is emerges from a close interaction between firms and knowledge providers, around incremental, customer-centred innovation processes. And those processes demand knowledges that are not always interesting for a university under pressure in different ways to demonstrate its international standing and prestige. What is needed are active incentives that allow UJEP to participate in regionally useful activities without forcing the university to make a trade-off between regionally relevant and internationally excellent research. This may involve for example providing the university with resources to participate in collaborative research activities with firms, and to develop long-term strategic relationships with those firms; at the same time there is the need to develop a regional level body that can demand and support systematic university regional engagement independently of electoral cycles. The unavoidable issue here is that of funding, and that the university needs to be able to access substantive funding from regional development plans that are relevant for firms and universities together. It is unrealistic to expect that the Usti region can immediately launch large-scale internationally competitive research partnerships within the region, but one step towards that is the creation of multidisciplinary projects encouraging co-operation between firms as well as between firms and industries, to help to create a regional 'knowledge pool' that can serve as the basis of a wider specialisation.

Conclusions

The historical path of Usti locked the region into a position of being an old industrial region and resulted in rigid, largely outdated industry, weak social composition of population, low education of the workforce, and damaged ecology. For Usti, the two main ways in which new pathways can be created to escape technological lock-in following the scheme of Lester have been firstly to diversify/transform existing industries, and secondly to revitalise/upgrade existing industries (Lester, 2003, 2006). The university has at least partly determined this, because of its relative youth as an institution, but also its strategic focus on improving its international profile and the crowding-out that this has on the strategic scope within the university to prioritise regional engagement more widely. These two path-creation processes revolve around regional innovation activities that are incremental and customer-driven, rather than being driven by the science base. These processes accord to the university an important role in providing the higher-level skills necessary for that innovation, whether masters-level engineers, knowledge exchange with firms through student placements, internships, and staff exchange processes. Certainly, UJEP has performed very strongly in terms of providing graduates in economic-, social-, and environmental-related professions, despite the persistent problem of brain-drain of graduates from Usti to other regions with more buoyant labour markets.

The regional role of the university in this case is rather to provide these more personnel-based knowledge exchange activities rather than creating science-based knowledge as the basis for regional development. The challenge for UJEP is in ensuring that these knowledge exchange activities are delivered as widely in the framework of activities that are organised according to a different logic, namely by staff who rationally concentrate on publishing papers in internationally referred journals. The accreditation requirements obstruct professionals from business teaching at the universities, and this undermines the involvement of practitioners in teaching, and in the absence of strategic prioritisation of this approach to teaching, there is a natural tendency to downplay this regional relevant goal. The provision of lifelong learning is also discouraged by government funding formulae to encourage the provision of degree programmes, which whilst useful for raising the education level do not necessarily always provide the most fertile source of these more informal knowledge exchange activities. And it is here that the greatest potential exists for the regional co-operation fund to give the university the necessary encouragement (financial, moral, and political) to embed engagement activities more thoroughly into its core teaching and research activities.

The situation of UJEP and Usti are not unique within Europe, because there are many old industrial regions seeking to become more innovative through customer-driven incremental innovation, and yet are host to potentially relevant higher education institutions that are themselves under overwhelming pressure to become internationally successful. What the Usti–UJEP case suggests is that it is necessary to create a strategic regional space that provides the university with the opportunity to undertake the range of activities necessary for regional knowledge exchange more thoroughly. At the heart of this lies a regional plan, reflecting both regional needs whilst realistically mapping the manifold ways in which the universities may contribute to them. There needs to be a co-operative forum that extends beyond individuals, and in particular beyond different kinds of electoral cycles, that guarantees the progress of the interactions. The role played by finance is unavoidable, and in these cases, regional funds are needed to encourage universities to undertake activities of regional relevance that nevertheless reinforce and strengthen their core teaching and research activities. The final element appears to be a strong demand from firms for the knowledge from the university, and contributing in various different ways to these knowledge exchange processes. If these elements can be resolved, then there is indeed considerable potential within these universities to help to create new developmental paths and contribute to regional upgrading more generally.

Acknowledgements

This case study is a part of the project 'The Contribution of Higher Education Institutions to Strengthen Socio-Economic Development of Peripheral Regions in Norway and the Czech Republic' financed by the Czech-Norwegian Research Program through Norwegian financial mechanism 2009–2014 (PERIF project).

Notes

1 Czech Invest is the governmental agency supporting foreign investment in the Czech Republic.
2 The average commute from Prague and Dresden to Usti and Labem is approximately 50 and 25 minutes by car, respectively.
3 The institute of pedagogy, on the basis of which the first faculty was created, existed in the region from 1961.
4 UJEP is thus no exception among Czech public HEIs; even Palacký University in Olomouc, considered a traditional research-oriented university, gets approximately 0.6% of its annual budget from contractual research (UPOL case study, 2016).
5 Very often people participating in these discussions do not live in the region themselves, which lessens their interest in actually implementing the results of the discussions.

References

Arnold, E. (2011). *International audit of research, development & innovation in the Czech Republic: Final synthesis report.* Brighton: Technopolis.
Arthur, W. B. (1989). Competing technologies, increasing returns, and lock-in by historical events. *The Economic Journal, 99*(394), 116–131.
Bathelt, H., Malmberg, A., & Maskell, P. (2004). Clusters and knowledge: Local buzz, global pipelines and the process of knowledge creation. *Progress in Human Geography, 28*(1), 31–56.
Battilana, J. (2006). Agency and institutions: The enabling role of individuals' social position. *Organization, 13*(5), 653–676.
Battilana, J., Leca, B., & Boxenbaum, E. (2009). How actors change institutions: Towards a theory of institutional entrepreneurship. *Academy of Management Annals, 3*(1), 65–107.
Benneworth, P., Pinheiro, R., & Karlsen, J. (2014). *Leadership, strategic actor-hood and institutional change: Deconstructing the role of university senior leadership in regional development.* Paper presented at the Regional Science Association, Annual Conference. 15–18 June, Izmir, Turkey.
Capoccia, G., & Kelemen, R. D. (2007). The study of critical junctures: Theory, narrative, and counterfactuals in historical institutionalism. *World Politics, 59*(03), 341–369.
Cerny, A. (2016a, 17 August). Dostal dotaci 300 milionů. Teď venkovský technologický park krachuje. *IDNES.* Retrieved 23 September 2016, from http://ekonomika.idnes.cz/insolvence-technologickeho-parku-nupharo-fil-/ekonomika.aspx?c=A160817_094636_ekonomika_rny.
Cerny, A. (2016b, 18 August). Stát chce dotaci od krachujícího NUPHARO Parku zpět. Šance je mizivá. *IDNES.* Retrieved 20 September 2016, http://ekonomika.idnes.cz/stat-pujde-do-insolvence-o-300-milionu-dvi-/ekonomika.aspx?c=A160817_182654_ekonomika_rny.

Chakrabarti,A.K.,& Lester,R.K.(2002).Regional economic development: Comparative case studies in the US and Finland. In *Engineering Management Conference, 2002. IEMC'02. 2002 IEEE International* (Vol. 2, pp. 635–642). IEEE.

Drahoš, J. (2012, 20 December). Milardy pro průmyslové podniky mě rozčilují. *Technet. cz*. Retrieved 15 January 2017, from http://technet.idnes.cz/jiri-drahos-rozhovor-05t-/veda.aspx?c=A121219_104415_veda_mla.

Etzkowitz, H., & Leydesdorff, L. (2000). The dynamics of innovation: From national systems and 'Mode 2' to a triple helix of university–industry–government relations. *Research Policy, 29*(2), 109–123.

File, J., Weko, T., Hauptman, A., Kristensen, B., & Herlitschka, S. (2006). *Country note– Czech Republic: OECD thematic review of tertiary education*. Paris: OECD.

Gonzales, L. D. (2012). Responding to mission creep: Faculty members as cosmopolitan agents. *Higher Education, 64*(3), 337–353.

Gonzales, L. D. (2013). Faculty sensemaking and mission creep: Interrogating institutionalized ways of knowing and doing legitimacy. *Review of Higher Education, 36*(2), 179–209.

Jürgens, U., & Krzywdzinski, M. (2009). Changing east–west division of labour in the European automotive industry. *European Urban and Regional Studies, 16*(1), 27–42.

Kohoutek, J. (2011). Fond rozvoje vysokých škol a Rozvojové programy v české vysokoškolské politice. *AULA, 19*(3/4), 5–25.

Koutský, J. (2011). *Staré průmyslové regiony – vývojové tendence, možnosti rozvoje*. v Uisti nad Labem: Univerzita J. E. Purkyne.

Lester, R. K. (2003). *Universities and local systems of innovation: A strategic approach*. ESRC Workshop on High-Tech Business: Clusters, Constraints, and Economic Development. Robinson College, Cambridge, 28 May 2003.

Lester, R. K. (2006). *Universities, innovation, and the competitiveness of local and national economies*. Centre for Business Research 10-year Anniversary Summit on Innovation and Governance, University of Cambridge, 29 March 2006.

Leydesdorff, L., & Etzkowitz, H. (1996). Emergence of a triple helix of university-industry-government relations. *Science and Public Policy, 23*(5), 279–286.

Linková, M., & Stöckelová, T. (2012). Public accountability and politicization of science: The peculiar journey of Czech research assessment. *Science and Public Policy, 39*(5), 618–629.

Martin, R., & Sunley, P. (2006). Path dependence and regional economic evolution. *Journal of Economic Geography, 6*(4), 395–437.

OECD. (2007). *Higher education and regions: Globally competitive, locally engaged*. Paris: OECD.

Owen-Smith, J., & Powell, W. W. (2008). Networks and institutions. In R. Greenwood, C. Oliver, S. Kerstin, & R. Suddaby (Eds), *The Sage handbook of organizational institutionalism* (pp. 593–623). Thousand Oaks, CA: Sage Publishers.

Padgett, J. F., & Powell, W. W. (2012). *The emergence of organizations and markets*. Princeton, NJ: Princeton University Press.

Pierson, P., & Skocpol, T. (2002). Historical institutionalism in contemporary political science. *Political Science: The State of the Discipline, 3*, 693–721.

Piknová, I. (2014, 10 November). Ústecký kraj trápí negativní image. *Teplický deník.cz*. Retrieved 24 January 2017, from http://teplicky.denik.cz/zpravy_region/ustecky-kraj-trapi-negativni-image-20141110.html.

Powell, W. W. (1998). Learning from collaboration: Knowledge and networks in the bio-technology and pharmaceutical industries. *California Management Review, 40*(3), 228–240.

Smilor, R. W., Dietrich, G. B., & Gibson, D. V. (1993). The entrepreneurial university: The role of higher education in the United States in technology commercialization and economic development. *International Social Science Journal* (February), 1–12.

Sujan, K. (2016, 11 September). Dražba NUPHARO Parku nepřipadá v úvahu. *Ústecký deník*. Retrieved 21 September 2016, from http://ustecky.denik.cz/zpravy_region/drazba-nupharo-parku-nepripada-v-uvahu-20160911.html.

UPOL case study. (2016). *Case university report: Palacký University, Olomouc (UPOL)*. Prague: Centre for Higher Education Studies. Retrieved 19 April 2018, from www.perifproject.eu/results/wp2/.

Vorlicek, J. (2013, 28 November). Vědecký park je investicí na desítky let. *Ústecký deník*. Retrieved 23 September 2016, from http://ustecky.denik.cz/zpravy_region/vedecky-park-je-investici-na-desitky-let-20131128.html#vybrat-mesto.

9 Higher education institutions at the periphery of the periphery

Creating sustainable economic development in Estonia

Anne Keerberg

Introduction

There is a fairly wide consensus among researchers and policy-makers that the presence of higher educational institutions (HEIs) stimulates economic development. The role of HEIs has been explored by many authors (e.g. Asheim, Boschma, & Cooke, 2011; Etzkowitz & Leydesdorff, 2000; Foray, David, & Hall, 2009; Rutten & Boekema, 2012). HEIs have a significant impact on businesses and organisations of the region through both formal and informal communication (Vaessen & van der Velde, 2003). HEIs may serve as the intermediaries of global pipelines and contribute to regional buzz (Bathelt, Malmberg, & Maskell, 2004), create favourable conditions for social and economic networking, and may take on an expert role in local decision-making bodies (Arbo & Benneworth, 2007). Braczyk, Cooke, and Heidenreich (1998) elaborated the concept of a regional innovation system (RIS). Lorenz and Lundvall (2006) made a distinction between STI (science, technology, innovation) and DUI-based innovation modes (doing, using, interaction) and Isaksen and Karlsen (2012) added the CCI type (complex, combined innovation). This distinction is particularly important in the small and peripheral Nordic and Baltic regions with their limited human and knowledge resources, located far away from large university cities. Their RIS usually cannot afford STI-type knowledge support systems. CCI and particularly DUI type RIS support company-based innovation through an experienced labour force and business services (Isaksen & Karlsen, 2012).

In this chapter we are specifically concerned with what we call 'the periphery of the periphery', that is to say regions within countries and territories that are themselves in various ways peripheral as a whole. The underlying problematic remains framed by the underlying fact that there are increasing returns to scale for knowledge capital, and peripheral countries would seem best encouraged to concentrate what knowledge resources they have in their capital and core regions rather than diffuse them into their peripheral areas. At the same time, there have been, particularly in the Nordic countries, serious attempts in recent years, to find creative institutional combinations that can support HE provision in these peripheral places. In peripheral spaces, low densities and limited access mean that learning has a different and less favourable character. However, smallness and the remoteness associated with closeness and friendliness might also be advantages. An area with capable people, high knowledge levels as well as reasonable accessibility may utilise the benefits of smaller places: less commuting and more time resources, less stress due to higher safety and smaller competition, a more relaxed and creative environment, more physical space and nature, the possibility to have more spacious and better living conditions, and a potentially good and lively community life and buzz that is often a breeding ground for social capital and innovation.

In this chapter we specifically ask the overall research question of how does the presence of HEIs impact the agency of a peripheral region in these regions at the periphery of the periphery? Setting up a new institution that involves considerable human resources, interpretive and network power (Sotarauta, 2009) in a relatively small place should have considerable potential to shape existing routines. A HEI as an organisation and a nest for talented individuals may not only interact with other institutions but also proactively create new and modify existing ones (DiMaggio, 1988). So far, there is little knowledge of the inner processes of these regional HEI units. Who initiated the establishment of HEIs and the ensuing institutions? What was the motivation behind these decisions? And how it can influence the development of the region?

We explore these questions with the use of an example of the case of a new HEI created in Estonia, itself a peripheral European country, the Kuressaare College of the Tallinn University of Technology (KC), located on Saaremaa, an island in Estonia's periphery. This case involved interviews with 27 actors in the period 2014–2016 that were involved in the establishment of regional colleges in Estonia, focusing on the Saaremaa example. We also briefly describe the economic situation of Saaremaa and the impressive structural change that took place there in the 2000s. On the basis of this case study, we try to identify the critical processes that emerged when setting up this institution, focusing in particular on the case of the Regional Competence centre that was created specifically to stimulate regional development.

The role of universities and regional development in the periphery of the periphery

This volume is concerned with the roles of universities in regional development, an issue that has attracted increasing interest from researchers, policy-makers, and regional development professionals in the last 15 years (Benneworth, 2017; OECD, 2007; see also Chapter 2 of this volume). These benefits can be distinguished at three levels of activity. Firstly universities provide inputs to regional development processes, whether this is through their own expenditure, the creation of human capital in skilled graduates, or indeed through providing knowledge services to businesses that improve their competitiveness (Florax, 1992; Hermannsson, Lisenkova, McGregor, & Swales, 2013). Secondly, Gunasekara (2006) distinguishes those generative contributions from what he calls developmental contributions, in which universities upgrade the quality of elements of regional economic structure, by creating new businesses and sectors, bringing new technologies and techniques to the region, and supporting new forms of governance, strategy, and policy (Gunasekara, 2006). Finally, a more transformative role is being recognised where universities contribute to evolutionary processes of path creation and path-breaking as part of creating new regional futures (Goddard, 2011).

Indeed it was said in our presence by a pioneering Italian professor of innovation that the one public policy investment that no regional president would ever reject from the centre was a university, because the benefits of a university, unlike an airport, power station, or factory, were unambiguously positive, even transformational for the region. And yet, a key theme in the volume has been that this remains the thinking that underpins much of the presence of universities in peripheral regions, as a stand-alone investment that will create its own new sectors, replacing rather than upgrading the old industrial and service sectors in these places (see for example Chapter 4 in this volume). In recent years there has been an emergence of new conceptual and policy paradigms emphasising the importance of creating broad-based coalitions that harness knowledge actors to create new opportunities out of existing strengths (Asheim *et al.*, 2011; McCann & Ortega-Argilés, 2013). Yet there is evidence that many of the universities specifically created in the periphery as part of wider modernisation projects remain too embedded within national structures and priorities (e.g. excellent research) to properly engage with regional actors in ways that create new economic opportunities in these regions.

In this chapter we are specifically concerned with a particular class of peripheral regions, and the contributions which higher education can make in these regions, namely the most remote regions, what we here call 'the periphery of the periphery'. These are the regions that are located in peripheral territories, and are themselves peripheral in that territorial context, in the case of this chapter Saaremaa in the European accession state Estonia. These regions have in many cases not received their own university through the previous waves of expansion of higher education. And today, with an increasing premium being set on investing in internationalisation, globalisation, and excellence, higher education ministries remain reluctant to grant these places their own institutions because of their inability to create their own critical mass. And yet, the presence of higher education in some form remains important for these places to help stimulate regional development and provide access to the knowledge capital to create new development pathways and ultimately contribute to regional upgrading.

Despite the improbability of creating effective higher education for regions in the periphery of the periphery, there have been a range of policy experiments to find ways to allow these regions to access knowledge. We are here not concerned so much with distance learning activities that provide teaching to students from core locations, such as the Open University in the UK or the Netherlands, but experiments that have involved creating some kind of activity with staff present in these regions. The University of the Sunshine Coast was formed to serve a remote part of rural Australia with a network of rural centres in the main employment centres, to allow local residents to achieve higher qualifications without having to emigrate (OECD, 2007; see also the case of the University of the Highlands and Islands in Scotland, the UK). Finland experimented with the idea of University Centres, where a number of universities 'pooled' new chairs in new centres created in locations lacking higher education, with these new chairs' profiles being oriented to upgrading the regional economic structure (Sotarauta & Kosonen, 2004). Charles (2016) explores how a number of Scottish universities have inherited rural campuses through structural change and merger and the ways that they have sought to ensure that this is a positive benefit rather than leading to a delocalisation.

These examples show how in some cases these doubly peripheral HEIs can become part of the mainstream higher education system (as the creation of the University of the Highlands and Islands demonstrates). But at the same time their experimental nature leaves them vulnerable, and kind of regional mission only increases their vulnerability by reducing their perceived academic excellence. Indeed Zeeman and Benneworth (2017) point to the effects that this has had on rural campuses in Wales where mergers have increased the financial viability of the organisation. But this organisational viability has come at the expense of a delocalisation as these campuses have been placed within institutions that disinvest in their remoter locations to focus on creating research excellence and attractive student environments in their core regions. And that is the challenge of higher education in the periphery of the periphery, being sufficiently open to its local environment to be able to contribute meaningfully to upgrading without becoming too diffuse and losing its academic credibility and hence support from the centre.

An introduction to regional higher education in Estonia

The first ever university was established in Estonia in Tartu under Swedish Rule, named Academia Gustaviana after the Swedish monarch Gustav Adolf II. Following the declaration of the Republic of Estonia in 1918, other higher education institutions were also established in the capital city, Tallinn, including a special technical college, a higher music school, and a teacher training seminar. During the Soviet period, there were six national higher educational institutions in Estonia, two in Tartu and four in Tallinn. Following its declaration of independence in 1991, educated specialists were in high demand in Estonia, creating a demand for establishing new higher educational institutions, with much of the need being met by new private institutions. In 1995, there were 26 institutions providing higher education in Estonia and by 2001 the number had increased to 49 (Table 9.1), clearly too many for a country with a population of 1.3 million. During the following years, quality control was tightened around private institutions resulting in several closing or merging.

Table 9.1 Institutions providing higher education curricula, 1995–2016

	1990	1995	2001	2010	2016
HEI TOTAL	6	26	49	33	24
Universities	**6**	**7**	**16**	**9**	**7**
public	6	6	6	6	6
private	0	1	10	3	1
Professional HEIs	**0**	**18**	**17**	**22**	**15**
state	0	8	7	10	8
private	0	10	10	12	7
Vocational schools★	**0**	**1**	**16**	**2**	**2**

★ Some vocational schools have the right to provide professional higher education programmes in their specific field if their curricula and teaching staff comply with the criteria set by the Standard of Higher Education.
Source: Statistics Estonia.

Table 9.2 Number of students at institutions providing higher education curricula, 1995–2014

	1990	1995	2000	2010	2016
Universities	25,899	20,786	41,847	51,205	37,755
Professional HEIs		2591	4000	16,392	10,039
Vocational schools		131	4963	1516	0
TOTAL	**25,899**	**23,508**	**50,810**	**69,113**	**47,794**

Source: Statistics Estonia.

In 2016, there were 24 institutions in Estonia providing higher education: one private and six public universities, along with eight national and seven private institutions of professional higher education. Two vocational schools continued with higher education curricula but new admissions were discontinued.

Between the years 1995 and 2000, the number of students in Estonia doubled, reaching its peak in 2010 but showing a decline in recent years (Table 9.2) because of the more rigorous quality requirements and due to the decline in the number of institutions of higher education, as well as due to the demographic situation.

At the end of the 1990s, three major universities – Tartu University, Tallinn University, and Tallinn University of Technology – started establishing their regional units in smaller towns of Estonia (Figure 9.1). The process was facilitated by several actors: demand for highly educated specialists, demography, new management systems and the introduction of market principles in education, *zeitgeist* of the transition period, and new governance. There was no national policy to regulate the process of establishing such colleges; the decisions were mainly born as a result of the agreement between the local initiative and the universities. This process was driven by local demands and a mission to engage with the community

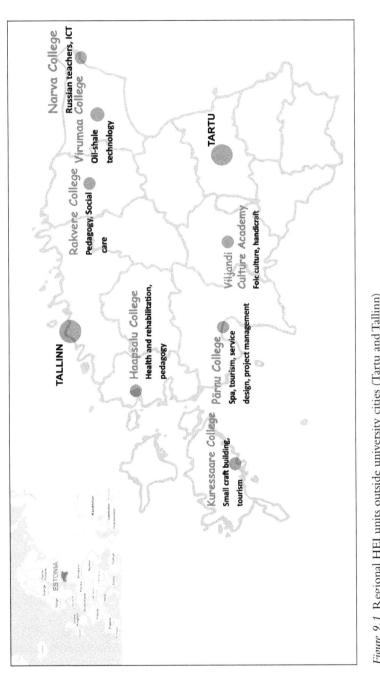

Figure 9.1 Regional HEI units outside university cities (Tartu and Tallinn)

Source: Author's own elaboration under a Attribution–ShareAlike 4.0 International licence (CC BY-SA 4.0).

(Garlick, 1998). There was a political will to support engaged HEIs with invest-ment by national and/or local partners and from the revenues associated with additional student places (Arbo & Eskelinen, 2003). However, there was no national legislation or policy to regulate the process of establishing regional HEIs in Estonia; the decisions were mainly borne out as a result of the agreement between local initiative-takers and the universities. The process was supported by strong regional partners, county and/or city governments who lobbied for the establishment of regional units at both national and university level.

In these local coalitions, support tended to be homogeneous, not reflecting different political positions but rather in empowering the socio-economic devel-opment of counties. In the interviews, university senior managers confirmed their interest in and readiness for extending into regions. However, from the point of view of regional representatives the process was intense, involving parallel negotiations with multiple universities. For small towns, having access to higher education locally was of vital importance to increase their overall attractiveness and development potential and although this expansion provided opportunities also for universities, it was clearly not their most urgent priority.

Universities were autonomous and national government institutions did not interfere at political level. As the first colleges emerged, the Ministry of Education held a neutral position, within its desire to manage the education landscape more transparently, and improved higher education quality by closing or merging weaker schools and moving higher education provision out of further educa-tion colleges. The initiative groups establishing colleges involved representatives of county and local governments, whilst the main process leaders were still the future directors of these colleges, with vocational schools and other educational institutions involved: the connection with the business sector was weaker, with business needs considered but subordinate to public-sector interests.

In 1996–1999, six regional colleges were established of which three were associated with Tartu University, two with Tallinn University, and one with the Tallinn University of Technology. A year later, in the industrial region of Ida-Virumaa, TTÜ established another college which assumed the higher educa-tion curricula from the vocational school which had previously taught them to create a small school of professional higher education that had critical mass to support regional-specific entrepreneurship activities. The latest college to be established was Viljandi Culture Academy in 2005, formed from an inde-pendent higher educational institution already operating for over 10 years: its management regarded joining Tartu University as a good opportunity for securing the quality of studies. The smallest among the colleges was the Tartu University Türi College, established in 1997 at the initiative of enthusiastic local leaders: due to the lack of local academic staff as well as a weak connection to local entrepreneurship, Tartu University closed the college in 2011.

Almost decades after the first college formed, as of 2018, there are seven units of public universities outside Tallinn and Tartu (the biggest cities in Estonia), which form a regional network with considerable human capital (367 employees, 3229 students; Table 9.3), through which the universities direct their

Table 9.3 Main characteristics of Estonian public universities' regional colleges, 2015–2016

	Year of establishment	Town population	Students	Personnel (total)	Personnel (academic)	Revenues (€)	R&D revenues (€)
TLÜ Haapsalu	1998	10,146	252	19	10	924,831	361,946
TLÜ Rakvere	1999	15,747	225	1	1	353,589	63,549
TÜ Pärnu	1996	39,828	637	53	29	1,570,680	80,270
TÜ Türi★	*1997*	*5257*	*136*				
TÜ Narva	1999	58,204	659	56	17	1,766,282	42,814
TÜ Viljandi	2005	17,860	694	115	59	3,543,000	118,000
TTÜ Virumaa	2000	35,928	555	101	33	2,242,000	444,000
TTÜ Kuressaare	1999	13,449	207	22	7	1,501,500	420,800

Notes:
TLÜ – Tallinn University; TÜ – Tartu University; TTÜ Tallinn University of Technology.
★ Türi College was closed in 2011, data from the year 2010.
Source: EHIS, Statistics Estonia; interviews 2016.

regional activities and are partners to entrepreneurs, local governments, and development institutions throughout Estonia.

However, the declining student numbers, fragmented and under-financed local administrations, and still sectorial project-based development policies set for these HEIs an unclear perspective. There is a desperate need for a policy adjustment. In order to sustain and guarantee the role of regional HEIs in Estonian region innovation systems, the role of regional colleges in national and regional innovation policy needs to be specified.

Indeed, in our previous studies (Raagmaa & Keerberg, 2017; TIPS, 2015), we found that regional HEIs located in the peripheries act not only as educators and technology transfer units but also as institutional entrepreneurs. Estonian regional HEIs could increase the state-wide continuing education and retraining they offer in the key areas of national innovation policy; further develop competence centres on the basis of the knowledge needed by the enterprises in the region; and more closely participate in social innovation and in developing the regional identity and self-awareness. The key issue is the strategy and priorities of universities as autonomous institutions. In the process of centralisation, setting sectorial focuses, and saving costs, regional units inevitably take the first blow as their activity requires more resources and their results are marginal in economic scale.

Higher education in the periphery of the periphery: the case of Saaremaa University College

Saaremaa is an island in the Baltic Sea, with a surface area of 2,673 km^2; together with several surrounding small islands it constitutes Saare County that makes c. 7% of Estonian territory, and with 33,000 inhabitants representing 2% of the country's population. Its population density of 11.4 residents/km^2 is one of the lowest amongst Estonia's 15 counties and the population is declining, its working age population decreasing most. The distance between the cities of Kuressaare on the island and Tallinn is 217 km, a journey of some 4 hours with the seaway. Saaremaa's southernmost spot measured in travel times is the remotest place in Estonia from the capital timewise. The life of the county's residents is greatly influenced by the sea as there is no fixed link with the mainland, limiting connections as well as the accessibility of outside markets and jobs. Current regional development strategies are attempting to make better use of sea-related resources, competencies, and activities to drive development of the county (Eesti regionaalarengu…, 2014). Saare County's economy is dominated by services although its share is decreasing whilst the share of manufacturing in regional GNP is increasing, some 40% in 2015, with more than 70% of industrial production being exported sales. The key branches are food, machinery, rubber and plastic industries; these four sectors account for more than 90% of the sales and more than 80% of employment (Keskpaik & Terk, 2013).

As of 2017, the county consists of 14 local governments, Kuressaare city (13,0000 inhabitants), and 13 rural municipalities. Administrative reform is driving mergers with a recent decision by local authorities to create a single local government with a population of some 31,500. The small islands of Ruhnu and Muhu will continue as independent local governments. The Development Strategy of Saaremaa County has identified small craft building and health tourism as regional smart growth areas. The smart growth directions in building work and leisure boats are research-based product management, application of new technologies, developing own brands, and entering new markets. Estonia's shipbuilding companies are concentrated in Saaremaa, with the regional sector accounting for one-third of companies, 90% of turnover, and 80% of employees in the national sector (Hartikainen & Nõgu, 2016).

Saaremaa has an active community of entrepreneurs. Despite or perhaps because of this, Saaremaa is logistically and resource-wise less well equipped than the mainland counties; entrepreneurship is much more active here and works on a pragmatic basis, including in co-operating with HEIs and vocational schools. The activeness and foresight of Saaremaa entrepreneurs is reflected in the fact that an HEI has been established in such a small economic region. Many companies list the presence of locally trained specialists as the main reason for basing their activities in Saaremaa. It has been the cooperation and demand of local entrepreneurs that led to establishing KC in 1999, whose profile reflects Saaremaa's companies' needs, an initial focus on training business and tourism managers evolving towards electronics and small craft engineering specialists. A key founding actor in establishing all the regional colleges was an enthusiastic local community; in the case of KC, emphasis was laid on Saaremaa's traditions of education and research. Alongside this was mentioned the existing academic structures (Saaremaa University Centre, Institute of Islands, and the branch offices of private schools). The development of colleges in Estonia, including KC, was at its fastest in 2010–2012 (TIPS, 2015). In the case of Kuressaare College, all three required components (Charles, 2016) were present: its activity was in correspondence with the county demand on small craft building, a field of regional smart specialisation, strategic support from university, and a parallel desire from the local government to support the college projects, notably the establishment of the competence centre.

Today, Kuressaare College is active in applied higher education, applied research, and technology development. KC is part of the Tallinn University of Technology, and as part of a central restructuring of the university, was placed within the Estonian Maritime Academy in January 2017, with an R&D & competence centre in the field of small craft operating in synergy with teaching activities. Although the will to establish a higher education unit in the county was unanimous, the local vocational training school was keen to incorporate it into its existing activities, following the Nordic model. Nevertheless, county decision-makers favoured a university above a vocational school, and today, there is strong public support from the local community for "their university" (KC), with people arguing it adds to the reputation and human resources of Saaremaa: "Raising the awareness of key people could be an important role for the college." Larger enterprise representatives noted: "The innovative factor of a HEI need not be there locally. Entrepreneurs can reach it themselves." However, since small enterprises begin their technological searches on a much more general level, an HEI can be of great help to them: "It is important to know how to talk to a small enterprise in order to find out what they really need. When their needs are greater than our capacity, the college can lead the enterprise to the right booth at the university" (TIPS, 2015).

Regional competence centres as drivers of regional development

The idea of developing regional competence centres goes back to 2006 when the Minister for Regional Affairs initiated a national programme to support university colleges as regional centres of expertise. Under that programme the broad meaning of the competence centre was used, integrating university education, continuing education as well as co-operation and development activities with entrepreneurs and the public sector (Reidolf, Keerberg, & Hartikainen, 2011). In 2008, the rectors of public universities of Estonia signed a joint agreement with the strategic objective of developing a network of regional centres of expertise, covering the country for facilitating lifelong learning and regional entrepreneurship (Ülikoolide…, 2008). With this act universities expressed their readiness to implement regional policy tasks and they assumed that the planned EU measure would support reaching the goal. A year later, the EU programme to develop competence centres was launched but with a severely restricted definition of 'competence centre' mainly covering services to entrepreneurs. The programme initiated in 2006 did not solve the problems as anticipated and so was discontinued. Universities adapted to the rules of the EU programme and reached their development goals, although less than had been planned, by fostering regional entrepreneurship. Out of six approved applications for developing competence centres, four were submitted as co-operations between universities and colleges.

KC, Kuressaare Regional Training Centre (vocational school), some municipalities, and 11 entrepreneurs signed a contract for developing the small craft cluster in 2008. An important step in the cluster development project preparation was a joint expression of interests by the enterprises. The common will to create a test laboratory in the region was deemed relatively hard to realise because of investment intensity. Instead, workforce development and symbiotic marketing became the main areas of co-operation.

The Saaremaa regional competence network, initiated by KC, was created in 2009. The College assumed the leadership of the network as there was no other strong partner in the county at that time, the County Development Centre did not have enough capacity, and the county government's development unit had other priorities. The network's purpose was to gather and share the regional development knowledge and experiences. In 2009, the network had monthly meetings where potential common projects and other joint activities, not only small craft building, were discussed. At first, the discussion partners identified the bottlenecks in their own areas of activity that could potentially be tackled by a targeted development support (e.g. fishing industry, ecological agriculture, tourism, timber processing, etc.). Eventually it was agreed that from the point of view of smart specialisation, small craft building was the most promising area as this field of activity distinguished Saaremaa from the rest of Estonia and the development of small craft building had a positive impact on other related fields of activity.

As a result, some of the network partners and the Association of Estonian Boatyards signed a cooperation agreement to develop the Small Craft Competence Centre (SCC) in Saaremaa. Its purpose was to accumulate and develop small craft building-related knowhow and to provide better facilities to train boat builders and meet entrepreneurs' need for local and proximate R&D services. It was not possible to start with exclusively local financing and therefore external help was essential. The proposal to develop a competence centre in Kuressaare was approved and, in early 2011, the SCC was officially established as part of KC. The Kuressaare City Government and the Association of Estonian Boatyards co-financed the project. Although had KC started its activity due to the development needs of tourism industry, a key regional sector, it was able to extend into a technological field because its parent university was a technology university, and had the required competence. The County also supported the proposals because they believed that from the perspective of the sustainability of Saaremaa's economic development, it was vital to develop a manufacturing sector alongside the service sector.

In parallel with the competence centre's development, the development process for curricula took place. KC started with Tourism and Catering Management, and then to meet the needs of regional businesses also developed courses in electronics and business management. In 2009, a project group started piloting the Small Craft Building curriculum that was launched as a joint curriculum of Tallinn University of Technology and Estonian Maritime Academy (until 2014, when EMA was joined to TTÜ). The tourism management curriculum has by now been directed further to experience management. At the time of the research, KC had 194 undergraduate students and a full-time staff of 22 (1.10.2016); from the academic year in 2017, this was expanded to incorporate two courses, namely Marine Engineering and Business and Experience Management.

A little over 50% of KC students come from other regions, meaning that its activity is directed not only to the island's inhabitants, with the fields of study not being so specialised as to leave them inapplicable to students then seeking work elsewhere. The courses are in any case provided in the form of distance learning, thus also allowing working people to study. The study process includes a considerable part of practical activity in enterprises that on the one hand allows the students to test applying their theoretical knowledge and is beneficial to enterprises on the other hand. In their final thesis, students provide solutions to actual challenges of enterprises or product development. Final thesis preparation is supervised by university lecturers, and these student theses provide an important mechanism for transferring knowledge to enterprises. As a substantial number of students have jobs, they, in turn, bring their knowledge and experience into the studies. Engineering students are able to execute their product projects in the up-to-date materials lab and towing tank and build up contacts with businesses that use the services of the centre. The personnel policy of the competence centre included recruiting college students, with one student and two graduates being employed in 2017 in the centre, the graduate developing a device required in the centre's work as his final thesis.

The competence centre's activity is aimed at R&D activity and rendering high technology services. From a sustainability point of view, the synergy with study activity is highly important and this difference of other research centres covering small craft building in the Baltic Sea region was explicitly identified in the competence centre's development strategy development strategy (Väikelaevaehituse…, 2016). Given the absence of large numbers of high level specialists and scientists in the field of shipbuilding in Estonia and the practical limitations upon increasing their number very quickly, it is reasonable to involve them in advising businesses, research activity, and as lecturers in educational establishments simultaneously, although it makes financing issues more complicated. Creating synergies between activities may have formed part of the overall centre programme's goals but in practice, the simultaneous use of different measures is extremely difficult. Because development and innovation policy is project based, and dependent on competition, this tends to give an advantage to larger centres as well as to undermine collaboration between centres.

During recent years, universities have started reconsidering their strategies and the aspect of regional activity is clearly becoming overshadowed by other priorities. Although Estonia's Regional Development Strategy regards universities and their regional colleges as making important contributions to regional policy, implementation is insufficiently strong, there is a lack of political will and of strong regional partners to drive regional development. Current administrative reforms foreground the importance of regional policy goals, and the notion of developing regional centres of expertise in different regions of Estonia as broader region development centres has been raised. To secure HEI units' sustainability, the presence of positive actors is required (as was required for establishing colleges): regionally (business or public sector related) focused area of activity, regional partners (both in business and public sector), appreciation of universities, the leadership of a local unit, political support at state level (and cross-ministerial). The critical mass of activities is created in an interaction of these actors.

The overall effect of competence centres on Estonia's peripheral periphery

As regional colleges were established during the 1990s, Estonia's political parties had yet to reach a solid stage of distinction, with little political rivalry in choices. At this time, regional representatives represented a common interest, the county governments had more powers, and Parliamentary members were more supportive of regional development. Universities established regional units to expand their markets into regions where higher education was not easily accessible at the same time as there was political support for creating regional centres. By 2010, the number of students in Estonian universities was at an all-time high as the result of a baby boom some 18 years previously. Since then birth rates had halved over a 10-year period (25,100 births in 1988, 12,200 births in 1998; Statistics Estonia), making it hard for universities to fill places and rewarding universities that understood the demand for lifelong learning that provided flexible study forms, distance learning, and open studies for retraining and refresher training.

The programme for developing competence centres aimed at facilitating smart specialisation of regions, a better utilisation of a region-specific potential in co-operation with businesses and educational and research institutions. These centres proved to be sustainable where the co-operation was successful. In Rakvere, for example, where the established competence centre was weakly connected to universities, there was no connection to the local college and today the centre is in difficulties. This contrasts with the centres established at Kuressaare, Haapsalu, and Virumaa colleges which have thrived as a result of close co-operation with their universities and businesses, clear focus, and coherence between the competence centre's research work and a college's educational courses. The regional colleges face problems from having a limited scope of activity and securing a critical mass of students, but they can still be successful in a precisely identified field of activity, close to regional growth sectors, if supported by research activity.

Today, Estonian regional HEIs lack capable regional partners, with public administration siloised and the more pragmatic politics now riven by party political divides. There is certainly more scope to consider how the human resources of regional colleges could also be used in more significant roles in planning the development of regions. The regional colleges of universities dispersed across Estonia could potentially be key institutions within regional innovation systems, fulfilling multiple roles simultaneously, as providers of training, centres of excellence related to region-specific entrepreneurship, and centres of innovation and creativity. Their sustainability depends on building internal synergies but also in contributing to a region's development needs, and ensuring the region contributes to Estonia's balanced development. In these conditions, a strong college leadership is necessary, to bring together the university and local community, build political support for the university college's activities, and translate that to the national level.

Conclusions

In this chapter we have asked the question of how does the presence of HEIs impact the agency of a peripheral region in these regions at the periphery of the periphery? There are different approaches to delivering universities' third missions, although they tend always to be closely aligned with or integrated into universities' main teaching and research activities. HEIs have also realised that providing wider access to their resources and infrastructure can provide the possibility for universities to increase their income. But they always face the tension between these regional missions, which may generate income, and guaranteeing the quality of their teaching and research activities. This has particular salience given recent emphasis on universities' roles to drive balanced regional development and knowledge-based entrepreneurship in peripheries. Whilst part of this impact comes simply through the presence of an HEI, and its staff, students, and expenditures, the greatest impacts from HEIs come in contributing in a co-ordinated way with regional partners to combined development trajectories. Smart policy-makers need therefore to ensure that universities can reach these potentials, and at the national level, there may be a strong case for ensuring that universities have appropriate resources to achieve these priorities.

There are various mechanisms by which HEIs can drive regional development, and these are evident in the case of the Estonian university colleges. There are a set of first order effects, where universities are active directly communicating with regional businesses, their local staff conveying various kinds of knowledge demanded by the community. In return, the community provides feedback and input for education courses and ongoing research activities. Therefore, at the heart of realising these benefits appears to be place-based initiatives, regional network and capacity for leadership, the will and agreement by the community to develop a certain sector with the university support. And it is necessary to emphasise that this may in turn bring a need for regional partners to find additional resources for the university to ensure that universities are not expected to make losses on their regionally beneficial activities. In the 1990s localities were more active in finding the resources for setting up their HEIs, but later because of weakening county governments and fragmented local governments the support depended more on project fundings.

This is illustrated by the mismatch seen in the centres of competence programme in Estonia where the universities declared themselves supportive but the government did not make resources available as the discussions became bogged down inside the machinery of government. The programme that was finally launched differed significantly from the preparatory stage, focusing more on technology development and leaving the educational component aside. It was only in 2014 when the Estonian Regional Development Strategy endorsed this cross-sectoral co-operation with universities that resources were made available. Ironically enough by this point regional co-operation was no longer such an urgent priority for the universities, influenced by the new financing scheme and with increasing pressure for excellence alongside other urgent political issues around administrative reform. Despite this unpropitious start the network of Estonian regional colleges has had a significant role in increasing the development capacity of different regions (TIPS, 2015). These cities with regional colleges have been growth centres for future-oriented industries because of the accumulation of competences and institutions that are able to support this industrial transition.

In isolated peripheral regions, the scope of curricula and research activity cannot be wide, and in Estonia the regional colleges have had to be focused on their region's leading sectors with future growth potential. The factors that have contributed to regional colleges being successful are regional embeddedness, strong business and community links, and integration with other teaching and research activities. Difficult to replicate from the Estonian example has been the close connection with the parent universities in terms of these regional focus sectors, but at the same time it illustrates how a degree of creativity in HEI organisation can help to find ways to improve universities' regional contributions, even 'at a distance'. The need for additional finance is important here to ensure that there is not a tension between the different centres of gravity, each with their own logic. The key message from this chapter is that synergy and creativity can help promote universities' contributions to peripheral regions, but the conditions to deliver this synergy are easily disrupted, and a wide constellation of regional and national supporters are necessary to ensure that synergy can be delivered.

Acknowledgements

The author would like to acknowledge the comments and suggestions of the editor on three earlier versions of the manuscript. Any errors or omissions remain of course the responsibility of the author.

References

Arbo, P., & Benneworth, P. (2007). *Understanding the regional contribution of higher education institutions: A literature review.* OECD Education Working Papers, 9. Paris: OECD Publishing. doi:10.1787/161208155312.

Arbo, P., & Eskelinen, H. (2003). *The role of small, comprehensive universities in regional economic development: Experiences from two Nordic cases*, 43rd Congress of the European Regional Science Association: 'Peripheries, Centres, and Spatial Development in the New Europe', 27–30 August 2003, Jyväskylä, Finland. Retrieved 19 April 2018, from http://hdl.handle.net/10419/116240.

Asheim, B. T., Boschma, R., & Cooke, P. (2011) Constructing regional advantage: Platform policies based on related variety and differentiated knowledge bases. *Regional Studies, 45*(7), 893–904.

Bathelt, H., Malmberg, A., & Maskell, P. (2004). Clusters and knowledge: Local buzz, global pipelines and the process of knowledge creation. *Progress in Human Geography, 28*(1), 31–56.

Benneworth, P. S. (2017). The role of research in shaping global and regional engagement. In F. X. Grau, J. B. Goddard, B. L. Hall, R. Tandon, & E. Hazelkorn (Eds), *Higher education in the world 6: Balancing the global with the local.* Barcelona: GUNI. Retrieved 19 April 2018, from www.guninetwork.org/files/download_full_report.pdf.

Braczyk, H. J., Cooke, P. N., & Heidenreich, M. (Eds). (1998). *Regional innovation systems: The role of governances in a globalized world*. London: Psychology Press.

Charles, D. (2016). The rural university campus and support for rural innovation. *Journal of Science and Public Policy, 43*(6), 763–773. doi:10.1093/scipol/scw017.

DiMaggio, P. (1988). Interest and agency in institutional theory. In L. Zucker (Ed.), *Institutional patterns and culture* (pp. 3–22). Cambridge, MA: Ballinger.

Eesti regionaalarengu strateegia 2014–2020. (2014). *Regional development strategy for 2014–2020*. Retrieved 19 April 2018, from www.siseministeerium.ee/sites/default/files/dokumendid/eesti_regionaalarengu_strateegia_2014-2020.pdf.

Etzkowitz, H., & Leydesdorff, L. (2000). The dynamics of innovation: From national systems and 'Mode 2' to a triple helix of university–industry–government relations. *Research Policy, 29*(2), 109–123.

Florax, R. J. G. M. (1992). *The university: A regional booster? Economic impacts of academic knowledge infrastructure*. Aldershot, UK: Avebury.

Foray, D., David, P. A., & Hall, B. (2009). Smart specialisation: The concept. In *Knowledge for growth: Prospects for science, technology and innovation*. Selected papers from Research Commissioner Janez Potočnik's Expert Group (pp. 25–29). Retrieved 19 April 2018, from http://ec.europa.eu/research/era/pdf/knowledge_for_growth.pdf.

Garlick, S. C. (1998). *'Creative associations in special places': Enhancing the partnership role of universities in building competitive regional economies* (Vol. 98, No. 4). Evaluations and Investigations Programme, Higher Education Division.

Goddard, J. B. (2011). *Connecting universities to regional growth: A practical guide*. Brussels: DG REGIO.

Gunasekara, C. (2006). Universities and associative regional governance: Australian evidence in non-core metropolitan regions. *Regional Studies, 40*(7), 727–741.

Hartikainen, A., & Nõgu, U. (2016). *Ship and boat manufacturing in Estonia*. Small Craft Competence Centre of Tallinn University of Technology. Retrieved 19 April 2018, from www.scc.ee/wp-content/uploads/2016/12/Ship-and-boat-manufacturing-in-Estonia-2016-c.pdf.

Hermannsson, K., Lisenkova, K., McGregor, P. G., & Swales, J. K. (2013). The expenditure impacts of individual higher education institutions and their students on the Scottish economy under a regional government budget constraint: Homogeneity or heterogeneity? *Environment and Planning A, 45*(3), 710–727.

Isaksen, A., & Karlsen, J. (2012). Combined and complex mode of innovation in regional cluster development: Analysis of the light-weight material cluster in Raufoss, Norway. In B. Asheim and M. Parrilli (Eds), *Interactive learning for innovation: A key driver within clusters and innovation systems* (pp. 115 136). Basingstoke: Palgrave Macmillan UK.

Keskpaik, A., & Terk, E. (2013). *Saare maakonna majanduse ülevaade* (Survey of Economic Activity in Saare County). Retrieved 19 April 2018, from www.ttu.ee/public/k/Kuressaare-kolledz/Teadus/Saaremaa_majandusulevaade_2013.pdf.

Lorenz, E., & Lundvall, B. Å. (Eds). (2006). *How Europe's economies learn: Coordinating competing models*. Oxford: Oxford University Press.

McCann, P., & Ortega-Argilés, R. (2013). Modern regional innovation policy. *Cambridge Journal of Regions, Economy and Society, 6*(2), 187–216. doi:10.1093/cjres/rst007.

OECD. (2007). *Higher education and regions: Globally competitive, locally engaged*. Paris: OECD.

Raagmaa, G., & Keerberg, A. (2017). Regional higher education institutions in regional leadership and development. *Regional Studies, 51*(2), 260–272.

Reidolf, M., Keerberg, A., & Hartikainen, A. (2011). Universities' role in the region: The case of Saaremaa Small Craft Competence Centre. *University-Business Cooperation-Tallinn 2011, 5*, 38.

Rutten, R., & Boekema, F. (2012). From learning region to learning in a socio-spatial context. *Regional Studies, 46*(8), 981–992.

Sotarauta, M. (2009). Power and influence tactics in the promotion of regional development: An empirical analysis of the work of Finnish regional development officers. *Geoforum, 40*(5), 895–905.

Sotarauta, M., & Kosonen, K. J. (2004). Strategic adaptation to the knowledge economy in less favoured regions: A South Ostrobothnian University network as a case in point. In P. Cooke & A. Piccaluga (Eds), *Regional economies as knowledge laboratories*. Cheltenham, UK: Edward Elgar.

TIPS. (2015). *The research and innovation policy monitoring programme*. Retrieved 19 April 2018, from www.tips.ut.ee/eng.

Ülikoolide ühiste kavatsuste leping regionaalsete kompetentsikeskuste loomise kohta. (2008). *The agreement of common intent of universities on the establishment of regional competence centres*. Memorandum, Rectors' Conference, Tallinn, 24 November.

Vaessen, P., & van der Velde, M. (2003). University knowledge transfer through social and professional embeddedness: A case study. In R. Rutten, F. Boekema, & E. Kuijpers (Eds), *Economic geography of higher education: Knowledge infrastructure and learning regions* (pp. 87–109). London: Routledge.

Väikelaevaehituse kompetentsikeskuse strateegia 2015–2020. (2016). *Strategy for Small Craft Competence Centre*. Retrieved 19 April 2018, from www.scc.ee/ee/wp-content/uploads/2016/09/SCC-strateegia-2020.pdf.

Zeeman, N., & Benneworth, P. S. (2017). Globalisation, mergers and 'inadvertent multi-campus universities': Reflections from Wales. *Tertiary Education and Management, 3*(1), 41–52. doi:10.1080/13583883.2016.1243256.

10 Universities and regional economic development in cross-border regions

Jos van den Broek, Franziska Eckardt and Paul Benneworth

Introduction

In the 19th and 20th centuries, a strong textiles cluster emerged in the Dutch-German border region spanning Twente and West-Münsterland. From the 1950s, the industry – which had once accounted for a substantial share of the regional economy and employment – started the steady decline that would ultimately lead to its near disappearance by the 1980s. This process was accelerated by decreasing protectionism in Germany and the Netherlands, the rise of competitors in the global east and south, and, of course, the rise of the single European integrated market. This region was a forerunner in European cross-border collaboration having established the first cross-border territorial grouping, the EUREGIO, in 1957 (Haselsberger & Benneworth, 2010; Perkmann, 2007). The EUREGIO has since been active in trying to stimulate cross-border co-operation in order to encourage increased interaction and movement in a highly fragmented border region and help reverse the decline of these two remote, peripheral regions.

Since 2007, the EUREGIO has become increasingly interested in stimulating innovation policy, and cross-border policy has been active in attempting to create cross-border regional competencies to assist in this transition. Universities and universities of applied science (vocational higher education institutions) in the immediate region, as well as the extended policy space (corresponding to the INTEREG IVA East Netherlands–north-west Germany), have been active in these programmes as beneficiaries of these subsidy programmes. At the same time, there appears to be an absence of the kinds of cross-border innovation governance and strategy structures that characterise what might be regarded as the best-practice cross-border regional innovation systems (CBRISs) (OECD, 2013; Van den Broek, Eckardt, & Benneworth, 2018). In particular, there is a very limited history of cross-border co-operation in the area of innovation – with that being limited to a handful of examples of companies that collaborate with other companies across the border in the field of innovation. It is much harder to get a sense that there is a 'collective knowledge pool' (Lorenz, 1999; Maskell & Malmberg, 1999) building up in the EUREGIO that might help to improve the overall munificence of the innovation environment, and facilitate other companies to be more innovative and competitive.

This chapter explores the extent to which universities have been able to deal with this specific regional innovation problem, the persistence of the border hindering the development of effective cross-border innovation spill-over effects. We specifically ask the research question of how can higher education institutions contribute to building a CBRIS in a peripheral region? To address this we develop a theoretical framework in which universities contribute to structuration of CBRISs by building networks that over time begin to acquire more systemic properties. We explore this structuration model with reference to the EUREGIO. Specifically, we are looking at three network-building activities, one where two universities created a double degree programme, a second one where universities of applied science created a course oriented towards a cross-border labour market, and a final one consisting of a cross-border technology transfer programme between higher education institutions and small and medium-sized enterprises (SMEs). We identify that there are four tensions, which the higher education institutions experienced in developing these activities, relating to splits in the cross-border markets, differing cross-border regulatory frameworks, technical factors derived from cross-border funding, and cultural differences. We identify the kinds of solutions that the higher education institutions used to ensure they were able to work across the border, and identify that common to them is the role they play in constructing an informal fuzzy governance space for regional innovation in the EUREGIO. With more than 40% of Europe's population living in cross-border regions, and these regions suffering more than most from lower rates of economic development, innovation, and productivity growth, we conclude that ideas of 'fuzzy governance' may be useful in finally addressing this persistent European regional economic development problem.

Universities contributing to institutional gaps

Understanding regional innovation system problems as institutional problems

Systematic interaction between firms, universities, and other research institutes is important for innovation because firms need a variety of knowledge inputs to remain competitive in an economy characterised by short product life-cycles and increasingly complex products. In this chapter we conceptualise regional innovation environments following Cooke (2005) as regional innovation systems (RISs) composed of a knowledge exploitation and knowledge exploration subsystem. The functioning of a RIS depends for a large part on the presence and effectiveness of local institutional arrangements (Rodríguez-Pose, 2013). These institutional arrangements are "place specific customs and procedures that shape interaction, in general, and economic exchanges, in particular" (Rodríguez-Pose, 2013, p. 1042) which facilitate systematic interaction between actors in a RIS.

Flaws in the institutional arrangement of the knowledge production or exploitation or socio-political structure may hamper the functioning of a

RIS (Benneworth, Pinheiro, & Karlsen, 2016). Benneworth *et al.* (2016; after Rodríguez-Pose, 2013) distinguish between five sets of deficiencies which may impede systematic interaction (Benneworth *et.al*, 2016, p. 237):

1. A lack of collectively held new cultural–cognitive understandings of the role that regional actors can play in a globally oriented knowledge economy;
2. Missing structural elements in the RIS governance system allowing collective smart specialization/constructed regional advantage activities;
3. Lack of understanding of potential opportunities for better exploiting regional knowledge to drive innovation-based regional economic development;
4. A failure of local actors to collaborate collectively to position themselves in emerging high-technology niches with economic development potential;
5. A failure to mobilize collective/share resources and co-investments to underpin innovation-based economic development.

In CBRISs, our diagnosis is that although the requisite actors are present, the presence of the border means that there is not the automatic interaction between the actors that allows a territorial knowledge pool to build up. That is not to say that there is no interaction rather that the presence of the border works against that interaction. We use Garud, Hardy, and Maguire's (2007) concept of institutional entrepreneurship to represent the action of university actors seeking to interact across borders, and if that institutional entrepreneurship can succeed it can create networks that subsequently structurate to give systemic effects. The lack of interaction can be understood as an institutional failure, and it is that institutional failure that universities working across the border are seeking to repair by creating new institutions through this institutional entrepreneurship process. Institutional entrepreneurs can here be understood as actors who: "mobilize resources and actionable knowledge to create/transform 'institutions' [..] to address RIS inefficiencies" (Benneworth *et al.*, 2016, p. 237). Before looking at who these institutional entrepreneurs are, what they do, and how they do this we need to understand what the possible institutional gaps in CBRISs are and how universities might contribute to addressing them.

Institutional gaps in CBRISs

The specificity of CBRISs is that they span across two adjacent territories and are thereby embedded in institutional architectures of both regions which may lead to different kinds of institutional gaps occurring (Van den Broek & Smulders, 2014). We distinguish between three kinds of border barriers that may lead to institutional gaps that impede systematic interaction in a CBRIS and can be linked to the above RIS deficiencies (see Table 10.1).

First, the other side of the border is often not considered with regard to collaboration and innovation (Hahn, 2013; Van den Broek, Benneworth, &

Table 10.1 Possible university contributions to addressing institutional gaps in CBRISs

RIS deficiencies (adapted from Benneworth et al., 2016 after Rodríguez-Pose, 2013, p. 1036)	Institutional gaps in CBRISs	University contributions to CBRISs	Border-related barriers
A lack of collectively held new cultural–cognitive understandings of the role that regional actors can play in a globally oriented knowledge economy.	Missing CB strategy and shared imaginary of cross-border research and innovation potential (Van den Broek, Rutten, & Benneworth, 2015).	Creation of CB courses to support cross-border orientation of students and employees (Caniëls & van den Bosch, 2011).	Joint programmes often hindered by national frameworks for education (OECD, 2013).
Missing structural elements in the RIS governance system allowing collective smart specialisation/ constructed regional advantage activities.	Lack of CB governance mechanisms (Trippl, 2010). Institutional hindrances resulting from differences in national governance systems (Van den Broek & Smulders, 2015).	Universities participating in working groups, governance structures, and innovation platforms (Cooke, 2007).	CB regional governance involvement has low priority. Dominance of municipal authorities in CB governance (Perkmann, 2007).
Lack of understanding of potential opportunities for better exploiting regional knowledge to drive innovation-based regional economic development.	Lack of knowledge and ignoring of CB opportunities (Hahn, 2013; Van den Broek et al., 2016).	Universities working together with firms and/or universities on other side of the border (Hansen, 2013).	Lack of shared identity impedes collaboration and promotes competition rather than collaboration (Hahn, 2013).
A failure of local actors to collaborate collectively to position themselves in emerging high-technology niches with economic development potential.	Difficult to calculate inputs and outputs resulting in inactivity. Focus on getting back what one puts in (OECD, 2013).	Universities can function as global pipelines and contribute to cross-border buzz (Bathelt, Malmberg, & Maskell, 2004).	Universities' international outlook does not always align with cross-border development activities (Goddard et al., 2013).
A failure to mobilize collective/share resources and co-investments to underpin innovation-based economic development.	Lack of structural and long-term CB resources (Nelles & Durand, 2014; Perkmann, 2007).	Structural universities' investments in public-private CB initiatives. Sharing university infrastructure cross-border (OECD, 2013).	Most initiatives co-funded by Interreg remaining short-term and project-based. Lack of game-changing interventions (OECD, 2013).

Source: Authors' own elaboration.

Rutten, 2018). On the one hand actors in respective regions seem to first consider regional and national opportunities for interaction even when cross-border opportunities may be closer and more easily accessible. This lack of interest can be seen as a mental border which leads to a neglect of the opportunities on the other side (Klatt & Herrmann, 2011; Van Houtum & van der Velde, 2004). On the other hand, opportunities on the other side of the border might be lacking due to different economic development paths which have led to distinct economic specialisations and leave limited room for innovation-driven collaboration (Trippl, 2008).

Second, there is a lack of cross-border governance mechanisms directed at innovation and knowledge exchange (Trippl, 2010). Whilst regional governance mechanisms like economic boards and triple helix constellations in which firms, universities, and governments work together have seen a large increase over the last decade, this trend has not yet been transferred to cross-border regions. Governance in these regions is merely focused on providing information and mediating differences (Klatt & Herrmann, 2011).

Third, the availability of resources (time, money, and knowledge) for cross-border systematic activities is often lacking and cross-border activities remain thus often project-based rather than becoming a regularity (Nelles & Durand, 2014; Perkmann, 2007). Most cross-border projects and Euroregions are highly dependent on Interreg funding and have difficulty diversifying their resource base (Nelles & Durand, 2014) which makes cross-border co-operation vulnerable for shifting priorities on other levels.

University contributions to addressing institutional gaps

Universities can contribute to the functioning of a RIS through the activities of teaching and research as well as in a broader role as regional animateurs (Pugh, Hamilton, Jack, & Gibbons, 2016). Exemplar contributions are courses which fit regional labour demands and collaborative research with regional firms but also connecting global and local networks and acting as a neutral intermediary in the region (Pugh *et al.*, 2016). The way in which universities contribute and the extent of it depends on the regional configuration of the innovation environment (Trippl, Sinozic, & Lawton Smith, 2015) which is different in a cross-border region.

Thereby we need to keep in mind that the university is not a single coherent regional actor (Charles, Kitagawa, & Uyarra, 2014; Pinheiro, 2013), rather it is a loosely coupled system with different interests and several inherent ambiguities (Pinheiro, 2013). This means that strategies and goals of university management might not tell the whole story of the activities of universities in CBRISs. Other actors, individuals or coherent units, within the university might contribute to the RIS with or without strong support by the university management. We focus upon how these actors operate and what kinds of actions they undertake in contributing to the CBRIS.

Universities in a border region can function as a bridge between two border regions and as a pipeline to other regions but are also confronted with border-related barriers. First, national frameworks of education might hamper the development of cross-border courses and programmes (OECD, 2013). Second, because of a lack of cross-border governance mechanisms the development of collective strategies to strengthen the region's innovative potential is difficult. Third, there is a risk of a low road development path (Trippl, 2010) when the respective regions merely exploit differences and as result engage in competition rather than collaboration (Hahn, 2013). Fourth, there can be a tension between the aspirations of international excellence in research and education and engagement with the cross-border region (Goddard, Kempton, & Vallance, 2013). Finally, the funding of cross-border initiatives of universities often depends upon short-term project funding which makes it vulnerable for shifting priorities and hinders the build-up of structural collaborations (OECD, 2013). Table 10.1 summarises how universities can possibly contribute to addressing institutional gaps in CBRISs and how border-related barriers possibly impact upon these activities.

A short introduction to the cross-border region EUREGIO

As the first and oldest CBRs in the European Union, the EUREGIO covers an area of 13,000 km² reaching from the Dutch provinces Overijssel, Gelderland, and Drenthe to the German federal states Nordrhein-Westfalen and Niedersachsen.[1] Within approximately 140 local authorities, it has a total population of 3.37 million inhabitants (Perkmann, 2007). As two old textile regions, both border regions are typical examples of 'rustbelt regions', which refers to those regions across Europe that suffered heavily from a radical decline of the traditional industrial sectors, textiles and metals, during the 1950s (Cooke, 1995). As a result of this, both border regions invested comprehensively during the 1960s in regional renewable activities. They aimed to develop new development paths through the creation of innovative local assets, networks, and sectors as a strategy to attract more global resources.

The European Community Initiative Interreg established the EUREGIO in 1958 with the aim to foster territorial integration through investments in regional economic growth and development as part of the European cohesion policy (or regional policy).[2] However, beside Interreg's and city-regional actors' efforts to enhance regional innovation within the EUREGIO, cross-border co-operation is still hampered at the border, although officially removed, due to for example language and legislation barriers. In order to stimulate more co-operation between universities and other partners at both sides of the border, Interreg started to financially support more co-operation between public- and private-sector partnerships across the border in the field of research and education during the 1990s. According to Perkmann (2005), especially during the Interreg II period (1994–1999), higher education institutions accounted for a "total of 28% of the total EU expenditure" (p. 167).

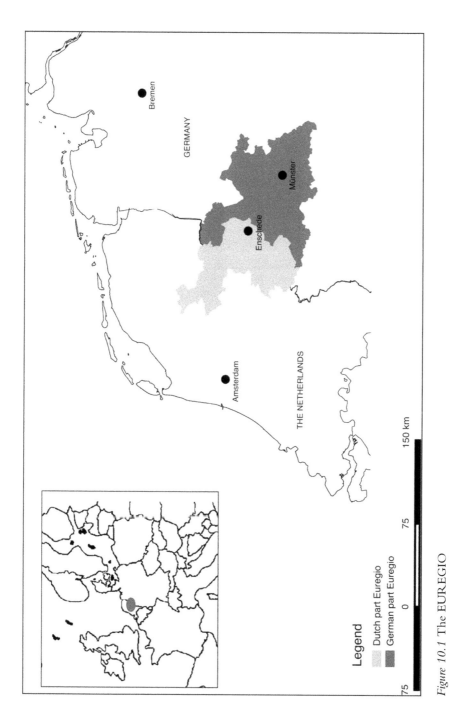

Figure 10.1 The EUREGIO

Source: Authors' own elaboration based on GeoBasis–DE/BKG 2017; CBS/TopGrenzen CCBY CBS & Kadaster.

Regional attempts to build cross-border capacity

In this chapter we are concerned with attempts to build up innovation capacity in cross-border regions, and in particular to establish connections. A RIS is a way of conceptualising how regularities build up over time; in RISs, innovators have regular contacts in which various kinds of knowledge and resources are exchanged, and over time, other actors can access these resources more easily through the networks without necessarily having to invest the resources required to initially establish those connections. This is a kind of structuration process, in which individual contacts form regularised networks that gradually over time acquire systemic properties, and we have identified three activities in the case study region where this structuration has taken place, where there are four higher education institutions (Twente and Münster), two universities and two universities of applied science (Saxion and Münster). The first is in the creation of a joint degree between two universities in the EUREGIO, which has facilitated student mobility as well as serving as the first step towards a yet-to-be-realised deeper collaboration. The second was the creation of a cross-border vocational degree programme which has contributed to integrating the labour market, and mobilising knowledge networks, around a single sector, social work. The third was a cross-border innovation resource centre in the field of mechatronics that sought to facilitate SMEs to access mechatronics support services across the Euregional border.

Double/joint degree 'public governance across borders'

The first initiatives to collaborate on the theme of public governance and European integration started around 1998 with two professors establishing a joint seminar series addressing debates in both countries regarding European integration in the Netherlands and Germany. After several successful seminars at the Rothenberge estate midway between Münster and Enschede, resulting in a number of publications, the professors proposed to develop the seminar into a joint educational course. At that point, Dutch students could voluntarily participate in the courses, but could not acquire credits for the teaching; in response, the professors explored setting up a full degree course, organising a conference inviting people from different accreditation organisations, EUREGIO policy-makers, colleagues from other higher education institutions with cross-border experience, with representatives from the Dutch and German academic exchange service. This conference revealed that a joint degree would be practically impossible, because of the high costs of a pan-European accreditation, but what was possible would be a double degree.

The University of Twente hired a former University of Münster employee to develop this double degree using their knowledge of both HE systems and their connections to both. The five-year double degree was launched in 2001 as a Bologna-compliant separate bachelor and master degree. In the end, it was accredited in Germany (somewhat unusually) by the government of North Rhein-Westphalia as the national German accreditation agency felt uncomfortable with the idea of accrediting a double degree. When a new accreditation became necessary in 2013, the bachelor course was developed as a joint degree, the master remaining a double degree.[3] The joint degree is only developed for the bachelor programme, reflecting the reality that it was a single programme that awarded two certificates as a historical fix for an accreditation problem. The joint degree was also politically popular with the Dutch Minister of Education and the German State Minister of Innovation and Science attending the signature ceremony to emphasise the political desirability of further cross-border collaboration.

Case: Euregional bachelor of social work

Saxion has always had a considerable share of German students, partly due to a shortage of places for certain professional higher education courses in Germany, but also reflecting Saxion's ongoing recruitment efforts in Germany. Being located in Enschede, a city at the German border with a direct train connection to Germany, Saxion is an accessible study location for German students. One course that has long had a high proportion of German students is Social Work, reflecting the fact that access to such courses is strictly controlled in Germany, and so Dutch border universities of applied science are a natural location for those unsuccessful in Germany. It also reflects a different orientation – a more practical focus – in the Netherlands in which graduates are better oriented to the labour market. The one barrier to German students accessing the course is language, because in preparing students for social work, involving high levels of interaction with the local population, it is natural that this course is in the local language. It is therefore noteworthy that the popularity of the study with German students led to a part-time bachelor stream completely taught in German, although graduates typically returned to Germany after their study rather than having a cross-border dimension.

The unease that this triggered amongst the teachers led to a discussion in which the teachers decided that their students – studying social work in a cross-border region – should be educated as such and be prepared to work on both sides of the border, helping integrate a cross-border labour market. This shift in mindset also reflected a growing unease in Dutch universities in teaching German students for German labour markets using Dutch taxpayers' cash; social care in the Netherlands as a result of the triple decentralisation has undergone drastic austerity, with vacancy rates lower and unemployment rates higher than immediately across the border. This was addressed by starting an Euregional bachelor of social work, educating both Dutch and Germany professionals for a Euregional labour market. However, from 2017 this course was closed to new recruitment because the whole Dutch provision of social work was reorganised in a way that made the continuation of that course impossible.

Case: Mechatronics for SMEs

The Mechatronics for SMEs project built on earlier projects in this border region around mechatronics, which started around 2000 with a project called Mechatronics Innovation Center. Most project partners participated from the beginning giving lengthy collaboration experience. However, the focus of these projects evolved in parallel with the evolution of the Interreg programme that was funding them. Initially, the EUREGIO had had its own Interreg programme, and the funding focused on technology centre activities. From 2007, the focus shifted towards supporting SMEs across a much larger cross-border region running from Groningen-Oldenburg in the north to Maastricht-Aachen Liège in the south. As the scope of the cross-border region was extended, there was an increasing emphasis on flagship projects that covered the whole Dutch-German border region. This meant that from 2007, the Mechatronics Innovation Centre was forced to seek out partners in a much wider hinterland and integrate them and new activities into existing partnerships.

The driving force behind these various projects was two intermediary organisations, one on each side of the border, who jointly developed the project, searched for partners, and drafted the proposals. The regional higher education systems were only marginally involved in the project development, but their involvement was necessary to win the funding because they represented a significant element of the cross-border knowledge base; both the two universities and the two universities of applied sciences were involved. An additional complication was a need for a balance in partner numbers alongside a fair split of funding. The universities played two roles in the Mechatronics for SMEs project, firstly in providing knowledge for universities to work with SMEs on shared mechatronics problems based on a framework funding system to guarantee a certain amount of predefined consultancy activity. There was a separate funding stream available for incidental collaborations with SMEs to provide feasibility studies or for developing prototypes. The project was deemed successful with 180 consultancy activities undertaken, 91 feasibility studies undertaken, and 106 development projects carried out, involving 131 Dutch and 125 German SMEs.

Tensions in the regional partnership approaches

The first set of tensions arose when there were clear differences in markets for various kinds of factors between the two countries, which undermined the necessity or the dynamic of building up these connections, and hence preventing an institutionalisation of these activities. One example of this was seen in the Social Work course, where there was a very strong demand for Dutch employees from the German health sector, and that led to a willingness for German organisations to allow training placements for Dutch students in Germany, in the hope that those students would then be sufficiently enthused and knowledgeable about the German system to bring their work-facing training to the German labour market. A second example of this was around the mechatronics sector, where there were differences in the respective strengths of the industrial and higher education institution sectors in mechatronics, reflecting the greater domestic strength of the German market for mechatronics products. For Dutch partners, working with a German knowledge supplier was helpful in accessing the German market, and particularly in acquiring German TÜV accreditation, whilst the German firms saw no comparable advantage in working with Dutch knowledge institutions. In the Mechatronics project, although the virtual centre was notionally a cross-border institute, the majority of the collaborations that were funded remained located within the nation-state.

The second set of tensions were those that arose because of differences in the regulatory frameworks across both sides of the border. Innovation, research, and education in both countries tend to be regulated in ways that have an implicit primacy for national interests. There are substantial public investments and therefore the primary regulatory concern is in ensuring national benefits, and this may create a framework in which it can be difficult for cross-border activities to find a way to regularise themselves beyond incidental collaborative projects. This was clearly evident in the evolution of the double degree in European Studies: the Dutch system effectively prioritises maximising student numbers, whilst the German system is primarily concerned with maximising quality, partly through keeping strict limits on student numbers. This created a tension when the Dutch partner experienced pressure dealing with dwindling student numbers elsewhere by expanding places on the double degree. The double degree programme also fell down a bureaucratic hole related to accreditation; in the Netherlands, the Dutch accreditation agency sets standards and carries out accreditation, whilst the German accreditation council (*Akkredietierungsraat*) sets standards whilst state-level institutions carry out that accreditation. Although the Dutch accreditation agency and the *Akkredietierungsraat* developed mutual recognition of standards, this created problems for the state-level accrediting institutions. There were likewise also tensions because of the different divisions of labour between the universities and universities of applied sciences on each side of the border; in Germany, the universities of applied sciences (*Fachhochschulen*) are more theoretically oriented and geared up to providing technology transfer support to SMEs, whilst in the Netherlands, the *Hogescholen* have only in the last 10 years seriously developed any kind of (applied) knowledge generation and transfer capacity and there is a strong private sector in technological consultancy (including technological services provided by companies that began life as university spin-offs).

The third set of tensions arose out of what might be considered as the technical artefacts of different kinds of funding arrangements that differ across borders, and which make it hard to create cross-border activities aligning resources from different national funding regimes. These manifested themselves in various different ways. The double degree suffered from the fact that funding systems pushed the two institutions towards different recruitment strategies, and there were differential fees across the border that made the course relatively expensive for German students (where fees were at the time of the research €400 compared to €2000 in the Netherlands). The EUREGIO bachelor was continually faced with the problem about accounting for funds that were used to educate foreign students for foreign labour markets which undermined its legitimacy despite a strong commitment from institutional managers to the programme, and in the end, was eventually undermined by a national decision to streamline social work training around three profiles specific to the Dutch situation.[4] The Mechatronics project involved different partners receiving very different kinds of funding although all were expected to respond to SME queries in a similar way. The Dutch university spent its funding on a PhD student, the Dutch universities of applied sciences had to find ways to link SME questions to their applied research staff, and the German universities of applied science employed bespoke technology transfer officers; perhaps unsurprisingly it was only the German universities of applied science who were interested in continuing the project after its initial funding.

The final tension arose because of what might be described as cultural differences, although following Iyer, Kitson, and Toh (2005), we are aware of the risk of reifying a kind of cultural residual variable that we imbue with the power to explain all the other things that we cannot explain. One tangible element of this is the issue of language, which came particularly to the fore in the case of the Social Work degree, with a large number of Germans being recruited to a Dutch language course; the choice was made to allow students to take exams in German but at the same time that further added to the questions that were raised about the validity of a course taught to foreign students for foreign labour markets. In the double degree programme, the final dissertation project was marked twice against two different and mutually incompatible schemes, the German (0.7–6, 0.7 is best and relatively common) and the Dutch (1–10, 10 is best but exceptional). A special conversion chart had to be developed to compare the two but it was always left to the two defence representatives to negotiate individually which grade felt correct within their own system for the single thesis.[5] In both these courses, there were clear differences in the attitudes of students from the different national secondary education systems, where the German system has an expectation of excellence whilst the Dutch system steers towards sufficiency. Likewise, German students were used to large classes with remote teachers and little individual attention, and had difficulties reportedly in adjusting to the more informal, smaller, and more discursive classroom settings.

Emergent solutions for building cross-regional collaborations

In this chapter we have conceptualised the problem of cross-border innovation as one of building up cross-border regional innovation networks, and what these three cases do is give some insights into the way that these processes can operate. The first set of tensions emerged when there were clear differences in different kinds of factor markets, and it was clear in these cases that these tensions could not be completely straightforwardly addressed. What did permit progress under certain circumstances was when the value of a cross-border collaboration could be demonstrated despite the clear differences in markets. An example of a solution was in the Social Work bachelor degree programme where the focus of the course was shifted from the German labour market to the cross-border labour market, thereby making it also attractive for students seeking work in the Netherlands. In the Mechatronics case the solution on the German side was found in close collaboration with economic development agencies (*Wirtschaftsförderung*) whose close pre-existing ties to firms left them able to convince some firms that they could benefit from working across the border. A solution emerged through the provision of subsidies for firms willing to work across, although in the Mechatronics case this was not necessarily coupled with cross-border collaboration (because collaboration between firms and knowledge institutes within the respective countries was permitted).

The second set of tensions emerged around the different regulatory framework, and it was found that effectively operating across the border involved two dimensions. These were firstly stretching the possibilities of creatively interpreting and using the existing frameworks and secondly simultaneously working on building frameworks that bridge across the border. In the double degree programme the accreditation issue was first solved by an incidental accreditation by the state of North Rhein-Westphalia itself instead of the organisations that were normally hired to carry out such an accreditation. In the latter stage when the collaboration existed between the Dutch accreditation agency (NVAO) and the *Akkredietierungsraat* the university administrators on both sides were very experienced in dealing with their differences so that they could assist both accreditation organisations in interpreting and dealing with the differences in regulatory frameworks. The tensions between the different capacities of universities of applied sciences and universities in both countries in the Mechatronics case were not solved but rather exploited in the projects as their competences were constructed within the project to be complementary. This was partly successful, and led to collaboration between Dutch firms and German universities of applied sciences in the Mechatronics case (although less so in terms of German firms working with Dutch universities of applied sciences).

Regarding the differences in funding systems solutions were found in both practical solutions and attempts to change programme structures. In the double degree case the tension around differences in fees was solved by letting both German and Dutch students enrol in Germany for the first year and in the Netherlands for the next two years, whilst for all three years the German students would get a free public transport ticket included in the German fee. The Euregional bachelor solved the problems of funding foreign students for a foreign labour market, because of its dual labour market focus, and indeed, the number of Dutch students rose over the latter years of its opportunity. The language issue was thorny and solved in different ways. In the double degree programme the courses were mainly taught in English and a voluntary Dutch language course was offered to German students. Conversely the Euregional bachelor courses were taught in Dutch and German with students expected to freely switch as required, excepting exams where students could use their preferred language. Cultural differences regarding class sizes and expectations were partly addressed in both cases by organising information meetings to prepare German students for the Dutch system.

Universities contributing to building cross-border regional innovation systems

In this chapter we have been concerned with the question of how can higher education contribute to building a cross-border RIS in a peripheral region? In the various kinds of solutions which emerged above out of attempts to contribute to creating cross-border institutions, we see some answers emerging to this question more generally. The first set of solutions involved constructing activities which appealed on different sides of the border, albeit in different ways and with different legitimacy within these different systems. Tensions emerging from the regulatory frameworks were enabled by the higher level development of fuzzy cross-border governance spaces which facilitated these informal regulatory approaches, both in terms of accreditation but also for innovation projects (as Interreg acquired an increasing emphasis on innovation). The third tension of funding was a substantial hurdle in the first instance, but once a solution emerged and it was seen to work, whether the rail season ticket or Interreg funding, then it became regarded unselfconsciously as part of the system. Finally, regional cultural differences were not insurmountable by any means and were dealt with by a process that might be thought of as a 'growing together across the border' and building various kinds of cross-border communities within which code-switching between the two languages and cultures was regulated.

What was common about all these regional solutions was that they were all creative, flexible, and bespoke to the particular situation, and in particular we identify three common characteristics which provide a useful starting point for reflecting on how universities can contribute to stimulating the development of cross-border regional innovation systems. Of course, creativity, flexibility, and a capacity to develop bespoke solutions were not characteristics that were automatically present in the EUREGIO, and therefore what appear to be more salient to us are the preconditions and drivers for these three characteristics, which we regard as the exercise of agency, through regional leadership, the construction of mutual benefits, and a sense of small steps of progress towards an overall desirable goal (in this case the creation of a Euregional innovation 'system').

The first element was the exercise of agency and the importance of regional leadership in this whole process in the Benneworth, Pinheiro, and Karlsen (2017) sense. Before these activities were created, they appeared to be totally impossible, and yet despite that, they were created. There were various roles played by individuals in this process, whether the institutional entrepreneurs who actually proposed and realised the ideas, the mentors and supporters who allowed ideas to progress into experiments, the early adopters – the students and firms who engaged with these newly created activities – and the consolidators who saw the promise of the experiments and provided additional support to allow them to continue. These various actors together worked to create what has been seen more widely across Europe, what Allmendinger and Haughton (2009) call fuzzy governance spaces that facilitate the necessary kind of collaboration.

Secondly, the construction of mutual benefits was necessary and not necessarily self-evident, sometimes involving substantial investments. This gave the various activities a hybrid nature because there were very different things demanded and expected across different sides of the border. There is often an assumption that the benefits of collaboration for innovation speak for themselves when partners are connected, but the issue here was not one of connection but of articulating the case for how these strange new hybrids could serve a particular need. In the EUREGIO case, each managed to achieve this by playing to things that had their own political salience on both sides of the border, in particular in regional policy and media discourses. But they retained the capacity to justify themselves and validate the activities in terms of these discourses which broke sharply across the border.

Finally, there was a sense of progression in these various experiments which endowed the activities with a sense of momentum that helped hold the coalition, and their dual sense of benefits, together. The fragility of this progress was demonstrated by the ease with which the Euregional social work bachelor programme was terminally disrupted by changes at a national level to the Dutch regulatory system. But nevertheless, these activities evolved by steps that were quite small when considered individually but added up to an overall direction of travel; the double degree evolved into a joint degree and loose collaboration into a Euregional technology transfer programme. The activities had value on two levels, at the micro-level in terms of creating coalitions of beneficiaries able to work together, and at the macro-level, representing symbolic progress to the long-standing goal of a 'hard' EUREGIO.

These lessons more generally illustrate the point that building innovation systems in cross-border regions is not a simplistic task, nor is involving universities in this task always straightforward. Here we see that the strength of higher education institutions in making regional contributions, namely their plurality and diversity of communities, faces additional pressures. Elsewhere in this volume we have seen the message that national systems create local tensions for universities, and that universities need sympathetic national partners to optimise their regional contributions. Here we see an additional dimension to this problem; these cross-border activities find themselves squeezed between two sets of national tensions, and have to find ways to mediate these.

'Fuzzy governance spaces' as a solution to this problem is conceptually satisfying, but as it formed no part of our analytic framework at the start, we must be modest in proposing this as the answer to the issue of cross-border solutions. Nevertheless, this fuzziness does appear to be substantively part of the ways by which the higher education institutions can contribute to the necessary creativity and flexibility to deliver cross-border RIS solutions. And this is the overall contribution we seek to make here, calling attention to this question of 'fuzziness' in CBRISs, something which currently is not accounted for in either the theory or practice of cross-border innovation. Only when the contours and dynamics of this fuzziness are better elucidated can we start to finally unlock the innovation potential of Europe's universities in cross-border regions.

Notes

1 See: www.euregio.eu/en.
2 See:http://ec.europa.eu/regional_policy/en/policy/cooperation/european-territorial/.
3 A Master's programme in the Netherlands for a social sciences degree may only last 1 year and in Germany it must last at least 2 years; within the double degree structure, it is possible to set up a 1.5-year programme compliant with both German and Dutch law.
4 This is related to a huge streamlining in Dutch social work as a result of the 'triple decentralisation' of 2016. In this process, large numbers of tasks were devolved to municipalities without a corresponding increase in funding. The social work training was therefore reorganised to deliver specific profiles for these tasks, relating to care work, youth work, and local coaching (community work).
5 One of the authors participated in one of these negotiations as a supervisor of a double degree bachelor thesis in 2015.

References

Allmendinger, P., & Haughton, G. (2009). Soft spaces, fuzzy boundaries, and metagovernance: The new spatial planning in the Thames Gateway. *Environment and Planning A, 41*(3), 617–633.

Bathelt, H., Malmberg, A., & Maskell, P. (2004). Clusters and knowledge: Local buzz, global pipelines and the process of knowledge creation. *Progress in Human Geography, 28*(1), 31–56.

Benneworth, P., Pinheiro, R., & Karlsen, J. (2017). Strategic agency and institutional change: Investigating the role of universities in regional innovation systems. *Regional Studies, 51*(2), 235–248.

Caniëls, M. C. J., & van den Bosch, H. (2011). The role of higher education institutions in building regional innovation systems. *Papers in Regional Science, 90*(2), 271–286.

Charles, D., Kitagawa, F., & Uyarra, E. (2014). Universities in crisis? New challenges and strategies in two English city-regions. *Cambridge Journal of Regions, Economy and Society, 7*(2), 327–348.

Cooke, P. (1995). *The rise of the rustbelt*. London: UCL Press.

Cooke, P. (2005). Regionally asymmetric knowledge capabilities and open innovation. *Research Policy, 34*(8), 1128–1149.

Cooke, P. (2007). To construct regional advantage from innovation systems first build policy platforms. *European Planning Studies, 15*(911796916), 179–194.

Garud, R., Hardy, C., & Maguire, S. (2007). Institutional entrepreneurship as embedded agency: An introduction to the special issue. *Organization Studies, 28*(7), 957–969.

Goddard, J., Kempton, L., & Vallance, P. (2013). The civic university: Connecting the global and the local. In R. Capello, A. Olechnicka, & G. Gorzelak (Eds), *Universities, cities and regions: Loci for knowledge and innovation creation* (pp. 43–61). London: Routledge.

Hahn, C. K. (2013). The transboundary automotive region of Saar-Lor-Lux: Political fantasy or economic reality? *Geoforum, 48*, 102–113.

Hansen, T. (2013). Bridging regional innovation: Cross-border collaboration in the Øresund region. *Geografisk Tidsskrift-Danish Journal of Geography, 113*(1), 25–38.

Haselsberger, B., & Benneworth, P. S. (2010). The Euroregional planning approach: Strategy making and policy delivery in multi-area 'Euroregions'. *disP: the Planning Review, 138*(4), 80–94.

Iyer, S., Kitson, M., & Toh, B. (2005). Social capital, economic growth and regional development. *Regional Studies, 39*(8), 1015–1040.

Klatt, M., & Herrmann, H. (2011). Half empty or half full? Over 30 years of regional cross-border cooperation within the EU: Experiences at the Dutch-German and Danish-German border. *Journal of Borderlands Studies, 26*(1), 65–87.

Lorenz, E. (1999). Trust, contract and economic cooperation. *Cambridge Journal of Economics, 23*, 301–315.

Maskell, P., & Malmberg, A. (1999). Localised learning and industrial competitiveness. *Cambridge Journal of Economics, 23*, 167–186.

Nelles, J., & Durand, F. (2014). Political rescaling and metropolitan governance in cross-border regions: Comparing the cross-border metropolitan areas of Lille and Luxembourg. *European Urban and Regional Studies, 21*(4), 104–122.

OECD. (2013). *Regions and innovation: Collaborating across borders.* OECD reviews of regional innovation. Paris: OECD Publishing.

Perkmann, M. (2005). *The emergence and governance of Euroregions: The case of the EUREGIO on the Dutch-German border.* Conference paper. Retrieved 20 April 2018, from https://dspace.lboro.ac.uk/2134/743.

Perkmann, M. (2007). Policy entrepreneurship and multilevel governance: A comparative study of European cross-border regions. *Environment and Planning C: Government and Policy, 25*(6), 861–879.

Pinheiro, R. (2013). Bridging the local with the global: Building a new university on the fringes of Europe. *Tertiary Education and Management, 19*(2), 144–160.

Pugh, R., Hamilton, E., Jack, S., & Gibbons, A. (2016). A step into the unknown: Universities and the governance of regional economic development. *European Planning Studies, 24*(7), 1357–1373.

Rodríguez-Pose, A. (2013). Do institutions matter for regional development? *Regional Studies, 47*(7), 1034–1047.

Trippl, M. (2008). Ökonomische verflechtungen und innovationsnetze im wirtschaftsraum Centrope [Economic linkages and innovation networks in the Centrope area]. *Wirtschaft und Management, 9*, 29–48.

Trippl, M. (2010). Developing cross-border regional innovation systems: Key factors and challenges. *Tijdschrift Voor Economische En Sociale Geografie, 101*(2), 150–160.

Trippl, M., Sinozic, T., & Lawton Smith, H. (2015). The role of universities in regional development: Conceptual models and policy institutions in the UK, Sweden and Austria. *European Planning Studies,* (June), 1–19.

Van den Broek, J., Benneworth, P., & Rutten, R. (2018). Border blocking effects in collaborative firm innovation. *European Planning Studies, 26*(7), 1330–1346.

Van den Broek, J., Eckardt, F., & Benneworth, P. S. (2018) The transformative role of universities in regional innovation systems: Lessons from university engagement in cross-border regions. In K. Erdös & A. Varga (Eds), *Handbook of universities and regional development.* Cheltenham, UK: Edward Elgar (forthcoming).

Van den Broek, J., Rutten, R., & Benneworth, P. (2015). Innovation and SMEs in Interreg policy: Too early to move beyond bike lanes? (Paper presented at the RSA European Conference 2015). Piacenza.

Van den Broek, J., & Smulders, H. (2014). Institutional gaps in cross-border regional innovation systems: The horticultural industry in Venlo-Niederrhein. In R. Rutten, P. Benneworth, D. Irawati, & F. Boekema (Eds), *The social dynamics of innovation networks* (pp. 157–175). London: Routledge.

Van den Broek, J., & Smulders, H. (2015). Institutional hindrances in cross-border regional innovation systems. *Regional Studies, Regional Science, 2*(1), 115–121.

Van Houtum, H., & van der Velde, M. (2004). The power of cross-border labour market immobility. *Tijdschrift Voor Economische En Sociale Geografie, 95*(1), 100–107.

11 Constructing regional resilience in a knowledge economy crisis

The case of the Nokia-led ICT industry in Tampere

Heli Kurikka, Jari Kolehmainen and Markku Sotarauta

Introduction

Tampere may be Finland's second largest city-region (after Helsinki) but from a European perspective it is at most a middle-sized city located far north. This makes it intriguing that Tampere was a key site for the Nokia corporation's tremendous expansion via mobile telephony. Tampere became part of this success story, because of its strong educational and research basis and ability to grow in tandem with Nokia's expansion, with local and national economic and innovation policies being tailored to support this development. However, the era of dominance ended when Microsoft acquired and finally closed Nokia's whole mobile business. This caused thousands of redundancies and lay-offs in Tampere, fundamentally restructuring the city's entire ICT industry landscape.

Tampere is now at a point where a new ICT industry is emerging, and local development policies appear to have some purchase on research and education to stimulate this re-industrialisation. This chapter seeks to explore the extent to which the Tampere cluster, and particularly its universities, contributed to building a resilience which outlived Nokia. The chapter seeks to examine how the different development phases of the local ICT industry are connected to the evolution of its resilience capacity. Exploration of the ways resilience was constructed in Tampere allows specific scrutiny of the universities' roles through industrial development. Drawing on a case study based on local statistics, an analysis of local newspapers, interviews and focus groups,[1] this chapter argues that resilience is not a predefined character of a city, but it can be developed through strategic, collaborative measures actively involving universities. Universities can play a positive role in these developments, but only if they are able to ensure that the pursuit of engagement activities does not lead to an excessive short-termism, so that they can contribute effectively to path-breaking and not to the extension of lock-in activities.

Path creation, extension, branching and exhaustion

In this chapter, we are concerned with the issue of regional economic resilience, which according to Martin (2012: 12) consists of a region's ability to resist recessionary shocks, its ability to recover, to renew growth path and to re-orientate. David (2001: 26–27) suggests that sometimes when endogenous development ceases an external shock is required to shake the region out of its lock-in. Martin and Sunley (2006: 406) see this as an overly radical interpretation and it is true that such a shock is not always needed – resilience turns a shock into a shift of economic trajectory. In this chapter, as with Chapter 8, we draw on Lester's (2007: 17–18) typology of industrial transformation process distinguishing four different ways of transformation: 1) indigenous creation (new technologies and competences); 2) transplantation from elsewhere (technologies and competences new to the region); 3) diversification into technologically related industries (new functions of technology and competences); and 4) upgrading of existing industries (incremental adjustments in technologies and competences). In all these cases, regions that are locked into old industries facing path exhaustion are able to create new pathways and/or extend existing pathways. Resilience therefore depends on a region's capacity to perform path creation, extension and branching, and ensure that lock-in does not lead to path exhaustion.

Hassink (2010b) describes **path exhaustion** as a state where the innovation potential of local firms has been reduced or innovations are restricted to a certain technological path. A regional industry has a low adaptability with regard to technological and market changes. Martin and Sunley (2006: 415) describe lock-in as a situation where a technology, industry or regional economy has become stuck in a particular trajectory or path that has become inefficient in some way. Martin and Sunley (2006: 400) summarise the views of path dependency that can emerge from the ossification of these structures: 1) technological lock-in; 2) dynamic increasing returns where positive feedback reinforces existing paths; and 3) institutional hysteresis where formal and informal institutions, social arrangements and cultural forms self-reproduce themselves.

Path creation can be described as "establishment of new firms in new sectors for the region or firms that have different variants of products, employ new techniques, organize differently, etc. than what hitherto have dominated in the region" (Isaksen 2015: 588). These industries can be either new to the region or totally new industries (Tödtling and Trippl 2013). Path creation usually has two main streams: it may be caused by inward investments and/or sectoral diversification of existing firms through path branching or it can be research driven focusing on commercialisation of research results (Henning *et al.* 2013: 1353). Path creation may also require building of new knowledge organisations and institutional change (Tödtling and Trippl 2013).

There is a bridge here from path creation into **path extension**, "in which increasing returns and positive externalities reinforce local industrial dynamism" (Martin and Sunley 2006: 415). In path extension success is based on incremental innovations in existing industry (Hassink 2010a). Established ways of doing things started to emerge, with logics of "increasing returns" and "positive lock-in" where current circumstances receive positive feedback and seem productive, creating a self-reinforcing circle (Arthur 1989: 127; Martin and

Sunley 2006: 401–402). **Path branching** refers to existing local firms and industries shifting to different, but related sectors (Boschma and Frenken 2011). Regions usually branch into industries that are technologically related to the pre-existing industries in the regions (Neffke *et al.* 2011: 237). Path branching is often seen as industry driven (Neffke *et al.* 2011: 237).

By linking the concept of resilience to the conceptual framework provided by path dependency we might be able to add analytical leverage in the efforts to understand how regions may escape their past and open new paths. Drawing upon Garud *et al.* (2010), we want to emphasise the power of reflexive agency and cumulative processes of gradual change as forces in path creation, and thus also in resilience. As Garud and Karnøe (2001) highlight, initial conditions are not given, as assumed in path dependency studies, but are constructed by actors. Therefore, various incidents shaping paths ought not to be approached as exogenous and manifesting something unpredictable, non-purposive and random but as emergent and serving as embedded contexts for agency. Garud and Karnøe's framework stress the role of entrepreneurs but, as Djelick and Quack (2007) maintain, path creation is also political by nature, and new paths may emerge due to entrepreneurial efforts of science and policy actors despite the lack of business entrepreneurs (Sotarauta and Mustikkamäki 2015; Sotarauta and Suvinen 2018). As Bristow and Healy (2014: 97–98) point out, the networked and polycentric nature of governance and policy is critical in resilience.

This brings us to the issue of universities, long an important resource in innovation policy but perhaps they even have a greater role as long-term competence builders from this framework. Universities' role in building human capital for the region in general cannot be underestimated. For example Crescenzi *et al.* (2015) have stated that human capital, especially tertiary educational attainment, is a strong predictor of regional growth, innovation and also resilience. It is this issue that this chapter specifically addresses, asking the question of whether universities can positively contribute specifically to path creation, extension and branching activities, countering path exhaustion in old industrial regions and therefore contributing to this territorial resilience.

An introduction to the case study[2]

This case presents a study of Tampere, founded in 1779, Finland's second largest city-region with a population of 380,000. It was one of the first Finnish regions to industrialise, driven by cotton mills and paper factories, and later expanding to include textiles and mechanical engineering (see Haapala 2005). These industries drove economic development until the 1970s, when textile industry began to disappear, and the 1990s, when Finland was hit by a deep recession, which drove deep changes in industrial structure and policy strategies, towards developing new high-tech industries. Within a decade Finland moved from being one of the least ICT-specialised countries to one of the most specialised ones in terms of exports, production and R&D (Boschma and Sotarauta 2007).

Finland's rapid shift to a knowledge economy involved many coincidental factors and good timing; a strong industrial structure began to emerge already in the twentieth century with the presence of foreign companies like Ericsson and Siemens (Boschma and Sotarauta 2007). Demanding customers (network operators), standardisation (Nordic Mobile Telephone Standard) and a culture open to new technologies contributed significantly to the evolution of the ICT cluster. Business and policy worked together well (Boschma and Sotarauta 2007: 169) to position Tampere as one of Finland's three ICT hotspots with Oulu and Helsinki. From the early 1990s, the ICT agglomeration grew very rapidly in Tampere; in 1996, there were 170 companies employing 5200 staff and with €770 million turnover (Häikiö 2002). By 2000 turnover had doubled to €1.5 billion, a growth driven by Nokia and attracting interest from local (business) development, innovation and higher education policy in the Tampere city-region. (Kolehmainen 2003).

The strong science and technology base and the educational institutions have been some of the major strengths of the ICT cluster in Tampere, with the Tampere University of Technology, the University of Tampere and Tampere University of Applied Sciences. *Tampere University of Technology* (TUT) has traditionally had very close relationships with local businesses both in terms of research and education. *The University of Tampere* (UTA) has its roots in social sciences, but today it is a diversified university with long traditions in computer science and other ICT-related fields of education and research as well, starting the first ever Nordic computer science degree in 1965 (Kolehmainen 2003). *Tampere University of Applied Sciences* (TAMK) is the smallest of the three higher education institutions (HEIs), oriented towards working life and RDI collaboration, one of Finland's most popular universities of applied sciences, and strongly international with its teaching supporting many regional ICT companies.

Tampere has many intermediary organisations that have been concerned with stimulating the emergence of a strong knowledge-based ICT sector with collaborations between HEIs and firms. Firstly, its local government is very strong, with a strong city government but also a regional council (general regional development authorities owned by regional cities/municipalities). Tampere Region Council has become very active in innovation policy promoting, e.g. innovation platforms and user-driven innovation. The national state owns the Centre for Economic Development, Transport and the Environment (ELY Centre) in Tampere offering a wide range of economic development activities, including business support and employment services (advisory, training and expert services and funding for investment and development projects, etc.). The ELY Centre also administers Tekes (the Finnish Funding Agency for Innovation) services in the region. The regional councils and ELY Centre will be amalgamated in 2020.

Cities and municipalities have also set up their own economic development organisations and networks. Tredea Ltd. or 'Business Tampere' (Tampere Region Economic Development Agency), was started in 2009 by the eight municipalities of Tampere city-region. It provides support to start-ups and potential inward investors and is active in the execution of international talent attraction activities. All the activities have been very important during the dramatic restructuring of the ICT industry. Hermia Group is more focused, established in 1986 as Tamlink, offering specific product development and innovation services through one of its two subsidiaries, being Finland's oldest technology transfer company linked to TUT both operationally and via ownership. The other subsidiary – Innovaatio Oy Uusi Tehdas Ltd – stems from the Tampere Technology Centre which was established in 1990 to develop the Technology Centre Hermia founded four years earlier (see Lehtimäki 2005).

Path creation and path extension in Tampere region

Path creation: roots grew into mature business

Tampere experienced path creation in ICT in the 1990s around the rapidly growing ICT industry, and in this section we explain its evolution as innovations, the existing knowledge base and structures laid the foundations for a new mobile industry. Nokia was an existing company that enlarged its product scale and invested heavily in research, tightly integrating it into the local research ecosystem. Tampere University of Technology was important in experimental basic research, standardisation and innovations (e.g. digital signal processing). In response to these developments, TUT began rapid growth in the 1990s, developing post-experience courses for businesses alongside diverse master and post-graduate degrees. Several courses provided important networking forums for local ICT professionals (Kolehmainen 2003), supported by the establishment of Tamlink and later Hermia Group (qv) as examples of institutional capacity being built to support the emergent path. From the early 2000s, the ICT cluster's structure was maturing, largely dominated by the business units of multinational ICT companies, such as Nokia, TietoEnator, Sonera and Fujitsu Invia. Nokia remained important, but these companies were all actively oriented towards R&D (Kolehmainen 2003). The dominant role of multinationals also brought negative consequences, such as undermining the entrepreneurial atmosphere, manifested in low numbers of fast-growing internationally oriented start-ups (cf. Autere 2000). In the context of the 'dot.com' bubble that hit Finland in the early 2000s, Tampere was relatively unscathed, but was bitten by deep restructuring a decade later.

Path extension: from the ultimate boom to first worrying signs

Alongside this path-creation activity, there was also path extension, with Nokia's global success creating a virtuous growth circle in Tampere based on Nokia's mobile technology. From our interviews it was clear that strong patterns of practice were emerging that provided a structure to this innovation activity. Tampere University of Technology (TUT) created a special relationship with Nokia, involving strong graduate recruitment to Nokia, many thesis projects with the company, modifying syllabi to reflect Nokia's needs, project funding from Nokia, and of course strong personal connections between TUT and Nokia. Indeed some years almost entire cohorts of Electronics and Communications Engineering graduates were recruited by Nokia. This special relationship was useful for TUT because Nokia funded research projects, and used its global connections to assist TUT's internationalisation process. However, this maturity brought the first sign of lock-in. TUT believed that it "didn't need anyone else" and it was "looking at the world through blue Nokia glasses", and this close relationship to Nokia overshadowed TUT's relationship building with other local businesses.

This had effects on the wider setting; TUT became a follower for Nokia providing qualified labour resources, just as Nokia started to focus more into product development than the basic research which had originally been important in the university collaboration. Engineering students ignored entrepreneurship because Nokia offered attractive job opportunities. Yet Nokia was not strongly locally embedded, with its own global Nokia community, networks and processes that involved closed traditional innovation processes. Nokia was positive but inactive towards regional development initiatives like the City Council's flagship information society initiative eTampere Programme, and most Nokia site managers in Tampere were not active in regional development networks despite Nokia's huge economic role in Tampere. As late as the early 2000s, this developing lock-in was not regarded as worrying because of the mutual (short-term) benefits to regional partners, ignoring the deteriorating resilience from an overdependence on a strong, but weakly locally embedded partner.

Path exhaustion: considerable structural changes

Mobile phone business by Nokia and Microsoft hits the wall

The path exhaustion came through problems with Nokia: a firm that once held a 40 per cent share of the world's mobile phone market, and accounted for 4 per cent of Finnish GDP in 2000, one-third of R&D expenditure and 20 per cent of exports in its heyday. From 2007, Nokia began shrinking, with negative effects on the Finnish economy, employment and exports, particularly concentrated on cities where Nokia had its facilities (Ali-Yrkkö 2010; Ali-Yrkkö *et al.* 2016). The decline of ICT can be dated to the global economic crisis, with numbers of open ICT vacancies decreasing. In 2009 Nokia started to reduce employee numbers offering 'voluntary separation packages', the first signs of the deep trouble facing its mobile business; many of its more senior and knowledgeable staff realised the extent of the problems, and the outflow grew, with Nokia laying off several hundred staff over the next two years.

In 2011, Nokia's new CEO Stephen Elop began strategic changes, choosing a new technological platform, the Microsoft Windows Phone, to compete with Apple and Android, abandoning other technologies. This platform shift can be seen as a turning point, as the new Windows phones flopped world-wide as a whole mobile ecosystem. Over the next four years Nokia and Nokia Siemens Networks ran several redundancy rounds, also outsourcing people to other companies, in total affecting several thousand employees in Tampere, and highlighting the risks of over-dependence on a single technology giant. Finally in 2014, after a three-year struggle, Nokia announced the sale of the mobile business to Microsoft, with its mobile phone development transferred to Microsoft. Following two more years of struggling, in 2016 Microsoft announced it was ending Windows phone production, the final strike for Tampere's mobile phone industry, with another 500 ICT jobs disappearing in Tampere.

Structural changes in the ICT sector of Tampere

Tampere's city and region unemployment rates had been above the national average since 2007 (Statistics Finland 2016), with Tampere City having the highest unemployment rates among Finland's six largest cities (City of Tampere 2016). As late as 2009 Tampere hosted close to 4000 employees in Nokia Ltd and Nokia Siemens Networks, making them the region's biggest employers (City of Tampere 2011). This number fell to 2650 people by 2011 and to 800 people by 2016 (Figure 11.1). ICT accounted for 8.7 per cent of all Tampere's employment in 2009 (Finland 6.3 per cent) falling to 7.0 per cent by 2015

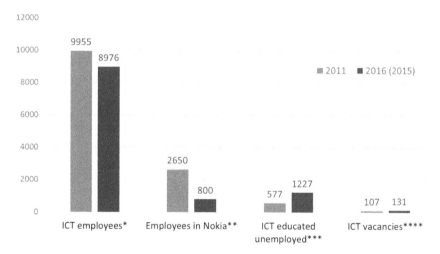

Figure 11.1 ICT employment changes in Tampere region

Data sources:
★ Statistics Finland (2016).
★★ 2011: Tampere Chamber of Commerce (2012: 2;); 2016: Aamulehti (2016); Tampere Chamber of Commerce (2016).
★★★ 2011 May and 2016 September by Neittaanmäki and Kinnunen (2016: 9)
★★★★ Ministry of Employment and the Economy (2016).

(Finland 5.6 per cent). This loss of ICT jobs had indirect employment effects in other sectors that provided services for ICT businesses.

In 2011 the ICT sector employed nearly 10,000 people. Five years later 3000 jobs had been restructured. About 40 per cent were employed relatively quickly, and 40 per cent undertook subsidised activities (coaching, re-training, entrepreneurship courses), while 20 per cent were in danger of long-term unemployment (Salkoaho and Ikonen 2015: 8). The two-thirds of unemployed ICT workers had only secondary level vocational education with new vacancies requiring high level technology competences. Another risk group were middle managers, employed in great numbers in Nokia (Neittaanmäki and Kinnunen 2016: 21). Alongside redundancies, a new wave of software SMEs and a few larger actors have emerged. ICT specialists were also employed by more traditional industrial sectors as they adopt smart technologies. Both local ICT firms and externally owned multisite ICT enterprises were continually recruiting during the recession, particularly software developers, sales and technical staff. Fast growing SMEs along with international enterprises were able to exploit this rapid restructuring, either by recruiting staff or establishing new sites in Tampere (e.g. Intel, Huawei).

The overall picture was of ICT industry transformation towards technologically intensive software, with a persistence of high unemployment in the region alongside unfilled ICT vacancies: in 2016, ICT companies were estimated to have recruited 700 new staff. The business structure of the ICT industry in Tampere region has also changed. There are more SMEs and focus has moved from hardware production (mobile phones) towards software development. The number of ICT companies or their local units has grown from 720 to 859 from 2007 to 2015 (Statistics Finland 2016). Exports have fallen dramatically and are only rather slowly recovering. New ICT businesses are diverse, with firms active in the games industry, web applications, cloud solutions, cyber safety, health technology, location-based services and digitalisation of all kinds of services and traditional industry. In comparison to the Nokia period, the overall production volume of current ICT companies (sum of turnovers) in the Tampere region remains low (Figure 11.2).

These changes had clear effects on Tampere's universities, with far fewer students interested in studying Electronics and Communications Engineering in TUT, whilst Electrical Energy Engineering grew in popularity. TUT faced a dramatic reduction in external funding because of Nokia's prior dominance as a research partner; these projects dried up over a two-year period, and TUT began competing more intensively for funds, actively seeking new project partners and collaborators. The new software firms have proven highly interested in working with the universities to access student potential as innovation resources.

Dimensions of Tampere's regional lock-in

Laamanen *et al.* (2016: 13–17) identified that Nokia's mobile phone division's decline after its huge success could be ascribed to four causes, including poor

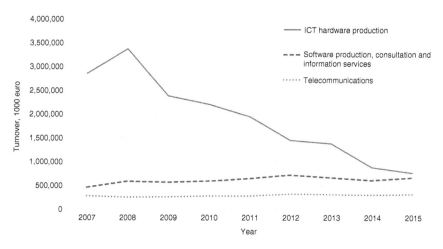

Figure 11.2 Turnover development of the ICT sector in Tampere region
Data source: Statistics Finland (2016).

strategic choices (e.g. technology, timing, leadership); a lack of capabilities to face new challenge; organisational problems (particularly inflexibility, where structures prevented efficient R&D); alongside general environment factors (market changes and an economic downturn). Faced with dominant iPhone competition, Nokia's organisation became too massive, bureaucratic and slow, had a traditional innovation process and finally there was a globally difficult economic situation. Interviewees argued that the "time of the dinosaurs was over", "it was time for new and more agile companies" and "creative destruction" was involved. This organisational failure drove path exhaustion, and as Nokia faltered, Tampere was unable to help it address the challenges despite the massive consequences this had for the regional economy.

The regional lock-in manifested itself in many ways. Interviewees argued that it was not just the failure of Nokia in the global market, but the excessive specialisation in the regional labour market with a failure to develop broader competencies and encourage entrepreneurship. Nokia was a highly attractive partner for many regional actors in the ICT sector, with the result that there was a very strong central node, and only limited interactions between the other partners. However, Tampere was not leaning only on ICT, but has been actively developing other industries, such as machine building and health technology. In any case, the structure of the local ICT industry undermined the regional resilience, something that became clear with the crisis and Nokia's rapid downfall with its highly disruptive effects as Tampere was forced to de-lock itself. After the event, one municipality development manager even said that the "Nokia and Microsoft downsizing and shutdowns were the best things that have happened to Tampere after all". The argument was that as that path had ended, it had at least created a space for the emergence of a new software businesses and the revitalisation of the machine building industry.

Path branching by deepening open collaboration

Not all the actions to reshape Tampere's industrial scene were reactive responses to the immediate crisis, particularly by the universities to promote innovation and entrepreneurship, with some work undertaken to promote innovation and SMEs beginning from 2008. Innovaatio Oy Uusi Tehdas Ltd. launched the 'New Factory', a business incubator and an innovation platform that aims to "connect entrepreneurs, students, researchers, mentors, investors and experts from various fields into value co-creation". In this respect, the concept called Demola has become quite prominent. Demola is a student innovation project platform on which multidisciplinary and often multinational student teams solve real-world challenges provided by companies and other organisations. Quite recently, TUT, UTA, TAMK and City of Tampere became the owners of Demola activities. New Factory also created the Protomo concept to facilitate the birth of start-ups by linking students and highly skilled unemployed people in anticipation of a coming crisis. In total there are more than 160 established start-ups and 1600 jobs created and €35 million funding raised by firms in Tampere's New Factory.

From 2011, as the depths of the Nokia crisis became evident, Tampere's universities also were active in working with development organisations and other regional actors to try to create new economic development paths for the region. The existing loose cooperation network made it relatively easy to mobilise a core group of actors; the City and Regional councils, Tekes, the ELY Centre, Hermia, the Region Economic Development Agency, the Chamber of Commerce, the two universities and at that time also Nokia. Operating through unofficial breakfast meetings, this core group sought to develop collaboration between public and private bodies amidst the ongoing structural changes (Salkoaho and Ikonen 2015: 9). The group built on its mutual trust and common will to functioned solutions, and Nokia passed confidential redundancy information to employment agencies to help with their planning. The group was called together by Tredea and despite the lack of formal leadership it was able to play a significant role in crisis management and coordination. One tangible outcome was the RecruIT event, started in 2011 to promote employment, but has since established its position as a meeting point for the ICT-sector companies and professionals.

We point to two activities that facilitated the emergence of new firms. The ELY Centre launched an upgrading programme 'Spirit – ICT Future in the Tampere Region'. Approximately 2000 people and 20 companies participated in the Spirit retraining and qualification upgrading activities (Salkoaho and Ikonen 2015: 8). This programme was the public counterpart of the Nokia Bridge programme, in which Nokia sought to avoid the damaging PR that had accompanied its Bochum factory closure. The Bridge programme offered five different paths: redeployment within Nokia; outplacement to another company; new companies foundation; retraining; and career coaching. The entrepreneurial path provided funded start-ups with grants of €10–25,000 and technology licences, with 100 businesses, employing 550 people with only 40 per cent of firms in ICT (Kiuru *et al.* 2013; Eskelinen 2015: 24–25). Microsoft also adopted a similar programme, Polku ('Path') for its redundancies, which was also positively received.

The City of Tampere and Tredea worked on an industrial development policy, with their 'Invest-in Tampere' programme, seeking to create new employment by supporting start-ups, providing growth services and promoting Tampere as an attractive site for global and national ICT companies, based upon qualified labour, high-quality physical infrastructure and research institutions. Some companies recruited whole development teams and located to Tampere, although some firms were not to stay permanently.

The path branching emerged as new companies were established from the ashes of Nokia and Microsoft pursuing strategies based on lack of hierarchical structures, openness and transparency, continuous learning, crowdsourcing, ethical and meaningful assignments (Kärki 2015: 16). The new ICT sector was more versatile than previously, covering the games industry, cloud solutions, cyber safety, health technology and digitalisation of traditional industry. Nokia did not entirely disappear but lost its dominant position in Finland's economy (Ali-Yrkkö *et al.* 2016: 3–4) nevertheless recovering to being the highest value added Finnish company with its network systems and patent portfolio. Nokia recently re-entered the mobile phone business, licensing the Nokia brand for phones and tablets to HMD Global Ltd, a low risk, but potentially profitable strategy.

The universities contributed to these path branching activities, most notably being active in Nokia's Bridge Programme and Spirit programme, and this stimulated new collaborative thinking amongst the universities. Tampere University of Technology, University of Tampere and Tampere University of Applied Sciences co-operated closely to coordinate their post-experience education offer, and also to compete against private providers for this training. The informal network was here important in helping the employment authorities to persuade the universities to participate in these shorter-term activities, despite the universities' general preferences for teaching larger and more general upgrading courses. Universities, especially TUT, needed to find new research partners to fill out the gap that Nokia had left. The issue of short-termism here was also a problem, and both university and regional firms devoted a lot of effort to building relationships which in some cases failed before a reasonably strong university-business network formed over recent years.

The path branching concept is useful to understand the restructuring of ICT in Tampere as the mobile phone industry diversified into other ICT sectors and also merged into traditional industries as smart technologies. It is easy to see that Tampere can be located into two latter categories of Lester's typology, namely diversification and upgrading. The university's resilience building role through university became evident with the employment rates of highly educated ICT employees being considerably higher than secondary level educated (Neittaanmäki and Kinnunen 2016: 21). In the regional management group, universities also contributed to the development of new approaches of collaboration and openness, away from supporting clusters towards driving processes of digitalisation. The universities have been active in reshaping the regional talent attraction policy to increase the human diversity and global linkages.

Looking to the future, this shared leadership contributed to the development of a new Smart Tampere programme (2017–2021) to produce a more transversal set of solutions to the cities' open, big, digitalization-related challenges. Innovative 'smart' solutions are provided by companies, universities and citizens, around seven themes that are health, education and know-how, industry, building, infrastructure, mobility and government and citizen. The City made the project funding contingent on this new way of working, and the universities have been willing to participate not only for projects in their own right, but in working with others to orient those projects and their other activities to the big, local challenges. Part of this programme seeks to develop new kinds of open innovation platforms, using existing infrastructures, such as the universities and larger businesses, to empower smaller groups, digitalising city life and promoting an agile approach which can later be upscaled to involve large companies, research institutions and the public sector (cf. Raunio *et al.* 2016: 5). The universities have been actively engaged with these platforms, drawing on their resources, competencies and highly skilled individuals. At the time of writing, the three regional universities had agreed to merge in 2019, intended to create a university with more than 35,000 students, and with new, modern procedures for the research, education and societal engagement.

Discussion: constructing regional resilience

This chapter has sought to look at the role of universities in the long-term development trajectory of a region and an industry at a time when it was dominated by a single company. In Tampere, the resilience capacity seemed to be rather high in the 1990s, when the ICT path was created and the system was in a flexible and creative state after a severe recession of the early 1990s. By the end of the 1990s Nokia and mobile phones had reached a tremendous growth and established their role as an engine of economic development in Tampere region. In the first years of the twenty-first century this appeared to continue, despite resilience deterioration through increasing dependence on one actor. As the crisis hit, the scale of lock-in became evident, with the first problems with the 2008 crisis, mass redundancies in 2011 and the closure of the mobile telephony industry in Tampere in 2016. What has happened since 2008 were various attempts by regional actors to construct resilience in ways that would minimise the damage done to the region by the de-locking process that hit as Nokia mobile telephony in Tampere entered its terminal decline. The universities have been important in that process, although unlike other chapters in this volume, one of the main issues the universities needed to address was solving their contribution to the lock-in problem, after an active role in earlier path creation.

Universities have had a significant role in different development phases of the ICT industry in Tampere. To begin with, we argue, the whole cluster would not have emerged without the initial efforts by both scientific universities. That is also the case concerning the rapid growth and the 'glorious days' of Nokia and its mobile phone business. At that time both educational and research activities were of great importance. However, quite intense university-industry inter-action between Nokia and TUT especially was not able to prevent the dramatic restructuring of the local industry. One could argue that the relationships were even too tight, or at least mental models were too homogenous. Later on, the universities were involved in the management of the acute crisis, but their role cannot be determined as crucial.

Consequently, the universities needed to relocate themselves to the new setting. For example, the 'open innovation platform approach' provides uni-versities with a quite different position to more traditional university-industry interaction modes. More generally the role of universities in this case study appears to have reasserted itself, both as a means of attracting highly tal-ented students but also in creating the channels to better embed them in the region. The adoption of an open innovation approach and the creation of new platforms was an attempt to facilitate that and to create an environment where experimentation was encouraged and failure permitted, a very different kind of regional culture to that prevalent under conditions of a large employer.

So what are the wider lessons we can learn from this case study of the involvement of universities in an attempt by an old industrial region to reinvent itself for the twenty-first century? The Tampere region is a quite extreme example because of the sheer size of the boom and bust the region experienced related to a single firm, and the effects that this had on a wider industrial sector, firstly as crowding out, and then providing potential productive assets for this. The most obvious example of this is that the universities have acted to have an ameliorating role on the boom to bust conversion, ensuring that as many of the resources that were built up in the 'gold rush' years were retained and retrained as the crisis built up. The retraining and upgrading programmes from the uni-versities are emblematical of this approach in explaining how universities can help to deal with these moments of evolutionary collapse.

But there is another more interesting story emerging from this case study again revealed by its extremity. Tampere's universities have been in recent years, as with other universities in this volume, under enormous pressure to succeed and compete in a range of national and international comparative frameworks. They have to compete for students, they have to produce highly rated research by winning prestigious and lucrative research grants. When faced with a single firm that was able to help them deliver so many of these goals it is unsur-prising that the university oriented a number of its activities towards that single firm. But at the same time, that orientation towards Nokia contributed to the sense of lock-in by reaffirming to other policy makers that the existing way of business was suitable. And the universities, and in particular TUT, had to find new ways to break that lock-in given these wider networks within which they were operating. Supporting new entrepreneurs with short courses and small research projects represented a very different way of working for TUT post-Nokia and required substantive learning activities within the university to realise the necessary internal changes to permit participation in the informal regional network.

And this we argue is the most interesting contribution to be made here, to place the role of the universities in the context of public organisations that nevertheless have strongly private interests, to compete and succeed in these wider knowledge networks. It is all too easy to assume that universities are able as 'ivory tower' actors to stand above the daily throng and take decisions with long-term perspectives at their heart. But these new global pressures drive universities towards the same short-term rationales that are at the heart of the emergence of regional lock-in. We contend that in the context of evolutionary approaches and resilience, it is this issue that requires additional research and reflection, how can universities be granted the necessary space and time to contribute to resilience, and not themselves exacerbate lock-in, crisis and the regional economic problems that ultimately result.

Notes

1 The case study uses various data sources including standard statistics (Statistics Finland), 73 daily paper articles (93 pages; *Aamulehti*, the main local newspaper), six extensive, thematic face-to-face interviews and two thematic group interviews, alongside other materials as referenced elsewhere. We have compiled the milestones of Nokia related events from local daily newspaper *Aamulehti* news archives and from regional employment authorities report (Salkoaho and Knuuttila 2015).
2 This section partly draws upon Kolehmainen (2003), but the description has been updated and revised.

References

Literature

Ali-Yrkkö, J. (ed.) (2010) *Nokia and Finland in a Sea of Change. Series B 244.* Helsinki: ETLA – Research Institute of the Finnish Economy.
Ali-Yrkkö, J., Seppälä, T. and Mattila, J. (2016) *Suurten yritysten ja niiden arvoketjujen rooli taloudessa. ETLA raportit No. 53* [The role of the largest companies and their value chains in the economy. ETLA reports No. 53]. Helsinki: ETLA – Research Institute of the Finnish Economy.
Arthur, W. B. (1989) Competing technologies, increasing returns, and 'lock-in' by historical events. *Economic Journal*, 99, 116–131.
Autere, J. (2000) Ohjelmistotuoteyritysten kasvuhakuisuus Helsingin, Oulun ja Tampereen seuduilla. In J. Kostiainen and M. Sotarauta (eds) *Kaupungit innovatiivisina toimintaympäristöinä*. Helsinki: Tekniikan akateemisten liitto TEK ry.

Boschma, R. and Frenken, K. (2011) Technological relatedness, related variety and economic geography. In P. Cooke, B. Asheim, R. Boschma, R. Martin, D. Schwartz and F. Tödtling (eds) *Handbook of Regional Innovation and Growth* (pp. 187–197). Cheltenham: Edward Elgar.

Boschma, R. and Sotarauta, M. (2007) Economic policy from an evolutionary perspective: The case of Finland. *International Journal of Entrepreneurship and Innovation Management*, 7:2–5, 156–173.

Bristow, G. and Healy, A. (2014) Building resilient regions: Complex adaptive systems and the role of policy intervention. *Raumforschung und Raumordnung*, 72:2, 93–102.

Crescenzi, R., Luca, D. and Milio, S. (2015) The geography of the economic crisis in Europe: National macroeconomic conditions, regional structural factors and short-term economic performance. *Cambridge Journal of Regions, Economy and Society*, 9:1, 13–32.

David, P. A. (2001) Path dependence, its critics and the quest for 'historical economics'. In P. Garrouste and S. Ioannides (eds) *Evolution and Path Dependence in Economic Ideas* (pp. 15–40). Cheltenham: Edward Elgar.

Djelic, M-L. and Quack, S. (2007) Overcoming path dependency: Path generation in open systems. *Theory and Society*, 36:2, 161–186.

Eskelinen, P. (2015) Bridge – ohjelma yhteiskuntavastuunotosta [Brigde – a social responsibility programme]. In U. Salkoaho and A. Knuuttila (eds) *Uuden edessä. Start. Up. Tuki, toimet ja tulevaisuus ICT-alan rakennemuutoksessa* [In front of something new. Start. Up. Support, activities and future of the ICT sector restructuring] (pp. 24–25) Tampere: The Centre for Economic Development, Transport and the Environment of Pirkanmaa.

Garud, R. and Karnøe, P. (2001) Path creation as a process of mindful deviation. In R. Garud and P. Karnøe (eds) *Path Dependence and Creation* (pp. 1–38). Mahwah, NJ: Lawrence Erlbaum.

Garud, R., Kumaraswamy, A. and Karnøe, P. (2010) Path dependence or path creation? *Journal of Management Studies*, 47:4, 760–774.

Haapala, P. (2005) History of Tampere: The very long road to informational city. In A. Kasvio and A.-V. Anttiroiko (eds). *e-City: Analysing Efforts to Generate Local Dynamism in the City of Tampere* (pp. 163–182). Tampere: Tampere University Press.

Häikiö, M. (2002) *Globalisaatio: Telekommunikaation maailmanvalloitus 1992–2000.* Helsinki: Edita.

Hassink, R. (2010a) Regional resilience: A promising concept to explain differences in regional economic adaptability? *Cambridge Journal of Regions, Economy and Society*, 3:1, 45–58.

Hassink, R. (2010b) Locked in decline? On the role of regional lock-ins in old industrial areas. In R. Boschma and R. Martin (eds) *The Handbook of Evolutionary Economic Geography* (pp. 450–468). London: Edward Elgar.

Henning, M., Stam, E. and Wenting, R. (2013) Path dependence research in regional economic development: Cacophony or knowledge accumulation? *Regional Studies*, 47:8, 1348–1362.

Isaksen, A. (2015) Industrial development in thin regions: Trapped in path extension? *Journal of Economic Geography*, 15:3, 585–600.

Kärki, T. (2015) Vähemmän ylhäältä johtamista, enemmän innokkuuden ja luovuuden ohjaamista ja tekemisen mahdollistamista [Less top to bottom management, more possibilising enthusiasm, creativity and doing]. In U. Salkoaho and A. Knuuttila (eds) *Uuden edessä. Start. Up. Tuki, toimet ja tulevaisuus ICT-alan rakennemuutoksessa* [In front of something new. Start. Up. Support, activities and future of the ICT sector restructuring] (pp. 14–15). Tampere: The Centre for Economic Development, Transport and the Environment of Pirkanmaa.

Kiuru, P., Handelberg, J., and Rannikko, H. (2013) *Bridge It Up – työntekijöille tarjottujen startup-palveluiden vaikuttavuus – Case Nokian Bridge-ohjelma* [Bridge It Up – the effectiveness of startup services for employees – Case Nokia Bridge Programme]. Helsinki: Aalto University.

Kolehmainen, J. (2003) *Territorial Agglomeration as a Local Innovation Environment: The Case of a Digital Media Agglomeration in Tampere, Finland.* MIT IPC Local Innovation Systems Working Paper 03-002. Accessed 28 February 2017 at http://ipc-lis.mit. edu/LIS03-002.pdf.

Laamanen, T., Lamberg, J.-A. and Vaara, E. (2016) Explanations of success and failure in management learning: What can we learn from Nokia's rise and fall? *Academy of Management Learning & Education*, 15:1, 2–25.

Lehtimäki, M. (2005) *Strategy Configuration of a Technology Center as an Innovation System – Historical Perspective on the Story of Hermia.* Tampereen teknillinen yliopisto, Julkaisu 578. Tampere.

Lester, R. K. (2007) Universities, innovation, and the competitiveness of local economies: An overview. In R. K Lester and M. Sotarauta (eds) *Innovation, Universities, and the Competitiveness of Regions* (pp. 9–30). Helsinki: Tekes.

Martin, R. (2012) Regional economic resilience, hysteresis and recessionary shocks. *Journal of Economic Geography*, 12:1, 1–32.

Martin, R. and Sunley, P. (2006) Path dependence and regional economic evolution. *Journal of Economic Geography*, 6:4, 395–437.

Neffke, F., Henning, M. and Boschma, R. (2011) How do regions diversify over time? Industry relatedness and the development of new growth paths in regions. *Economic Geography*, 87:3, 237–265.

Neittaanmäki, P. and Kinnunen, P. (2016) *Työttömyys IT-alalla koko Suomessa ja maakunnissa 2006–2015.* Informaatioteknologian tiedekunnan julkaisuja –sarja [Unemployment of the ICT sector in Finland and its regions. Publications of the Faculty of the Information Science]. Jyväskylä: University of Jyväskylä.

Raunio, M., Nordling, N., Ketola, T., Saarinen, J.P. and Heinikangas, A. (2016). *Open Innovation Platforms: An Approach to City Development.* Tampere: 6Aika.

Salkoaho, U. and Ikonen, J. (2015) Pelastuslauttojen rakentamiseen [Building life rafts]. In U. Salkoaho and A. Knuuttila (eds) *Uuden edessä. Start. Up. Tuki, toimet ja tulevaisuus ICT-alan rakennemuutoksessa* [In front of something new. Start. Up. Support, activities and future of the ICT sector restructuring] (pp. 8–9). Tampere: The Centre for Economic Development, Transport and the Environment of Pirkanmaa.

Salkoaho, U. and Knuuttila, A. (eds) (2015) *Uuden edessä. Start. Up. Tuki, toimet ja tulevaisuus ICT-alan rakennemuutoksessa* [In front of something new. Start. Up. Support, activities and future of the ICT sector restructuring]. Tampere: The Centre for Economic Development, Transport and the Environment of Pirkanmaa.

Sotarauta, M. and Mustikkamäki, N. (2015) Institutional entrepreneurship, power, and knowledge in innovation systems: Institutionalization of regenerative medicine in Tampere, Finland. *Environment and Planning C: Government and Policy*, 33:2, 342–357.

Sotarauta, M. and Suvinen, N. (2018) Institutional agency and path creation: Institutional path from industrial to knowledge city. In Arne, Isaksen, Roman Martin and Michaela Trippl (eds) *New Avenues for Regional Innovation Systems – Theoretical Advances, Empirical Cases and Policy Lessons.* New York: Springer.

Tödtling, F. and Trippl, M. (2013) Transformation of regional innovation systems: From old legacies to new development paths. In P. Cooke (ed.) *Reframing Regional Development* (pp. 297–317). London: Routledge.

Statistics and other material

Aamulehti news archives. *Suomen Media-arkisto*, www.media-arkisto.com/, 4 February 2017.

City of Tampere (2011) *Akseli. Tilastollisia tiedonantoja Tampereelta 1/2011* [Akseli. Statistical Review of Tampere 1/2011], www.pilkahdus.fi/sites/default/files/134_akseli_1_2011.pdf, 28 February 2017.

City of Tampere (2016) *Tampereen työttömyysaste kuuden suurimman kaupungin korkein* [Unemployment rate in Tampere highest among Finland's six largest cities], Tiedotteet [Releases], 2 August 2016, www.tampere.fi/tampereen-kaupunki/ajankohtaista/tiedotteet/2016/02/08022016_4.html, 28 February 2017.

Ministry of Employment and Economy (2016) Avoimet työpaikat kuukauden aikana ammatin ja toimialan mukaan ELY-keskuksittain/maakunnittain [Vacancies per month by sector and region], *Sector Online database*, www.temtoimialapalvelu.fi/en/mee_business_sector_services/sector_online, 1 February 2017.

Statistics Finland (2016) Alueellinen yritystoimintatilasto [Regional Statistics on Enterprises], *StaFin database*. http://pxnet2.stat.fi/PXWeb/pxweb/fi/StatFin/StatFin__yri__alyr/?tablelist=true&rxid=0a7dc93a-e71f-4e02-ad79-b82cd63e104d, 1 February 2017.

Tampere Chamber of Commerce (2012) *Kyselyt ja selvitykset 2011–2012* [Surveys and reviews 2011–2012], http://tampere-chamber-fi-bin.directo.fi/@Bin/a111dcebf0370b46f9752b48667a9265/1488269590/application/pdf/2512661/Kyselyt_ja_selvitykset_2011-2012.pdf, 1 February 2017, 28 February 2017.

Tampere Chamber of Commerce (2016) *Kyselyt ja selvitykset 2015–2016* [Surveys and reviews 2015–2016], http://tampere-chamber-fi-bin.directo.fi/@Bin/14c966576432a78b4035d4af342d67d7/1488272265/application/pdf/4605773/Kyselytjaselvitykset2015%202016.pdf, 3 February 2017.

12 Conceptualising the university-region economic development interface in peripheral regions

Paul Benneworth and Lisa Nieth

Introduction

In this volume we have been concerned with the way that universities contribute to regional development in the periphery. We have been particularly concerned with the tensions that arise when universities under many pressures to internationalise and compete seek to engage with regional innovation environments that are not inherently dynamic. In the nine empirical chapters, we have presented detailed case studies from nine regions where there is not a natural innovation pressure coming from these regions acting as a pull on universities to engage. What we have observed through these chapters is that there is often a demand for universities to engage from policy-makers, sometimes placing the universities in a slightly uncomfortable situation of dealing with the expectation of policy-makers that they can play a transformative role. We can therefore see in these nine case studies an interesting overview of the pressures that universities face more generally to engage with their territories from policy-makers and the difficulties there can be in realising those often extensive policy ambitions.

In Chapter 2, we identified that there were three main classes of tensions that appeared to be emerging in peripheral regions (see also Tödtling & Tripp1, 2005). The first of those related to the fact that peripheries are often institutionally quite thin, and there may not necessarily be very sophisticated regional policy coalitions who are in a position to work with universities and other regional actors to develop a 'smart mix' of policies involving university contributions (Flanagan, Uyarra, & Laranja, 2011). The second relates to the mismatch between university and regional knowledge competencies and the roles that universities play in creating new industries; if universities are placed in the situation of challenging lock-in that then may antagonise their regional partners whilst existing industries might not necessarily fit well with university competencies. Thirdly, a set of tensions can emerge because of the dominance of universities in their respective innovation systems (RISs); although cases have been identified of innovation systems that are dominated by firms, government, and non-governmental actors, much less consideration is given to those RISs that are dominated by universities; as well as carrying out their innovation roles they may also be expected to play regional leadership roles that do not naturally fit with their inherent inclinations (Benneworth, Pinheiro, & Karlsen, 2017).

These tensions are of course not exclusive to universities in peripheral regions, and we contend that the wider issue of universities' regional contributions can be given a depth of perspective by reflecting on these tensions more widely in contemporary debates about the roles of universities in their regions. We see that many of the framings of universities' roles are strongly normative in which the work of dealing with these tensions is done by the enthusiasm, strategic orientation, and commitment of the university to engagement. We see through our case studies that an alternative reading of these situations is possible, namely that it is those universities who manage to find practical ways to deal with these problems, and resolve the internal and external tensions that are raised, that are able to make themselves as institutions, enthusiastic about, strategically oriented, and committed towards regional engagement. Those institutional characteristics are themselves a consequence of finding these practical pathways towards building regional engagement rather than a precondition towards them.

That is something that we believe is misunderstood in the contemporary debates around universities and their regional engagement, and providing a corrective to that view is that is the overarching message that we seek to make in this volume. This inverts the relationships as they are usually understood – universities that are able to develop a strategic vision are able to find all kinds of ways to construct regional activities that deliver both regional benefits but at the same time also support the key missions specific to the regional universities or HEIs. What was perhaps striking in this volume was that even very applied research institutions, polytechnics, *Fachhochschulen* in Germany, *Hogescholen* in the Netherlands experienced a range of pressures around internationalisation and competition that worked against their regional engagement. The general tendency of academic drift, for more applied institutions to become more research-intensive in the long-term (see Collini, 2011), was also evident in these contributions, adding an additional layer of complexity to this issue. In all three Norwegian chapters, for example, mergers along with pressure to academic excellence drove disinvestments from more peripheral campuses to create core nodes capable of attracting these substantia investments (see also Zeeman & Benneworth, 2016).

In the final diptych of chapters, we therefore reflect in more depth on these tensions and their consequences for university-regional engagement more generally. In this chapter we reflect on the conceptual consequences of these tensions and bring them back to three core literatures (regional innovation coalitions, evolutionary economic geography, regional leadership) for understanding universities' regional contributions. In institutionally thin regions, universities can represent not just one actor within regional coalitions with a single corporate interest, but many actors all exerting agency simultaneously. The strategic challenge for universities (what drives effective engagement) therefore becomes finding appropriate ways to coordinate and shape these many diverse actors towards common goals and playing what we call a transformative goal to deliver effectuative entrepreneurial discovery processes within regional innovation coalitions. The notion of the third mission here may even be unhelpful because it suggests a commonality between actors within universities that are not present or indeed may in reality better be understood as conflicts and differences.

In the final chapter, we reflect on what this unruliness of the third mission concept means for policy-makers and practitioners seeking to stimulate universities' transformational contributions to their regional environments and produce effectuative entrepreneurial discovery antecedent to regional path-switching. We make recommendations at a variety of levels:

- national policy-makers must allow room in their higher education systems for engagement not to be neglected;
- regional policy-makers should look to support institutional entrepreneurs within HEIs;
- university senior managers need to create permissive environments for effectuative institutional entrepreneurs; and
- individual engaged academics should look more closely at creating links between their teaching/research activities and their societal duties.

Regional innovation coalitions in institutionally thin environments

The first set of tensions that emerged in this volume were the challenges of mobilising and exploiting what we have called regional innovation coalitions in institutionally thin regions. Although we have chosen the coalitions approach, our argument is that the coalition notion has become increasingly central in contemporary innovation policy, but at the same time assumes that these coalitions will find it relatively straightforward to identify areas of common interest and develop and implement shared strategies. However, the 'thinness' of peripheral regions creates a set of tensions for these regional coalitions, and we argue that more cognisance needs to be taken of these issues, and the ways that they can be addressed, if what McCann and Orteges-Argilés (2013) call modern regional innovation policy is to be effectively realised. The first is that achieving agreement in institutionally thin environments is not particularly straightforward, even where there are relatively few actors, because of these divergence of interests. Secondly, there can be sub-regional divisions in coalitions, and with universities bringing both local and regional benefits, these splits may also be salient for university engagement. Thirdly, regional partners may be primarily outward looking without strong regional orientation specifically because they have few ways to derive institutional advantage from regional co-operation. Finally, the thinness may create urgency and pressure, but universities need to ensure that they do not bow entirely to this local pressure and thereby undermine their wider knowledge connections from which these wider advantages are produced.

It may seem perverse but in institutionally thin environments, there can be a tension that arises from the over-importance of universities to regional innovation coalitions that added an additional dimension of complexity to achieving consensus, legitimacy, and implementation. In Algarve, for example, the internal strength of the HEIs led them to impose their perspective in shaping regional economic development policies. In Agder, the lack of regional demand for knowledge allowed quick decision-making, but between policy-makers and HEIs without necessarily bringing along the regional businesses whose involvement was vital to achieve the desired change. In the EUREGIO, the existence of the border imposed a hybridity to strategies, to meet the expectations and regulations across the different sides of the borders, bringing with it additional costs and convolutions to the regional innovation strategy process. In Estonia, the regional colleges quickly aligned themselves to particular sectors, which ran the risk of reducing their flexibility to react and evolve in ways that more comprehensive HEIs in more diverse regions may have been able to do.

Related to this first set of tensions was a second set that emerged as a consequence of the fact that universities deliver their societal benefits at a range of scales that do not neatly map to political boundaries but are instead related to the places at which these interactions happen. Tödtling and Trippl (2005) identified that peripheral regions can suffer from internal fragmentation, and because universities can produce both regional and urban benefits, in regions with many small urban centres, then coalitions sometimes faced a fragmentation because universities were seen more as local-urban partners than as fully regional partners creating benefits for the region as a whole. Perhaps the most obvious case of this was the EUREGIO, where the HEIs were seen as primarily identified with their local region (Twente or Westmünsterland) and it was not a simple task for them to make cross-border engagement seem legitimate to any stakeholders. In Finnmark, tensions emerged because of the urban locations of the college branches, in parallel with a strong urban/rural split in the context of a huge region; one would likewise expect these tensions to further grow with the merger with UiT, a comprehensive university in the capital of Northern Norway. Indeed, mergers have foregrounded these tensions, particularly where the notional scope of the university college is not the same as the region, something which Norway had accentuated with its merger programme, with similar effects for all three studied Norwegian regions.

The effects of the nationally driven mergers in Norway lead to the third issue about regional innovation coalitions, namely that because these coalitions are thin, more dynamic regional actors tend to be more outward facing and hence exposed to different kinds of external pressures making these coalitions inherently less stable. The case of Algarve highlighted an additional dimension here namely that HEIs operate in frameworks that are often determined by the needs of the most powerful universities in the most successful regions; national higher education policy in Portugal as elsewhere is based on a presumption that universities operate in core regional environments, and therefore make no allowance for the problems that arise in operating in peripheral regions.

The case of Estonia illustrated an extreme example of where national party political splits and turbulence can undermine universities' efforts to engage with their regions, by creating a volatility that denies universities the long-term certainty to build up potentially beneficial assets in peripheral regions. In such cases, these regional colleges became highly focused on particular activities, and although beneficial for the individual sectors with which they were aligned did not deliver the broader synergy-based benefits that are sometimes expected from universities. Something we have seen in all the countries were the effects of national higher education ministries emphasising excellence by universities, judged against national or international standards, reducing the possibilities for local flexibility in reacting to regional partners' needs.

The final set of tensions that emerged came through the imminence of regional partners' demands being at odds with HEIs' needs to develop a more general perspective on knowledge. There were several examples of where regional coalitions had made specific efforts to ensure that regional HEIs were spared this undue pressure. Sometimes this was very informal, based on a mutual understanding of the needs to avoid this pressure, as in Telemark. In Tampere, this was a central part of the style of regional innovation, where there was a long-term history of regional partners coming together and openly negotiating shared plans whilst foregrounding their separate needs. In Usti the need for this institutional space emerged because it was clear that the local situation was too volatile for the regional college to engage seriously with. In the EUREGIO, a system of fuzzy governance spaces provided the flexibility to deal with the needs of partners operating in very different environments across regional borders.

Universities' evolutionary contributions to their regions

The second set of tensions that emerged is related to the role of universities as evolutionary institutions, and in particular the roles they could play in path-creation and path-renewal. There was a huge amount of evidence within the chapters that universities could contribute to both of these processes in various different ways, from generating new technologies to contributing social capital. An additional if underappreciated element of universities' contributions came in terms of the way they contributed to what might be considered as the resilience of a place, in providing anchors for highly skilled people at moments of crisis that retained sufficient foundations for the basis of later diversification and growth. But at the same time, universities faced the tension of being drawn into lock-in, path-extension, and path-extinction processes, and worse, even facing benefits from misguided policy investments. More generally, there was little policy understanding of how to optimise universities' evolutionary contributions without providing the perverse incentives that encouraged these less positive university contributions. Universities are naturally sources of great diversity and synergy and *can* promote evolutionary repertoires, but there are likewise various ways that they may hinder regional path-switching.

It is important to note at this stage that this volume has provided substantive evidence that universities can contribute in various different ways, and in various different scales, to positive evolutionary path-switching processes. Although the focus of this chapter is to further explore a particular set of tensions, it is necessary to note that one of the tensions that has emerged has been almost a luxury problem of the fact that HEIs do have enormous potential to contribute to evolutionary processes, even in the most extreme examples of peripheral regions we have presented in this volume. What might be considered a best-practice example here is Tampere, where the three HEIs are so interwoven with the regional fabric that they have been at the heart of the birth and rebirth of ICT in the forms of mobile telephony and industrial digitisation; we give the caveat that Tampere is so *sui generis* that one must be careful in using the example more widely.

Certainly, elsewhere, the roles of HEIs and indeed of path-switching, have been more modest. In Usti, we have seen what one might consider as the classical path-switching process, with universities contributing to diversifying and transforming existing industries, along with revitalising existing industries; in this case the university has not been the lead actor for this process. Likewise, in Finnmark, the relatively small size of the university has limited its scope to drive rapid transformation, although given the limitations in absorption capacity, it is not clear that creating a diverse, research-intensive university would drive regional transformation. HiF has had a substantive place-making effect on the town of Alta and remains critical to its long-term sustainability, but in part because of a lack of functional relationships between Finnmark's sub-regions there has not been a rippling outward effect from HiF to create new trajectories. An interesting case here was seen in Vysočina where the entire regional development strategy was about creating activities de novo, thereby skipping heavy industrialisation, and avoiding the despoliation of one of the region's strongest assets, its standard of living and environment quality. A final aside came from the case of the EUREGIO, where the activities of the HEIs were part of the very first tentative steps towards trying to encourage more structural cross-border cooperation, and the projects created became part of a more generally held acceptance of the value of cross-border innovation activities.

There was one element that emerged strongly in the case studies that we do not recognise from an account of evolutionary path-switching from more munificent regional innovation environments. The HEIs had a greater longevity and anchoring in the regions during moments of crisis than firms, and were capable of undertaking activities that helped to retain human capital resources within the regions and help those people to develop appropriate skills that in turn contributed to post-crisis reconstruction and path-creation. Although we are extremely wary of simplistically evoking ideas of resilience, universities seemed to play a key evolutionary role in providing temporary sanctuary for people (and hence retaining their human capital) during moments of path-extinction. There were many examples of universities providing appropriate skills to create new industries, such as through the regional colleges in Estonia or locally focused campuses in Telemark, and assist with path-diversification in Usti. But we also see that universities in Tampere, Telemark, and Usti facilitated creating related variety by helping to retain skilled people at moments of crisis and helping to restore their agency once the crises or declines had passed.

We are aware here that we are letting the example of Tampere do a lot of work for us in this section, and mindful of warnings about the 'dark side' of university engagement (Bozeman, Fay, & Slade, 2013), we also see that university engagement can evolve a 'dark side' that undermines path-renewal and creation processes. The case of Tampere is a good example of the problems that can emerge when universities become locked into existing technological and policy networks in regions. Just as the region faced an economic rupture when the industry died out, Tampere University of Technology faced the challenge of suddenly reorienting its research and teaching activities away from a large, sophisticated user towards a much more diverse array of smaller businesses. In the Algarve, the lack of clear opportunities hindered the policy imagination, making new opportunities seem too improbable to be worth chasing, and leading to a repetition of existing interventions that whilst they certainly strengthened the regional HEIs were less effective in creating new economic development trajectories.

In both these cases, we emphasise that these examples all covered agents acting in good faith, seeking to engage regionally to create regional benefits as well as strengthen their individual capacities. One clear issue here did lie in the capacities of policy structures to incentivise the right kinds of behaviour, regional collaboration that created new pathways, creating new shared territorial knowledge assets through these collaborations. In the Algarve, the sheer dominance of the HEIs in the policy networks meant that they could not fulfil roles of outsiders and critics but instead led to a continuation of the existing suboptimal policy arrangements. In Vysočina, although regional partners knew what they sought to promote, social capital and quality of life, these benefits were too remote from the immediate knowledge base and interests of policy-makers, and in the absence of well-developed policy repertoires for stimulating these developments, a policy stasis emerged. That policy-makers are part of the problem is something widely recognised in regional evolutionary economic geography (e.g. Hassink, 2005), but we are here mindful that innovation need not become an explanation for 'too difficult' categories. In particular, the mere involvement of universities in regional innovation coalitions is no guarantee that they will break lock in and stimulate path-switching activities.

Effective university leadership for regional innovation

The third set of tensions arise when universities attempt to exercise a regional leadership role. Regional innovation policy is a prime example of a reality in which regional leadership is informal, inter-institutional, and exercised in soft ways (see Ayres, 2014; Beer & Clower, 2014; Sotarauta, 2014 for a more detailed discussion). Effective regional leaders typically play two kinds of roles; firstly, they engage with other regional leaders to create regional platforms that oversee strategic policy delivery. But almost more important is the second internal role that they play, in creating the conditions under which people in their organisations are willing to collaborate with other regional partners, creating policies that allow external partners to use their facilities and assets, and in making regional engagement seem attractive and natural to people in the effective delivery of their roles. And it is an increasingly loud critique of much of the literature on the regional leadership roles played by universities that there is far too much emphasis of the former, and an almost total oversight of the latter. This latter dimension is highly important for universities as knowledge-intensive institutions hosting large numbers of Weberian bureaucrats with considerable latitude in organising their work processes (Benneworth *et al.*, 2017). And from the empirical evidence it is clear that there are a number of tensions emerging in effective university region leadership for innovation.

The empirical chapters present extensive evidence of universities playing a regional leadership role, sometimes delivering rather impressive results under challenging circumstances. But at the same time they also demonstrate that there are three areas where this regional leadership role is not straightforward. The first is that there were examples of a strategic mismatch, where university senior managers had an imperfect nature of what their engaged staff were doing and therefore were unable to exercise suitable strategic influence. A second issue was that, following Watson and Hall (2015), academic behaviour was more shaped by individuals' immediate incentives than by high-level university declarations about regional engagement. The third issue was that engaged academics often understood engaged practices in teaching and research to be intrinsically part of 'good' knowledge-creation practice, illustrating a symbolic dimension to regional engagement at odds with the idea of 'ivory tower' institutions that rarely emerges in strategic university management discourses regarding engagement.

The case studies did indeed illustrate how university leadership can stimulate regional engagement. In the case of Agder University, regional engagement was deliberately chosen by its leaders as a young, mid-sized university seeking a distinct identity and profile, and as a basis to get vocal (regional support) at the national level for its wider ambitions. In Estonia, the regional colleges were highly dependent on leadership to hold the many necessary elements together, the distant university, local communities, and politicians, and again to make a national case that these activities had value. In both cases, university leadership was active in inserting the role of the university in the region as contributing to the nationally desirable policy goal of balanced territorial development. In the EUREGIO, regional leaders encouraged their staff to construct joint projects, not being put off by their apparently ex ante impossibility, and realising the generally desirable situation of cross-border innovation cooperation. In Telemark, university leaders were able to take an existing strength in distance learning, and to refine and profile it in order to create an appreciation by regional partners of the regional potential of TUC. But at the same time these examples also neatly illustrated the tensions and problems universities facing in exercising this leadership function.

The first issue that emerged was where university strategic capacity actually fell behind what actors within the universities were themselves doing, that led to an inability or difficulty at the strategic level to promulgate an overarching vision. Perhaps the most obvious case of that was seen in Agder, which evolved into a two-campus university with two very distinct sites, each with their own faculties, and lead users. The campus at Kristiansand was primarily oriented towards supporting the public sector, whilst that in Grimstad was more oriented towards engineering, industry, and in particular the emerging mechatronics sector. Each of these two kinds of users required very different kinds of interactions and offered very different kinds of opportunities for the university. As a result, the university found it difficult to offer a specific strategic vision for regional engagement that went further than a bland statement of positive support (Benneworth, Normann, & Young, 2018). But it is also worth noting that this was more of a problem for the university strategic managers than it was for the engaged academics for whom engagement was embedded in their knowledge-production practices. And this echoes the point made by Feldman and Desrochers (2003) that academic regional engagement often happens in the absence of strategic management support; the question remains of what kind of strategic management support can positively encourage regional engagement. This is something that is dealt with at more length in the 'University senior managers' section in Chapter 13.

The second problem related to the fact that what appeared most important in determining behaviour around regional engagement was not the presence of a strategic interface between the university corporate centre and regional partners, but the incentives mechanisms that academic knowledge communities faced in their institutional environment. Following Watson and Hall (2015) it appeared that academic behaviour was more shaped by individuals' immediate incentives than by high-level university declarations about regional engagement. Strategic interfaces could potentially be important where they had immediate salience for academic decision-making, and were certainly important in terms of controlling the general benefits that universities brought to their host places, through their campuses, their accommodation, and services. In Tampere, the authors have been clear in admitting that the pressure to be perceived as globally excellent engendered lock-in as the mobile telephony trajectory underwent extinction; academics needed research partners and student placements/employment prospects so urgently that they often lacked freedom to experiment and create new paths. Both Czech universities suffered in gaining staff commitment because of the wider reform efforts within higher education that sought to raise the overall level of academic quality measured in terms of international publications and national accreditations for qualifications, thereby reducing individual flexibility to engage in regional experimentation processes. In all three Norwegian universities, the publication points model looms large in academics planning decision-making, creating an implicit prioritisation for English language publication over locally relevant engagement (Pinheiro & Stensaker, 2013).

The final issue for regional university leadership was diversity of the ways in which engagement practices were embedded within scholars' daily knowledge behaviours and the problems that arose from defining this as something exogenous to normal practice. In Agder, both campuses' teaching and research had extensive contacts with local stakeholders around activities such as placements, guest lectures, and consultations. But in each case they were highly specific in their appearance to the particular disciplines and subjects being taught, and defied a kind of easy standardisation into uniform policy documents. This situation can make it hard for academic leaders to consolidate these activities, build upon and upscale them in ways that make it easy for regional partners to interact with them. We saw in the case studies initially enthusiastic partners finding themselves getting lost in the maze of university internal architectures with no straightforward strategic solution to this overall problem.

Discussion and conclusions

In this first concluding chapter, we have sought to highlight the more general lessons emerging from three recurrent tensions within university regional engagement as a way of more effectively integrating three conceptual elements of universities' regional contributions. In Chapter 2 we set out what we believe to be the implicit model within evolutionary models of regional economic development, namely that a coalition of regional actors exerts leadership within and outside formal bodies, aligns resources, and produces switching of economic development trajectories. In focusing on peripheral regions, we have restricted our view to those regions where these processes do not naturally happen organically and spontaneously, but rather that there are regional actors who are seeking to do something differently, to construct regional advantages and create new kinds of pathways (Asheim, Boschma, & Cooke, 2011). This creates various kinds of tensions within regional coalitions that influence their operation and ultimately shape the way that HEIs are able to make their contributions.

One of the most fundamental tensions here is between the old and new paths that exist and must be created, and we contend that to date there has been little consideration of the effects that this has on universities beyond casting it as a kind of lock-in from which the regional coalitions must escape. But in our case studies, we see an additional dimension that arises through the tension between these old and new paths that universities face, which we relate to Gunasekara's (2006) distinction between generative and developmental contributions. In both these kinds of activities, universities contribute through a **positive additive** activity, filling a gap in the region, whether that is in terms of particular innovation services (generative) or the regional policy layer (developmental). But for universities to contribute to these path-switching processes, they are confronted with imagining a future that does not currently exist **and which conflicts with current generative and developmental activities**.

This tension we see here is fundamental to understanding 'new' regional policies around constructed regional advantage or smart specialisation, but it is almost entirely ignored and this has profound consequences for universities. These new perspectives ignore the difficulties of disinvesting in, neglecting, and unimagining the present and directing strategic energies to an as-yet unrealised future. Regional partners therefore face the devil's dilemma of killing off (or contributing to) existing activities without knowing if they are truly moribund, with no guarantee that these new future promising industries can in reality be realised. The modern university is not well equipped to deal with the nuances and shades of grey inherent in such a problem, which demands that universities have the certainty to make strategic choices and allocate resources to those focal areas. But these choices, between existing declining industries and potentially successful future industries, can never have certainty, and therefore this runs the recurrent risk, so poignantly underlined by Pugh (2014), that under such circumstances there is a perennial risk of simply reframing these old networks within the new paradigm, with all the risks that that brings.

What is demanded from universities under such circumstances is that they play a third role, which we tentatively term 'transformative' (because of its hyperbolic resonances), in which they assist in a well-informed process of nudging existing regional actors towards as yet unrealised futures. We analyse the specific policy implications that this brings for universities in the 'Regional policymakers' section in the following chapter but, at the same time, we note that this also provides a means to make a substantive intellectual contribution relating to how these regional innovation coalitions are able to deliver this transformative change. This happens when a regional innovation coalition is able to envisage a meaningful pathway to a genuinely alternative region that brings enough regional partners and with sufficient regional beneficiaries to mobilise the assets for change to ensure that the partners can proceed progressively through these change processes and not continually fall back on the trusted ways of doing things (Sotarauta & Saarivirta, 2012).

We here see an interesting analogue with Sarasvathy's (2001) notion of effectuation in entrepreneurship. In this notion a distinction is made between entrepreneurs that organise their processes with a causal mindset in which they seek to achieve particular ends, and those that have an effectuative mindset, identifying what kinds of resource they have at their disposal and developing strategies that help build towards the defined end-goal on a step-wise basis (Dew, Read, Sarasvathy, & Wiltbank, 2009). This effectuative thinking appears to be at the heart of what a university's transformative contribution to a region might be, using knowledge of its resources in an effectuative way to contribute to a genuine process of constructing regional futures or entrepreneurial discovery. We therefore contend that serious thinking should be given to understanding more deeply how universities' transformative contributions to knowledge-based regional development can come through effectuative entrepreneurial discovery.

We here highlight two key elements which must form the basis for any future research agenda. The first is that there are strong overlaps between effectuative approaches and opportunism, in which an entrepreneur simply takes the most obvious and easy choice. Opportunism is common in innovation policy, as Pugh so compellingly shows, where regional actors facing a 'too difficult' problem simply declare that what they wanted to do anyway and have always been doing corresponds perfectly with this new paradigm. The question therefore emerges of how can effectuative entrepreneurial discovery avoid this opportunism, to navigate between opportunism and causation, to remain grounded without running aground in the past (opportunism), and to be novel without naivety regarding future possibilities (causation). This will guarantor the prospective effectuation in the regional entrepreneurial discovery process and prevent defaulting to retrospective opportunism. In the next chapter in the 'Introduction' and 'National policy-makers' sections we provide an initial reflection on the more immediate implications of this notion of effectuative new regional innovation policy for policy-makers seeking to harness universities' transformative potentials.

The second issue that emerges is around the role of the university as a complex assemblage of all kinds of resources that can contribute to various different ways to these effectuative entrepreneurial discovery processes. As Benneworth and Jongbloed (2013) convincingly demonstrate, a common misconception within university strategic management is that university managers are capable of knowing the capacities and resources within their institution, let alone can develop strategies to creatively combine them to create new regional assets. University strategic managers inherently tend towards more causation-based approaches to university strategy, and it is not an insignificant challenge to consider what kind of entrepreneurial architectures might be necessary within universities to allow this informed effectuation to take place. What is certainly necessary is following Benneworth *et al.* (2017) that universities' institutional entrepreneurs are unlocked to undertake effectuative institutional entrepreneurship and build new regional assets. We envisage that particular problems might emerge from the fact that the individuals with the tacit knowledge of the resources that might usefully be used might not necessarily as academic researchers identify closely with a goal of regional engagement, even if they would be in principle willing to act as knowledge gatekeepers within wider regional effectuation process. Although this challenge needs addressing conceptually, in the next chapter in the 'Regional Policy-makers' and 'University senior managers' sections we provide some first-cut implications that this raises for university policy-makers and academics.

Acknowledgements

The research leading to these results has received funding from the Norwegian Financial Mechanism 2009–2014 and the Ministry of Education, Youth and Sports under Project Contract No. MSMT-5397/2015. This chapter also reports findings from the RUNIN project (The Role of Universities in Innovation and Regional Development) that received funding from the European Union's Horizon 2020 research and innovation programme under Marie Skłodowska-Curie grant agreement No. 722295. Many thanks to Martin Stienstra for his useful discussions on effectuation and causation models of entrepreneurship. Any errors or omissions remain the author's responsibility.

References

Asheim, B. T., Boschma, R., & Cooke, P. (2011). Constructing regional advantage: Platform policies based on related variety and differentiated knowledge bases. *Regional Studies, 45*(7), 893–904.

Ayres, S. (2014). Place-based leadership: Reflections on scale, agency and theory. *Regional Studies, Regional Science, 1*, 21–24.

Beer, A., & Clower, T. (2014). Mobilizing leadership in cities and regions. *Regional Studies, Regional Science, 1*(1), 5–20.

Benneworth, P., & Jongbloed, B. (2013). Policies for promoting university-community engagement in practice. In P. Benneworth (Ed.), *University engagement with socially excluded communities.* Dordrecht: Springer.

Benneworth, P., Normann, R., & Young, M. (2018). Between rigour & regional relevance: Conceptualising tensions in university engagement for socio-economic development. *Higher Education Policy* (accepted 10 May 2017).

Benneworth, P. S., Pinheiro, R., & Karlsen, J. (2017). Strategic agency and institutional change: Investigating the role of universities in regional innovation systems (RISs). *Regional Studies, 51*(2), 235–248. doi:10.1080/00343404.2016.1215599.

Bozeman, B., Fay, D., & Slade, C. P. (2013). Research collaboration in universities and academic entrepreneurship: The-state-of-the-art. *The Journal of Technology Transfer, 38*(1), 1–67.

Collini, S. (2011). *What are universities for?* London: Penguin.

Dew, N., Read, S., Sarasvathy, S. D., & Wiltbank, R. (2009). Effectual versus predictive logics in entrepreneurial decision-making: Differences between experts and novices. *Journal of Business Venturing, 24*(4), 287–309.

Feldman, M., & Desrochers, P. (2003). Research universities and local economic development: Lessons from the history of the Johns Hopkins University. *Industry & Innovation, 10*, 5–24.

Flanagan, K., Uyarra, E., & Laranja, M. (2011). Reconceptualising the 'policy mix' for innovation. *Research Policy, 40*(5), 702–713.

Gunasekara, C. (2006). Reframing the role of universities in the development of regional innovation systems. *Journal of Technology Transfer, 31*(1), 101–111.

Hassink, R. (2005). How to unlock regional economies from path dependency? From learning region to learning cluster. *European Planning Studies, 13*(4), 521–535.

McCann, P., & Ortega-Argilés, R. (2013). Modern regional innovation policy. *Cambridge Journal of Regions, Economy and Society, 6*(2), 187–216.

Pinheiro, R., & Stensaker, B. (2013). Designing the entrepreneurial university: The interpretation of a global idea. *Public Organization Review, 1*–20.

Pugh, R. E. (2014). 'Old wine in new bottles'? Smart specialisation in Wales. *Regional Studies, Regional Science, 1*(1), 152–157.

Sarasvathy, S. D. (2001). Causation and effectuation: Toward a theoretical shift from economic inevitability to entrepreneurial contingency. *Academy of Management Review, 26*(2), 243–263.

Sotarauta, M. (2014). Reflections on 'Mobilizing leadership in cities and regions'. *Regional Studies, Regional Science, 1*(1), 28–31.

Sotarauta, M., & Saarivirta, T. (2012). Strategy development in knowledge cities revisited – the roles of innovation strategy in Helsinki Metropolitan Area explored. In H. C. Garmann Johnsen & R. Ennals (Eds), *Creating collaborative advantage: Innovation and knowledge creation in regional economies* (pp. 79–90). Farnham, UK: Gower.

Tödtling, F., & Trippl, M. (2005). One size fits all?: Towards a differentiated regional innovation policy approach. *Research Policy, 34*(8), 1203–1219.

Watson, D., & Hall, L. (2015). Addressing the elephant in the room: Are universities committed to the third stream agenda. *International Journal of Academic Research in Management, 4*(2), 48–76.

Zeeman, N., & Benneworth, P. S. (2016). Globalisation, mergers and 'inadvertent multi-campus universities': reflections from Wales. *Tertiary Education and Management 23*(1), 43–52.

13 Future perspectives on universities and peripheral regional development

Lisa Nieth and Paul Benneworth

Introduction

The volume has explored the implicit model for modern regional innovation policy in peripheral regions as a means of understanding how universities can contribute to regional development in those regions. We argued in Chapter 12 that universities are able to most effectively contribute in such places through what we tentatively name 'transformative' contributions, setting it up as a third class of contribution alongside Gunasekara's developmental and generative contributions (2006). We have argued that such 'transformative' contributions come when these constructive regional policy processes (whether constructing regional advantage or entrepreneurial discovery towards smart specialisation strategies) are able to contribute towards effectuative regional innovation policy-making (Sarasvathy, 2001). By effectuative regional policy, we mean identifying how on the basis of regional strengths and resources a series of steps can be taken both away from existing locked-in sectors and towards highly promising but as yet unrealised industries, a form of effectuative entrepreneurial discovery process.

Although there remains considerable work to be done on fleshing out the details of this overall concept, this outline in tandem with the empirical case studies makes it possible for us to reflect on the implications that this model has for a variety of stakeholders in universities making these transformative regional contributions through their participation in regional innovation coalitions. We further contend that because this effectuative assumption is present in a far wider range of regions than just those peripheral regions where it is most necessary because of the path switching, there are lessons that can be learned for stakeholders in regional innovation coalitions in all regions, not exclusively the periphery. This second concluding chapter therefore seeks to understand what implications are raised for four kinds of stakeholder, distinguishing:

- national policy-makers that determine the regulatory and financial frameworks within which universities operate;
- regional policy-makers who are most specifically concerned with stimulating these regional innovation coalitions;

- university leaders who seek to sincerely improve their universities' contributions to those regional coalitions; and
- active academic agents whose institutional entrepreneurship is vital in terms of creating resources which can feed into effectuative entrepreneurial discovery processes.

For each of these groups of stakeholders, we explore the most immediate implications of this effectuative innovation policy-making on their particular domain, with reference to the empirical material presented in chapters 3–11, in order to make recommendations to these stakeholders on how to optimise universities' contributions to their host regions. In the final chapter, we reflect on what this unruliness of the third mission concept means for policy-makers and practitioners seeking to stimulate universities' contributions to their regional environments. We make recommendations at a variety of levels:

- national policy-makers must allow room in their higher education systems for engagement not to be neglected;
- regional policy-makers should look to support institutional entrepreneurs within HEIs;
- university senior managers need to create permissive environments;
- actors involved in university engagement infrastructures need to think more clearly about how they can support new combinations of regional knowledge resources to assist regional development; and
- individual engaged academics should look more closely at creating links between their teaching/research activities and their societal duties.

In this final chapter, we turn to consider each of these in turn.

National policy-makers

We found very few examples where national governments had a clear perspective on how strong regional innovation coalitions as considered in this volume would have a wider national purpose. It is therefore perhaps unsurprising that there are very few examples of where governments have specifically sought to encourage regional activity and engagement by their HEIs. Although many governments say that regional innovation coalitions are necessary, what they do not do is set out a vision for how coalitions in less successful regions can contribute to national development projects. Those examples that have existed, such as the Northern Way or the Peaks in the Delta programmes in the UK and the Netherlands respectively, have been relatively short-lived policy cycles that have not influenced the overall policy frameworks. The overall result of this is often national higher education and economic policy that passes rewards to those already successful regions, and undermines the potential contributions that these less successful regions can make.

A key issue here is that of the rigidity of national systems in combination with an inability of universities in less peripheral regions to make claims of exceptionalism to validate and justify their own activities. National higher education systems can drive all institutions to behave in similar ways, and to seek to mimic the most successful HEIs rather than allowing them the space to work out how they are going to make their own contributions. Policy-makers are focused on achieving a particular set of national goals – whether defined as excellence, internationalisation, employability or quality – and these systems allow this to be achieved in an efficient manner. The regional vision for higher education therefore becomes defined as expanding and replicating those activities that are undertaken by universities in a country's core regions. The challenge here is then a recognition by policy-makers of the value of a diverse tapestry of universities contributing in different ways to their regions, but ultimately all in ways that strengthen the country as a whole.

A key way that national policy-makers can contribute to this process is by reducing the ridigity that exists, particular in the distinctions between excellent and engaged research within regions. The reality is that universities of all kinds in all kinds of places have research groups active in undertaking research across a broad spectrum from fundamental and excellent to local and applied. In reality these research groups and their researchers blend these activities in creative ways to create interesting and useful knowledge and package it up in different ways within different kinds of recognition and evaluation system. National policy-makers can therefore help by providing funding that stretches across these divides; the most obvious example of this would be the Norwegian Regional Research Fund (see Chapters 3, 5, and 6) which provides universities and university colleges who face a strong pressure from the research point system to be excellent to form regional business-university research networks to address these fundamental questions.

This could be part of a wider national conversation about how science contributes to these national systems and what it is economic to achieve. What is interesting more generally is that many of the institutions that are now seen as world-class and separate from their immediate locations were often created to generate specific place regional advantages. We are not just here thinking about the American Land-Grant Colleges, but also Massachusetts Institute of Technology which was initiated in the expectation that it would converge over time on Harvard's more humanities-focused approach. It is often the technical universities, created to drive local and national advantage, that have found themselves at the forefront of dynamic innovative regions, and have therefore redefined in the policy imagination what excellent engagement is. It is false to portray excellence and engagement as mutually exclusive, the more urgent question that requires addressing is under which conditions can these two end-goals be served, and what kinds of national policy-frameworks can promote them.

Ultimately, we argue that there needs to be a new approach to the business of higher education policy, away from the currently dominant models of new public management (Kickert, 1995; Kickert, Klijn, & Koppenjan, 1997). In these models, policy-makers set targets for the most important outcomes they

- Recognise the very diverse regional settings in which universities are embedded and the resulting varied contributions universities make to their regions.
- Do not copy 'best practice examples' from successful regions (one size does not fit all).
- Reduce rigidity in identifying what is excellent and what is engaged research (e.g. in national regulation systems) and identify how universities can support engaged academics.
- Develop policy frameworks and support activities (e.g. funding) that highlight the connectibility and mutual reinforcement of excellence and engagement.
- Encourage experimentation of researchers and record/communicate the experiences in order to advance the understanding for excellent engaged academics in peripheral regions.

Figure 13.1 Key take-away messages for national policy-makers

seek to address and leave managers to decide how to achieve them. The results of this for university engagement in the periphery have been evident in this book, a convergence on those models seen as being most successful nationally rather than those most effective for the region.

So what can a national policy-maker do to ensure that an engaged researcher, when faced by an approach from a regional partner or the opportunity to write for a highly cited journal, takes the former choice? The challenge lies in negotiating between the poles of the hypersensitivity to incentives, which currently exists, and placing no requirements. But what this volume shows is that there is already so much activity despite the presence of these huge disincentives sketched out here, that with a little positive support, it should be possible to create large substantive results. The next step in expanding this activity is in encouraging experiments to understand how these excellent engaged academics in peripheral regions are able to organise their activities, and the balances of incentives and barriers they face in this. National policy-makers should therefore seek to promote the national dialogue about the uses and benefits of science more generally by encouraging experimentation of these researchers, identifying how universities can best support them, and allowing their universities the space to encourage that activity in their national regulation systems.

Regional policy-makers

The examples we have presented make clear the variety of important roles that regional authorities play in shaping the operation of regional innovation coalitions. The key strategic challenge that peripheral regions face is, given their relatively underdeveloped regional innovation systems, how can they have a well-informed strategic dialogue. Most specifically, what do they need to do to ensure that the entrepreneurial discovery process does not lead to well-meaning regional strategies in which the first step is easily taken, but two years later no strategic capacity has been built up, leading to the initial step being repeated without leading to regional upgrading (described by Sotarauta, 2016 as falling into the 'strategic black hole'). We have here promoted the idea of effectual rather than causal mindsets being necessary to achieve these outcomes, and this raises the question of what can regional authorities do to allow regional partners to genuinely plan their own way rather than seek to mimic what has proven effective in more successful places. The issue we have identified is that innovation policy within economic development policy is often one of the genuinely regional competences that authorities have and so they tend to take a rather reductionist view of what kinds of innovation may work.

And in our reading, this has a view of imposing duality on the kinds of activities regional innovation may support, either the most immediately obvious activities supported by businesses, or those with the most attractive long-term potential. In short, the policy logic undermines the mobilisation of regional innovation policy coalitions by framing HEIs as suppliers of a set of immediate applied research outputs in return of the longer-term promise of a more demanding regional industrial base. But at the same time, this encourages an opportunism amongst universities, mobilising particular projects to access regional policy resources rather than trying to act as regional institutional entrepreneurs (as seen most explicitly in the case of the EUREGIO). In the case of Tampere (see Chapter 11) efforts were made to ameliorate these problems by operating more informal meeting activities where these new activities could be co-constructed between partners. Rather than acting as directors incentivising actors to individually deliver these projects, these cases illustrate universities and regional partners working together to work out how to join up and integrate their different assets into goals with wider benefits for the region, and ultimately supportive of regional development policy.

The challenge for smart regional policy-makers is to take a broader view and think of how they can mobilise these smart regional policy arenas (Flanagan, Uyarra, & Laranja, 2011). This involves finding ways to construct arenas where these effectual entrepreneurial discovery processes can take place: these processes happen when regional partners come together and combine their existing resources in new approaches that create new ways of working or thinking that go beyond individual projects but create something that has wider regional benefit. We saw in several of the regional cases that the partners were slowly feeling their way to creating a 'regional platform' that went beyond articulating a long-term regional vision in tandem with a short-term tactical plan. These examples highlight how informality is necessary here, to avoid overly restricting activities with different kinds of demands from the different sectors. However, the cases also illustrate that flexibility on its own is not sufficient: because individual actors all face different urgent demands, what can be collectively realised as acceptable to all is actually extremely limited.

One opportunity to deal with this is to formally support the flexibility with new forms of working, as we saw in Chapter 11, with fuzzy way of working. Although regional platforms are not formally part of the regional institutional structure, it is still possible for regions to give them tasks which reduce the interference that they face. All regions in Europe are tasked with constructing

- Define and support regional settings that encourage strategic dialogue between stakeholders.
- Recognise the risks of falling into vicious circles of strategic planning, consisting of strategies being redefined continuously (they are easy to follow, but do not bring long-term change).
- Communicate and support the role of universities as regional institutional entrepreneurs (instead of regional providers of specific outputs).
- Create arenas for entrepreneurial discovery processes that encourage the combination of resources, the communication of goals and achievements, and the development of new ways of thinking beyond individual interests, in so-called innovation platforms.
- Support regional platforms by transferring power and possibility of action to them (e.g. taking the leading role in RIS3 processes).

Figure 13.2 Key take-away messages for regional policy-makers

Research and Innovation Strategies for smart specialisation (RIS3) in return for being granted access to European Funds. Giving these regional platforms a leading role in something like a RIS3 process, which is not subject to the vagaries of regional political choices, is one kind of way that this fuzzy working can be institutionalised (other kinds of European activities are possible here, such as Interreg, or the Trans-European Networks strategies). By framing these platforms as meaningful sites of co-creation and effectual entrepreneurial discovery, regional policy-makers can reduce their capture by short-term lobby interests and improve the longer-term effectiveness.

At the same time as encouraging these platforms to operate, the other element for regional policy-makers is in supporting the work that they do. We saw that this was something that many of the weaker regions were good at, acting as powerful cheerleaders for successful experiments within these regional innovation coalitions. Part of this is internal, as was evident in the Czech Republic and Finland, in validating these experiments as successful to encourage partners to take the next step forward, and in particular to reduce resistance amongst those regional partners that are not the greatest winners. There was also an external element, that we also saw strongly in Finland and Norway, a willingness to use connections between regional and national policy networks to argue that the particular regional experiments had been successful or were a national precondition of successful regional policy (Norway).

We have seen that one of the problems that can arise is the imposition of different logics between regional partners, and there was one particular tension that we would here highlight as being something that policy-makers should pay attention to. A number of the HEIs had multiple regional campuses within which different colleges had been merged to build more efficient institutions. There is a risk that these larger institutions also seek efficiency between sites, and under pressure to internationalise and attract more international students concentrate their activities on a single site with the highest level of international connectivity (see also Zeeman & Benneworth, 2017). The campuses of the Norwegian universities were under pressure to rationalise, and even where this did not go as far as to lead to site closures (excepting the historical closures of Skien and some of the smaller Agder colleges), this could lead to a fragmentation in university interest with each campus having its own local partners. That is not of itself problematic, but that may introduce a local fragmentation between localities that undermines further collective action, and regional policy-makers need to find a way to accommodate and hold together these divergent local interests.

University senior managers

At the heart of the challenge for university leaders lie two inalienable features of university regional engagement, firstly that universities comprise a number of very different knowledge communities (Reponen, 1999) and regional leadership is an informal and negotiated process (Beer & Clower, 2014). Indeed, in the higher education literature, it is not uncommon to regard universities as 'loosely coupled institutions', whose core institutions are mainly about holding together knowledge producers that have beliefs about what constitutes good teaching and research that are diametrically opposite (consider theoretical astrophysics, water engineering, psychology and anthropology). Universities typically deal with these by ensuring that general policies fit with and can be tailored to the specific needs of teaching and research across these different fields leaving room for staff in those different fields to interpret those requirements in their own way. Requirements for promotion might say that a candidate has to publish at an internationally recognised level, leaving individual departments to make the choice about what that involves, and cross-disciplinary communities to be willing to accept each other's definitions and understandings in agreeing (in this case) promotions.[1] This allows these different communities to mutually and profitably co-exist without each community fully having to understand the detail of what each other does.

But what we see with universities seeking to promote regional engagement is that they often adopt strategies that are relatively unnuanced in terms of this remaining interpretative freedom. Universities say that they are going to create spin-off companies, or offer technology transfer, or do joint research projects, often on the basis of which are the most profitable activities for the universities. At the same time, these imply and validate particular kinds of knowledge transaction that might have no relevance for engaged academics in other disciplinary areas. These strategies often define in advance what the HEI does whilst it is impossible for the university to have full strategic knowledge of what the university is doing. The result is that this pushes universities towards emphasising those activities that are already taking place and which are known about at the strategic level. And our contention is that this has the effect of limiting the university contributions to the regional innovation coalition to a kind of generative input to the first step of a strategy rather than thinking about how to add up those various different kinds of steps into a transformative strategy.

- Develop a general understanding of engagement and create strategies of engagement that give room for interpretation for the diverse actors within different knowledge communities.
- Do not solely emphasise and report engagement activities that seem to be the most profitable (e.g. creation of spin-off companies) or most widely known. Instead, highlight and promote the broad range of activities of engagement.
- Acknowledge that there are many engagement activities that you, as a senior manager, do not know about and that can be just as valuable as the visible ones.
- Encourage institutional entrepreneurs.

Figure 13.3 Key take-away messages for university senior managers

The fundamental problem is that it is almost impossible for university senior managers to know everything that its staff do, particularly in an activity that is as diverse and peripheral as regional engagement (Benneworth, 2013). What we found in the empirical chapters is that this is not an activity problem, because there are hugely substantive developmental and even transformative activities being driven by universities in their regions. But it does appear that universities are not fully in strategic control of these processes, that universities achieve these benefits despite or at least not because of the efforts devoted by their senior management to engagement. Under circumstances where you are dependent on institutional entrepreneurs who are creating knowledge in ways that you don't necessarily understand to create uncertain future benefits, how can you strategically manage these processes?

Reflecting on the nature of the diverse regional engagement processes reveals the extent to which many of them are not really distinct activities or processes within universities. Many of the activities were integrated into teaching activities, and served the interest of enriching student education or as in the case of Telemark (see Chapter 6), in supporting student employability through a careers fair. However, the ones that are distinct transactions are often the ones that generate income for the university, and are therefore 'institutionally visible' and attract managerial attention in strategies. The answer here seems to lie in the same way that universities manage other divergent knowledge processes, which is to set common guidelines whilst allowing devolved interpretative freedom of what counts as valid regional engagement.

The heart of university engagement activities is not strategic managers, but the institutional entrepreneurs that come up with creative ways to combine activities in ways which serve the goals of both regional partners but also institutions. And the essence of what university senior managers can do to support engagement is in the first instance to find ways to encourage these institutional entrepreneurs. However, there is also the need to create a collective understanding of what constitutes valid institutional entrepreneurship in this context. Just as individuals from across a university or faculty can come to a shared understanding of what constitutes international publication or academic validity of a course, they can also develop common understandings of what constitutes valid engagement practice. This can allow the development of wider institutional frameworks for regional engagement, that in turn provide a more nuanced starting point for a common regional strategy.

University engagement activities

In this volume we have seen that a range of different activities within universities were notionally charged with taking responsibility for regional engagement. Yet at the same time, these activities did not always have the necessary authority to be able to encourage and support their academics and deliver the intentions of senior policy-makers. Those universities that were successful at engagement had been successful into calling into creation an institutional space – similar to what Clark (1998) called the 'extended development periphery' – within which the challenges and tensions of regional engagement in peripheral environments could be addressed. What was important here was the effect this had on what Vorley and Nelles (2012) call the entrepreneurial architecture of a university, ensuring that interesting experimental projects have a chance to add to university capacity. This entrepreneurial architecture ensures that projects do not just function as generative activities, but have a developmental impact, adding to the overall regional balance sheet in terms of the various capitals within the region available for socio-economic development.

This role is played – as Clark envisaged it – by linking core academic actors engaged in teaching and research and in particular in ensuring that academics are able to appreciate the benefits that occur through engagement. This is not in the generic sense of advocating engagement as being a good thing to do in its own right, but as something which is obviously beneficial for individual academics (see the next section). What is important here in this extended development periphery (EDP) is the way that it assists academics to benefit from synergies and that it brings its own resources with it to support academics. Many of these activities will not necessarily be immediately fee-earning or even profit-making for the EDP, but there is a need to understand how these activities have second-order benefits. By second-order benefits, we refer here to the ways in which a well-placed piece of regional engagement can cross-fertilise an important knowledge activity – a new teaching course or a new research stream that ultimately creates wider regional benefits and brings direct benefits into the university.

The big challenge this raises for the EDP is how to be proactive in this, and in particular to understand supporting which kinds of activity could potentially lead to longer-term benefits for the university. What these case studies have shown is the almost total impossibility, even in relatively small, focused, and new HEIs, of centrally knowing all the areas where universities can make a difference. At the same time, we see EDPs becoming centres of excellence and knowledge in their own right – the most obvious examples being in Estonia, where the regional colleges' core functions blended almost seamlessly into institutional development activities. Likewise, in other institutions, it was striking

- It is vital for all actors involved in the engagement process to understand the value of engagement and that second-order benefits might not be visible from the start.
- This risk of being locked in to engagement pathways of the past applies to all sides. Searching for new and innovative ways to engage is a task everyone should attend to.
- Empowering environments within the university setting give room for new networks to develop which in return can lead to engagement activities.

Figure 13.4 Key take-away messages for university engagement support activities

how often EDPs developed their profiles based on selling particular kinds of consultancy service bundles (Heydebreck, Klofsten, & Maier, 2000) to clients. That occurred even in circumstances where that reflected only one element important to those universities, or where the activities of one campus became instrumental in defining the way that the university collectively thought about and supported engagement.

So we see here a risk for technology transfer offices within universities, that of themselves becoming path-impregnated and oriented towards current ways of working, with the technology transfer 'tail' wagging the academic heartland 'dog', so to speak. In particular the case of Tampere highlighted the effort required to break the existing mindset within universities and begin searching for new activities when the dominant industry disappears. There is therefore a need for EDP activities to ensure that they do not themselves become part of the problem, part of the lock-in, by directing academics to existing partners with existing ways of working that ultimately may not lead to the emergence of new sectors. What is necessary here is that the EDPs instead are creating empowering environments where creative academics can build exciting new activities that contribute to creating new regional development pathways. We deal with this issue of engaged academics on their own engagement journey in the following section, but areas where EDPs can assist are in helping academics to build up networks, and in particular to work with key partners outside the university in attempting to deliver these creative activities.

A final element relates to the question of the diversity of university activities and the role of regional engagement within that. The question of whether engagement can benefit an HEI's teaching and research activities is an emergent one that relates to the region, the academics, and their respective research interests. As Callon (1999) makes clear, external engagement is not appropriate or mutually rewarding for all academics and all disciplines. The current strong normative position that actors should be engaging with regional partners undermines the issue that effective regional engagement is built as much upon the ability to build on the regional and the university balance sheets simultaneously as it is for the university to discharge its wider duties to societal partners (what Barnett, 2000 calls the social compact of universities). This strong normative position can lead to the pursuit of engagement activities for their extrinsic value – the symbolic recognition they bring from external partners or the direct investments they may enable. But at the same time this can lead to a neglect of consideration of how these activities lead to a capitalisation on the knowledge balance of the university, enabling this cross-fertilisation and creation of new knowledge pathways.

Engaged academics

The final group of stakeholders in university-regional engagement is the academics and scholars themselves who are active in building the linkages through which knowledge circulates between universities and regions, thereby creating new local capacities and ideally supporting constructive evolutionary processes. The most important observation is the huge diversity of practices that we have seen in the various regions. In the Algarve and Agder, there were examples of consultancy and technology transfer activities directly related to knowledge creation; in Finnmark and Telemark, university actors became involved in regional strategy making and vision-development; in Vysočina this was about helping support the development of the social, democratic, and environmental foundations of the region. The academics involved in those activities have very different views of the world, of what knowledge creation is, how knowledge is created, and how to apply that knowledge in practice. They have very different kinds of links with societal stakeholders, underpinned by very diverse kinds of transactions and interactions, all of which reflect as much the nature of those knowledge processes and the regional context as much as the policies and structures within which these academics operate. And following the final point in the last section, there appear to be a group of academics (although we did not focus on highlighting them in the chapters) that were for those very reasons not strongly engaged with regional partners and for whom there were few positive benefits from that regional engagement.

What these engaged academics all did have in common was the ways in which they built up activities which achieved effects and a lifespan beyond that of the immediate intervention. This was specifically the focus of the EUREGIO chapter (Chapter 10) which considered the extent to which universities could create cross-border networks and institutions in a cross-border region which has an institutional separating effect derived from the border. But these examples of what van den Broek *et al.* called institutional entrepreneurship are also evident and implicit in a number of the other chapters. In Tampere, for example, Kurrika *et al.* foregrounded the agency of a range of actors in adapting to the Nokia closure shock, and there clearly is a link between academics in the three HEIs seeking new regional partners and the emergence of new knowledge-intensive services around automation and content delivery. In Saaremaa, Estonia, it was institutional entrepreneurs that literally built the entire infrastructure for the regional college, supported by regional partners and its sponsor university in Tallinn, but involving building connections and an institutional structure bridging global knowledge in the capital city and local application in the island's marine engineering industry. In Vysočina, the HEI created a new class of useful education, vocational higher education outside the regulated professions, where all students undertake a mandatory semester placement in regional business, and arranging that new kind of education – with strong regional benefits – involved academics across a range of disciplines understanding how to fit that idea into their overall education activities.

This highlights an additional feature of university regional engagement and that there is a substantive element present here of what Sivertsen (2017) elsewhere has referred to as 'ordinary engagement'. Sivertsen (2017) is specifically creating a contrast here with what has become popular in policy discourses, the evocation of 'extraordinary impact', in which apparently titanic efforts by highly skilled academics manage against the odds to create an impressive societal impact. An example of this eye-catching impact might for example be the work that Lund University did in attracting the Ericsson mobile telephony research laboratory in the early 1980s, leading to a massive telecoms giant and a rash of spin-off companies in related activities (Benneworth, Coenen, Moodyson, & Asheim, 2009). Sivertsen's critique is that this frames engagement as rare, requiring tremendous effort and enormous luck, making it a hugely risky undertaking for those involved, whilst the reality is that universities as knowledge communities have all kinds of links back into their societies, into their regions (see Figure 13.5). His point is that there needs to be a much wider understanding of the extent to which regional engagement is normalised into the everyday practices of academics *who do not necessarily regard that as constituting something special*. Attempts therefore to promote 'regional engagement' run the risk of making that engagement seem external and unfamiliar, thereby downplaying the extent to which it is already embedded in academic practice.

The final issue here concerns this question of the wider value of impact and the normative pressure placed on academics to engage. Academics find themselves caught between two countervailing forces, between the tension to be excellent and the normative pressure that engagement is good in its own right. There is an increasing realisation that there are many kinds of circumstances under which engagement can be problematic by privatising knowledge in particular ways that subtract from rather than add to the overall societal knowledge balance. Bozeman, Fay, and Slade (2013) refer to this as the dark side of engagement, and we see here the way that this can happen in peripheral regions, in engagement reinforcing lock-in with existing partners instead of unlocking new pathways. At the same time, academics may feel that they are being urged to engage despite the risk and rewards being out of balance. This was particularly the case in regions where HEIs were the dominant innovation actors and therefore found themselves playing multiple roles within regional innovation coalitions including selling innovation support services that were relatively difficult to connect back to their core knowledge activities of teaching and (applied) research. There need be much more consideration for the needs of diversity amongst academics and the steps necessary to embed ordinary engagement as an everyday part of the academic task if scholars are to fulfil their potential to build transformatory networks and institutions in the sparse innovation environments of Europe's peripheral regions.

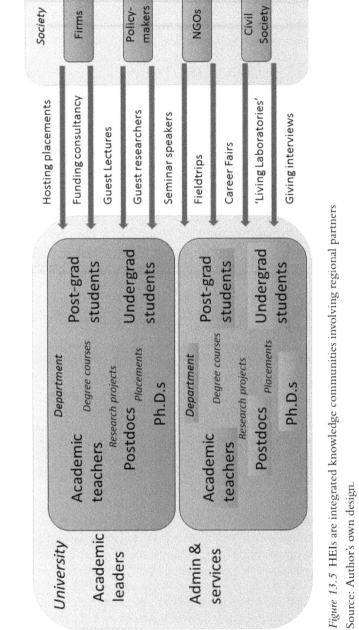

Figure 13.5 HEIs are integrated knowledge communities involving regional partners
Source: Author's own design.

- Be aware of the high diversity of possible activities/practices of engagement which are in line with the very unalike academics and scholars that exist in the HE landscape.
- Don't expect activities to always show immediate results or be of high impact resulting in extraordinary effort and above-average time and resource commitment.
- Open up for engaging practices that go beyond the lifespan of particular projects and result in long-term benefits, relationships, and knowledge creation.
- Engagement activities are often within the everyday practices of academics/scholars and do not need to be 'special or rare'.

Figure 13.6 Key take-away messages for engaged academics

Acknowledgements

This chapter received funding from the Norwegian Financial Mechanism 2009–2014 and the Ministry of Education, Youth and Sports under Project Contract No. MSMT-5397/2015. This chapter also reports findings from the RUNIN project (The Role of Universities in Innovation and Regional Development) that received funding from the European Union's Horizon 2020 research and innovation programme under Marie Skłodowska-Curie grant agreement No. 722295.

Note

1 We see here an important explanation for the rise of bibliometrics as a steering tool in higher education because it gives an apparent veneer of independence to decisions that were more commonly previously reserved for academic communities.

References

Asheim, B. T., Boschma, R., & Cooke, P. (2011). Constructing regional advantage: Platform policies based on related variety and differentiated knowledge bases. *Regional Studies, 45*(7), 893–904.

Barnett, R. (2000). Realising a compact for higher education. In K. Moti Gokulsing & C. DaCosta (Eds), *A compact for higher education*. Aldershot: Ashgate.

Beer, A., & Clower, T. (2014). Mobilizing leadership in cities and regions. *Regional Studies, Regional Science, 1*(1), 5–20.

Benneworth, P. (Ed.). (2013). *University engagement with socially excluded communities: Towards the idea of 'the engaged university'*. Dordrecht: Springer.

Benneworth, P. S., Coenen, L., Moodyson, J., & Asheim, B. (2009). Exploring the multiple roles of Lund University in strengthening the Scania regional innovation system: Towards institutional learning? *European Planning Studies, 17*(11), 1645–1664.

Bozeman, B., Fay, D., & Slade, C. (2013). Research collaboration in universities and academic entrepreneurship: The-state-of-the-art. *The Journal of Technology Transfer, 38*(1), 1–67.

Callon, M. (1999). The role of lay people in the production and dissemination of scientific knowledge. *Science Technology Society, 4*(1), 81–94.

Clark, B. (1998). *Creating entrepreneurial universities: Organizational pathways of transformation*. Oxford: Pergamon/IAU Press.

Flanagan, K., Uyarra, E., & Laranja, M. (2011). Reconceptualising the 'policy mix' for innovation. *Research Policy, 40*, 702–713.

Gunasekara, C. (2006). Reframing the role of universities in the development of regional innovation systems. *Journal of Technology Transfer, 31*(1), 101–111.

Heydebreck, P., Klofsten, M., & Maier, J. C. (2000). Innovation support for new technology based firms: The Swedish Teknopol approach. *R&D Management, 30*(1), 89–100.

Kickert, W. (1995). Steering at a distance: A new paradigm of public governance in Dutch higher education. *Governance, 8*, 135–157.

Kickert, W. J. M., Klijn, E. H., & Koppenjan, J. F. M. (Eds). (1997). *Managing complex networks: Strategies for the public sector* (1st ed.). London: SAGE Publications.

McCann, P., & Ortega-Argilés, R. (2013). Modern regional innovation policy. *Cambridge Journal of Regions, Economy and Society, 6*(2), 187–216.

Reponen, T. (1999). Is leadership possible at loosely coupled organizations such as universities? *Higher Education Policy, 12*(3), 237–244.

Sarasvathy, S. D. (2001). Causation and effectuation: Toward a theoretical shift from economic inevitability to entrepreneurial contingency. *Academy of Management Review, 26*(2), 243–263.

Sivertsen, G. (2017). *Frameworks for understanding the societal relevance of the humanities.* Presented to RESSH2017 – Research Evaluation in the Social Sciences and Humanities, Antwerp, 6–7 July 2017.

Sotarauta, M. (2016). *Leadership and the city: Power, strategy and networks in the making of knowledge cities.* London: Routledge, Taylor & Francis Group.

Vorley, T., & Nelles, J. (2012). Scaling entrepreneurial architecture: The challenge of managing regional technology transfer in Hamburg. In R. Pinheiro, P. Benneworth, & G. A. Jones (Eds), *Universities and regional development: A critical assessment of tensions and contradictions* (pp. 181–198). Milton Park and New York: Routledge.

Zeeman, N., & Benneworth, P. S. (2017). Globalisation, mergers and 'inadvertent multi-campus universities': Reflections from Wales. *Tertiary Education and Management, 23*(1), 41–52. doi:10.1080/13583883.2016.1243256.

Index

For Product Safety Concerns and Information please contact our EU
representative GPSR@taylorandfrancis.com
Taylor & Francis Verlag GmbH, Kaufingerstraße 24, 80331 München, Germany